War and Peace in the Gulf

War and Peace in the Gulf

Testimonies of the
Gulf Peace Team

Edited by

Bela Bhatia
Jean Drèze
Kathy Kelly

SPOKESMAN

Acknowledgements

Like the Gulf Peace Team itself, this book has benefited from the support of many good people over the years. First and foremost we would like to thank Curtis Doebbler for practical help at every stage, and also for useful suggestions concerning the introduction. Catriona Byrne, Reetika Khera, Ginnie Landon, Anuradha Madhusudhanan, Renata Marroum and Milan Rai helped us to assemble and organise the material on which this book is based. We are also indebted to Anthony Simpson and Anthony Arnove for valuable editorial advice, and to S. Sridhar for financial support.

Finally, we are grateful to Gulf Peace Team members for sharing with us their diaries, notes, photographs and other testimonies from the Gulf. They have been very generous in sharing this personal material with us. Due to space constraints, only a small selection of these contributions has been included in this book (the original contributions are available at the International Institute of Social History in Amsterdam, along with other archives of the Gulf Peace Team). We hope that it does justice to the Gulf Peace Team as a whole, and that this record of nonviolent interposition in a war zone will contribute – however modestly – to the prevention of future wars.

Bela Bhatia
Jean Drèze
Kathy Kelly

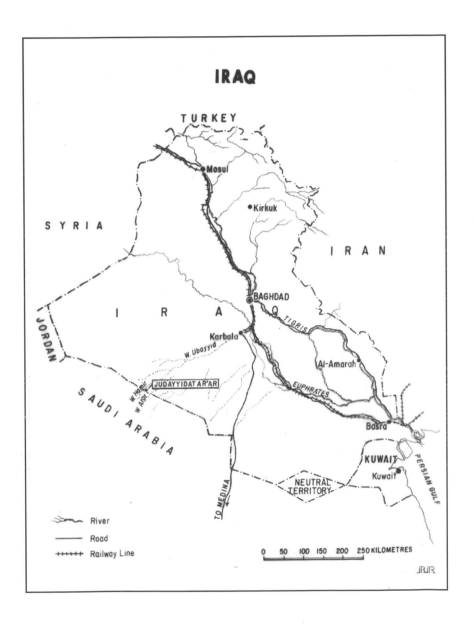

First published in 2001 by
Spokesman
Russell House
Bulwell Lane
Nottingham
NG6 0BT
Phone 0115 9708318. Fax 0115 9420433.
e-mail elfeuro@compuserve.com
www.spokesmanbooks.com

ISBN 0 85124 640 0

A CIP Catalogue record is available from the British Library.

Printed by Russell Press Ltd (phone 0115 9784505).

CONTENTS

PART II: THE WAR AND AFTER

PART III: VIEWPOINTS

PART IV: IN MEMORIAM

Foreword

Noam Chomsky

In the several years before the Gulf Peace Team established its camp in the Iraqi deserts in January 1991 in an inspiring effort to prevent a terrible catastrophe, significant events had been taking place that provide a background for thinking about the mission they undertook, and its potential significance.

As the Bush administration entered office in January 1989, it undertook a National Security Policy Review dealing with "third world threats." Parts were leaked to the press during the Gulf war — "Gulf massacre" might be a more appropriate term, considering the forces arrayed and the casualties suffered. The Review concluded that: "In cases where the U.S. confronts much weaker enemies" — that is, the only kind one chooses to fight — "our challenge will be not simply to defeat them, but to defeat them decisively and rapidly." Any other outcome would be "embarrassing" and might "undercut political support," understood to be thin.

The dilemma is conventionally traced to the "Vietnam syndrome," understood to be the unwillingness of the public to accept high casualties or to "undertake major burdens in foreign interventions" in the wake of Vietnam. This is the interpretation given to regular polls for the past 30 years, most recently in 1999, showing that a surprisingly large majority of the public has consistently described the Vietnam war as "fundamentally wrong and immoral," not "a mistake." That judgement stands in sharp opposition to elite opinion, which across the mainstream spectrum regards the war as well-intentioned but a mistake because its cost proved too high. In the characteristic words of one of the leading doves, Senator John Kerry, "our involvement was born in America's unique sense of mission regarding democracy and freedom" and what "so tormented our politicians and our people" was "the subsequent compounding of lies and arrogance," nothing more. What "our people" actually say about what "so tormented them" must therefore be recast, radically, to conform to elite demands, and has been within the intellectual culture.

The actual results are remarkable, not only because it is rare for people to recognise so clearly and honestly what has been done in their name, but also because these must have been individual judgements. It is not merely that they have received no support from media or other public sources.

Beyond that, they are strikingly contrary to the insistent message of mainstream doctrine, so much so that elite opinion simply cannot comprehend what the public is saying, as illustrated by the perverse interpretation assigned to it.

A few months after the Bush National Security Policy Review, the Berlin Wall fell, ending the superpower confrontation for all practical purposes. The disappearance of the Soviet deterrent opened new opportunities for decisive and rapid destruction of much weaker enemies. Not surprisingly, it led to more general shifts of military strategy, and modifications of doctrinal stance, which are instructive to trace.

In October 1989, a month before the fall of the Wall, a National Security Directive had called for "the use of U.S. military force" where "necessary and appropriate" to defend our "vital interests...against the Soviet Union or any other regional power...," specifically in the Middle East, where the Directive also recommended continued support for Washington's ally Saddam Hussein. In November the Berlin Wall fell: the Soviet Union could no longer serve as the alleged reason for the use of military force, and no longer posed a credible deterrent.

A month later, in December 1989, Bush invaded Panama over strong regional and international protests that required him to veto two Security Council resolutions and vote against a strongly-worded General Assembly resolution. The invading forces killed hundreds or perhaps thousands of people, and installed a puppet regime of bankers, businessmen and narcotraffickers so flimsy "that removing the mantle of United States protection would quickly result in a civilian or military overthrow" (Latin American historian Stephen Ropp). The specific target of the invasion was the local thug in charge, Manuel Noriega, who had been a U.S. favourite until he began to disobey orders in the mid-1980s, dragging his feet on cooperation with Washington's war against Nicaragua. He was kidnapped by the invaders. When brought to trial and condemned in a U.S. court, the charges against him, surely valid, were almost entirely from the period when he was a loyal CIA asset.

All of this is so familiar as to be a mere footnote to history, with two important innovations, one doctrinal, one strategic, both bearing directly on the Gulf war and its aftermath.

The doctrinal innovation was a change of pretexts. The U.S. was not defending itself from the Russian menace, as it had been since the origins of the Cold War. For example, when it declared a national emergency and attacked Nicaragua to protect itself from a Soviet-backed Nicaraguan invasion of Texas (as the President explained). Or when it conquered Grenada, "standing tall," in the President's words, as 6000 elite troops overcame a few dozen Cuban construction workers, receiving 8000 medals in honour of their achievement, and removing the imminent threat posed by this awesome outpost of Russian power to shipping lanes in the Caribbean, if not worse. A month after the fall of the Wall, however, the U.S. was defending itself against Hispanic narcotraffickers bent on undermining the country by corrupting the youth.

The strategic innovation, explained by former State Department official Elliott Abrams, was that the use of force is now more feasible, and the President therefore "probably is going to be increasingly willing to use force," because "developments in Moscow have lessened the prospect for a small operation to escalate into a superpower conflict." In short, the deterrent was gone.

In March 1990, the White House submitted its annual message to Congress on the military budget, and the Joint Chiefs of Staff presented a strategic assessment of the world situation. The message to Congress explained that we face ominous threats that require enormous military expenditures, dwarfing those of the rest of the world, namely, the "technological sophistication" of Third World countries. Previously, the threat had always been "the monolithic and ruthless conspiracy" bent on world conquest, in John F. Kennedy's words. This new threat to our existence requires that the U.S. maintain its military forces without substantial change and also the "defence industrial base," a code word for high-tech industry. Furthermore, the U.S. must maintain powerful intervention forces aimed, as before, primarily at the Middle East, where the "threats to our interests" that have required direct military engagement "could not be laid at the Kremlin's door," the White House informed Congress.

The shift of military strategy was broader in scope, directed openly against the South — which, in reality, had been the primary victim of subversion, military intervention, and U.S.-backed national security states throughout the Cold War. Russia was "weapon rich," the Joint Chiefs observed in their March 1990 assessment, but the South is "target rich," with "increasingly capable Third World threats." Assessing "deterrence strategy" at the same time, Pentagon planners called for a new "globality capability" that would extend to the South, given that the world "has now evolved from a 'weapon rich environment' to a 'target rich environment'." Targets are to include nations capable of developing weapons of mass destruction: that is, any country with laboratories, industry, and infrastructure. New tactics and military technology are required, including "mini-nukes" and technical innovations to allow rapid action "in response to spontaneous threats" from smaller countries.

The operative scope of the concept "spontaneous threats" was elucidated in 1999 by Secretary of Defense William Cohen, spelling out more explicitly President Clinton's doctrine, announced to the UN in 1993, that the U.S. will act "multilaterally when possible but unilaterally when necessary." In Cohen's words, the U.S. is committed to "unilateral use of military power" to defend vital interests, which include "ensuring uninhibited access to key markets, energy supplies and strategic resources." With the traditional objective now more clearly in view without the distortions of Cold War ideology, military doctrine and technology have to be reshaped to these ends, as has been illustrated in recent wars against much weaker enemies. In another innovation, in June 2000 the Navy announced a new class of warships designed for the first time "with the ability to influence events on land," extending the earlier use of cruise missiles against land targets in Iraq, Afghanistan, and Serbia. "We recognise that as U.S. interests abroad have strengthened in a global world," Secretary of the Navy Richard Danzig explained, "then frequently we want to use military power to protect those interests, and the most obvious choice is naval power." The reversion to the days of "gunboat diplomacy" was widely deplored in the South during the Kosovo war, but the voice of most of the world has not been allowed to interfere with the triumphalism and self-adulation of Western intellectual culture.

It is important to bear in mind, however, that the main thrust of strategy must remain, as Clinton's Strategic Command (STRATCOM) determined in a study of "post-Cold War deterrence." The U.S. "deterrence statement" must be "convincing" and "immediately discernible." To rephrase in standard terminology, it is important to establish "the credibility" of the United States — sometimes called "the credibility of NATO," the primary goal of the 1999 Balkans war, if official pronouncements are to be believed. The U.S. must retain "the full range of responses," STRATCOM advised, including weapons of mass destruction. The most important of these are nuclear weapons, because "unlike chemical or biological weapons," the weapons of the weak, "the extreme destruction from a nuclear explosion is immediate, with few if any palliatives to reduce its effect." The study concluded that "we are not likely to use nuclear weapons in less than matters of the greatest national importance, or in less than extreme circumstances," which is doubtless reassuring; but nevertheless, "nuclear weapons always cast a shadow over any crisis or conflict" and must therefore be available, and visible. Furthermore, the U.S. must "maintain ambiguity": "planners should not be too rational about determining... what the opponent values the most," all of which must be targeted. "That the US may become irrational and vindictive if its vital interests are attacked should be a part of the national persona we project." It is "beneficial" for our strategic posture if "some elements may appear to be potentially 'out of control'."

These elements of doctrine and strategy had been in place long before, but they acquired a new form and significance with the effective disappearance of the Soviet deterrent in November 1989, and have considerable import for the South. During the Kosovo war, military and political analysts outside of the "international community" (as NATO describes itself) observed that the reversion to the "colonial era" under the traditional "cloak of moralistic righteousness" is "a danger to the world," and is likely to lead to efforts to develop weapons of mass destruction as a deterrent against U.S. violence. The matter receives little public attention, but Western strategic analysts have been alert to the reaction, and have issued warnings about the likely consequences.

In early 1990, when doctrine and strategy were being reshaped for the post-Cold War era, Saddam was still a friend and ally of Washington and London, which (along with others) had been eagerly providing government-financed aid that enabled him to pursue his weapons programmes and to purchase great quantities of U.S. agricultural supplies. These Saddam desperately needed, particularly after he had destroyed agricultural regions in the course of his attack on Iraqi Kurds, including the poison gas attack at Halabja in 1988 which one Iraq scholar describes as "the single most enormous massacre of civilians in one place at one time since the Nazi atrocities" (Miron Rezun). In the midst of the Panama invasion, the Bush Administration announced new U.S. credits to Saddam. The goal was to increase "U.S. exports and put us in a better position to deal with Iraq regarding its human rights record," the State Department explained, perhaps having in mind Washington's stirring reaction to the Halabja massacre. In April 1990, a senatorial delegation visited Saddam in Mosul led by Republican leader Robert Dole, later Republican presidential candidate, who conveyed President Bush's greetings. Senator Alan Simpson joined Dole in assuring Saddam that his problems lay with the media, not the U.S. government, which was seeking "better relations with Iraq," and had even removed a Voice of America commentator who had criticised Saddam.

In August 1990, Saddam conquered Kuwait, either ignoring or misunderstanding U.S. orders. Disobedience is a real crime, unlike the gassing of Kurds, the torture of dissidents, and a long record of cruelty and brutality. Accordingly, Saddam underwent the familiar shift from favoured friend to reincarnation of Attila the Hun, following the pattern of Trujillo, Somoza, Marcos, Duvalier, Noriega, Suharto a few years later, and numerous other gangsters great and small who have outlived their usefulness. And plans were set in motion for the Gulf war.

The National Security Policy Review of early 1989 was accurate in its assessment of domestic political support for the resort to force. It remained thin through 1990, despite feverish propaganda depicting Saddam as a menace of Hitlerian proportions bent on world conquest. There were many indications of the limits of indoctrination. The Gulf war was the first in recent memory when huge protest demonstrations, involving hundreds of thousands of people, were organised before the war even began. Protests over the U.S. wars in Indochina did not reach a comparable scale until several hundred thousand U.S. troops were devastating South Vietnam, five years after the Kennedy Administration had initiated the intensive bombardment of South Vietnam along with use of napalm, crop destruction, and programmes to drive millions of people into concentration camps with the official goal of "protecting them" from the indigenous enemy, whom, it was conceded, they willingly supported.

The "Vietnam syndrome" is real, though its nature is far removed from the picture preferred by educated opinion. Centres of power and privilege are quite right to be concerned over the civilising effect of the ferment of the 1960s, the "crisis of democracy" as it was called by troubled liberal internationalist elites, notably in an important study with that title. They were deeply troubled by the fact that large sectors of the public were entering the political arena to pursue their interests instead of leaving such matters to their betters, and that the institutions responsible "for the indoctrination of the young" — their term for schools, universities, and others — were failing in their task. One element of the "crisis" was the markedly increased sensitivity of the general population to aggression and other crimes of state, recognised in its own way by Bush's 1989 National Security Policy Review.

By the time the Reagan Administration entered office in 1981, it was hoped that the crisis had been overcome by the massive propaganda campaigns of the 1970s, and that the population had been returned to obedience and passivity. Reagan's planners faced problems that were not unlike those that confronted Kennedy in South Vietnam, where the U.S. client state had killed tens of thousands of people by 1960, evoking indigenous resistance that it could not control. Twenty years later, the system of state violence and repression imposed and sustained by the U.S. in most of Central America was eroding in the face of popular organising and resistance. The Reagan Administration attempted to follow the Kennedy model, but was forced to back down by unanticipated public opposition, and to turn to large-scale clandestine terror instead of bombing and outright invasion. These attempts to contain domestic opposition had only limited success. The Central America solidarity movements were far broader in scale than the protests against the Vietnam war, and much more deeply rooted in the mainstream society. They also forged new paths of resistance. To mention only one case particularly relevant here, many people went to live with the victims of the U.S. assault, not only to offer constructive help but also in the hope of reducing, by their presence, the ferocity of the assault. To my knowledge, there is no analogy in the history of imperialism to the initiatives of Witness for Peace and others, coming from "middle America," often from church circles, some conservative, some inspired by the teachings of liberation theology.

These developments lie in the immediate background of the Gulf war, and bear directly on the mission of the Gulf Peace Team.

The last national poll taken before the bombing of Iraq, on 9 January 1991, revealed again that the "crisis of democracy" was alive and flourishing. Two-thirds of the population favoured Iraqi withdrawal from Kuwait in the context of a regional conference considering the Arab-Israel conflict and other security issues, a remarkable and significant figure, much as in the case of reactions to the Vietnam war. The poll question was designed to minimise this response, stating that the President opposed the proposal; and such "linkage" had been uniformly denounced in the strongest terms by the government and media for months. One can only guess what the poll results would have been if the public had been informed that an Iraqi proposal calling for a settlement in similar terms had been released a week earlier by U.S. officials, who took it to be a "serious prenegotiation position" that "signal[s] Iraqi interest in a negotiated settlement," and that it was flatly rejected by Washington. Or if the public had been permitted to know that the Iraqi democratic opposition, and most of the world, took a similar stand. But such information was carefully withheld; not by state censorship, but by the free press, with exceptions too rare to have an impact on democratic choice.

The problem of ensuring that this "much weaker enemy" would be crushed by force had been acute since Saddam's invasion of Kuwait. Washington feared that Saddam would quickly withdraw, leaving behind a puppet regime. In a high-level meeting shortly after the invasion, the Chairman of the Joint Chiefs of Staff, Colin Powell, argued that in "the next few days Iraq will withdraw," putting "his puppet in," and "everyone in the Arab world will be happy." If so, Saddam would have duplicated what the U.S. had achieved in Panama a few months before, except that in that case the region was far from happy: the puppet regime was expelled from the Group of Eight Latin American democracies on grounds that the country was under foreign military occupation. Four years after the invasion, Panama's own Human Rights Commission charged that the right to self-determination and sovereignty of the Panamanian people continued to be violated by the "state of occupation by a foreign army."

The Administration's quandary over Iraq-Kuwait was explained by *New York Times* diplomatic correspondent Thomas Friedman on 22 August. Washington insists that the "diplomatic track" must be blocked, Friedman explained, or negotiations might "defuse the crisis" at the cost of "a few token gains" for Iraq, perhaps "a Kuwaiti island or minor border adjustments." The "Kuwaiti island" would have been two uninhabited mudflats that had been assigned to Kuwait in the imperial settlement, leaving Iraq landlocked; the "minor border adjustments" presumably had to do with the Rumailah oil field, about 95% in Iraq, extending two miles into Kuwait over an unsettled border, and long a bone of contention.

From August 1990, information was being leaked from Washington about possibilities for diplomatic settlement. I know of only one newspaper that published the information, regularly and prominently: the suburban New York daily *Newsday*, which appears on every newstand in New

York, so that it took effort for the rest of the media to miss the opportunities that were being blocked by Administration planners who were bent on war to punish their lapsed associate and to demonstrate Washington's "credibility" to others who might be tempted to stray.

In late August 1990, front-page headlines in *Newsday* revealed that a proposal had been offered by Iraq in much the terms described by Friedman, and had been dismissed by the Administration. The Iraqi proposal, regarded as "serious" and "negotiable" by a State Department Mideast expert, called for Iraqi withdrawal from Kuwait in exchange for access to the Gulf (the two mudflats) and Iraqi control of the Rumailah oil field. The proposal reached Washington on 9 August, one week after the invasion, and was brought the next day to the National Security Council, which rejected it as "already moving against policy," according to the retired Army officer who arranged the meeting. Others, including former CIA chief Richard Helms, attempted to carry the initiative further, but got nowhere. "There was nothing in this [peace initiative] that interested the U.S. government," Helms said. A congressional summary, with an input from intelligence, concluded that a diplomatic solution might have been possible at that time. What the likelihood was we will never know, but we do know that such possibilities were kept far from the public eye, with the most marginal of exceptions.

With the war drums beating ever more furiously, the Gulf Peace Team assembled from many corners of the world. Its highest immediate goal, one participant explains, was "to prevent the outbreak of war by opposing it nonviolently *in situ* — that is, by interposing ourselves as a nonviolent human barrier between the two opposing forces" (Pat Arrowsmith). That goal was acknowledged to be far beyond reach, but a lesser one was not: to serve "as a catalyst, prompting more strenuous opposition to the war" at home (Arrowsmith). The lesser goal was realistic, as the state of public opinion indicates.

Success in achieving this goal requires, of course, a significant response in far wider circles. The degree of success cannot really be evaluated within the narrow context of the decisive and rapid demolition of a much weaker enemy in January-February 1991. The relevant context is much broader. It is indicated, appropriately, in the final words of this collection, which express the hope that the Gulf Peace Team has made a contribution to "the ongoing evolution of a more peaceful planet."

There have been many opportunities to test that hope since, not least with regard to Iraq. In March 1991, Saddam quickly reverted from Hitlerian monster to tacit ally as he was authorised to crush a Shi'ite rebellion in the South under the gaze of General Schwartzkopf, who permitted Saddam to use helicopter gunships and denied the request of rebelling Iraqi generals for access to captured arms. Washington adopted the same stance as Saddam moved to the north to crush a Kurdish rebellion, though in that case domestic and international pressure compelled Washington to make some moves to limit the slaughter. The reasons for the renewed support for Saddam were frankly explained. *New York Times* Middle East correspondent Alan Cowell attributed the failure of the rebels to the fact that "very few people outside Iraq wanted them to win;" the concept "people" refers to "people who count," not those who were appalled by Washington's reaction. The "allied campaign against President Hussein brought the United States and its Arab coalition partners to a strikingly unanimous view," Cowell continued: "whatever the sins of the Iraqi leader, he offered the West and the region a better hope for his country's stability than did those who have suffered his repression."

"Stability" is another code word, like "deterrence" and "credibility." A region is "stable" in the doctrinal sense not because it is stable, but if it is properly integrated into the U.S.-dominated world system. In the case of Iraq, *Times* diplomatic correspondent Thomas Friedman reflected, Saddam's "iron fist" had "held Iraq together, much to the satisfaction of the American allies Turkey and Saudi Arabia," not to speak of the boss in Washington, who had no serious objections to the means employed. In the post-war period, it was hoped, "if Iraqi society suffers sufficient pain, Iraqi generals may topple Mr. Hussein"; not, however, Iraqi generals who are leading a Shi'ite rebellion that might lead to Iranian influence in the region. If the right kind of generals appear on the scene, "then Washington would have the best of all worlds: an iron-fisted Iraqi junta without Saddam Hussein," restoring the "stability" that had been lost when the former guardian of order made his first serious error.

To be sure, Washington's "best of all worlds" is not quite that of the people of Iraq or of the region, as Iraqi dissidents were at pains to point out, eloquently and forcefully. But they were silenced. The State Department had banned contacts with the democratic opposition after the Halabja massacre, leaders of the democratic opposition report, so as not to irritate its friend Saddam; the ban was officially renewed in March 1991 as Saddam moved to restore "stability." They were virtually banned from the media as well, as they had been throughout the Gulf war and the critical period before it, because of their unwelcome message of opposition to a war that would destroy their despised enemy, but Iraqi society along with him.

The U.S. and Britain then turned to a harsh sanctions regime under the cover of the UN Security Council (which, as generally acknowledged, would not maintain it without their insistence), punctuated by occasional acts to demonstrate "credibility," as when Clinton launched cruise missiles at Baghdad soon after coming into office. Eight civilians were killed when missiles hit a residential area, among them the well-known artist Layla al-Attar and a man found with his baby son in his arms. The attack conformed to international law, Ambassador Madeleine Albright explained to the UN Security Council, falling under Article 51 of the Charter, which permits "self-defence against armed attack" until the Security Council responds; in this case, "self-defence" against an alleged Iraqi attempt to assassinate ex-President Bush two months before (for which Washington had no serious evidence, it conceded). The national press assured the nation's elites that the facts of this case "plainly fit" Article 51; after all, "Any President has a duty to use military force to protect the nation's interests" (*Washington Post, New York Times*).

There is no need to review the impact of the sanctions, which "may well have been a necessary [sic] cause of the deaths of more people in Iraq than have been slain by all so-called weapons of mass destruction throughout history," two hawkish military specialists observe in *Foreign Affairs* (John Mueller and Karl Mueller). Combined with the attack on civilian infrastructure during the war — in effect, a form of chemical and biological warfare — the consequences of the sanctions have been "genocidal," in the judgement of the humanitarian coordinator for the UN in Iraq, Denis Halliday, who resigned in protest, as did his successor Hans von Sponeck, and two days later, Jutta Burghardt, head of the World Food Programme in Iraq. After touring Iraq with Halliday and seeking "an independent assessment from some of the 550 UN people, who are Iraq's lifeline," John Pilger reports: "Among them, Halliday and von Sponeck are heroes. I have reported the UN at work in many countries; I have never known such dissent and anger, directed at the manipulation of the Security Council, and the corruption of what some of them still refer to as the UN 'ideal'"

As widely acknowledged, the sanctions have strengthened Saddam

Hussein. Meanwhile, "a once prosperous nation is being driven into the pre-industrial Dark Ages," British correspondent David Sharrock writes, confirming the judgement of others, which is not seriously disputed, though the U.S. and British authorities deny his conclusion that it is a "monstrous social experiment." Denis Halliday, who knows Iraq as well as any Westerner, observes further that "Iraq's younger generation of professionals, the political leadership of the future — bitter, angry, isolated, and dangerously alienated from the world — is maturing in an environment not dissimilar to that found in Germany under the conditions set by the Versailles Treaty," condemning Saddam as too "moderate" and likely to follow "the path of the Taliban and the fundamentalist right," in a climate of "death and despair," humiliation and anger.

In December 1998, the U.S. and Britain bombed Baghdad in defiance of the United Nations, signalling their contempt by sending the bombers just as the Security Council was meeting in an Emergency Session to deal with the problem of Iraq. The actions were undertaken in the certain knowledge that it would terminate the UN inspections system that had been far more successful in destroying Iraqi weapons capability than the war and subsequent bombing; what was left of the inspections system, that is, after it had been subverted by the U.S. by using it as a cover for spying. At the same time, Secretary of State Albright announced that "we have come to the determination" — in December 1998 — "that the Iraqi people would benefit if they had a government that really represented them." Since then, Iraq has been subjected to regular air attacks, killing hundreds of civilians, leaving "a lethal litter [of unexploded ordnance] that could claim civilian casualties for years," *Washington Post* correspondent Edward Cody reports from the scene. The official justification is that the bombing, from very high altitude to avoid air force casualties (while increasing "collateral damage"), is intended to suppress Iraqi air defences. But "the Clinton Administration also sees them as a tool to contain and degrade the Iraqi military, humiliating Saddam Hussein and perhaps generate opposition to his rule," Cody reports, though it is recognised that they are more likely to have the opposite effect, much like the harsh sanctions.

The official reasons for the sanctions have remained stable, and are regularly cited in mainstream commentary with approval, even some passion. They were reiterated in March 2000 in UN Security Council debate by Peter van Walsum, the Dutch representative and chairman of the committee on sanctions against Iraq:

> Iraq is the only country in modern history that has not
> only attempted to develop all categories of weapons of
> mass destruction — nuclear, biological and chemical —
> but has actually used such weapons, both against a for-
> eign enemy and against its own citizens. In doing so,
> Iraq has placed itself in a league of its own.

The statement is accurate, but incomplete. Missing are a few rather important words: Iraq committed these crimes with the support and assistance of the righteous avengers, who therefore belong in the same league. It also follows at once that these terrible crimes cannot conceivably be the reason for the sanctions imposed by the U.S. and U.K. (via a reluctant Security Council).

The moral cowardice of the omission is startling, another mark of shame for a compliant intellectual culture. One must seek explanations for the sanctions elsewhere: largely, I believe, under the broad concept of "credibility," construed in its doctrinal sense.

It may be recalled that in the 1980s, during the period of Saddam's gravest crimes, Iraq posed a far more serious military threat than today or for the foreseeable future, though it should also be recalled that even with the support of the West and the Soviet bloc, it was unable to defeat Iran, which had severely weakened its officer corps and military forces after the Khomeini revolution. The U.S. was compelled to come to Saddam's aid by direct participation. It was Washington's decisive support for Saddam that convinced Iran to capitulate to "Baghdad and Washington," Dilip Hiro concludes in his history of the Iran-Iraq war. The two allies had "co-ordinate[d] their military operations against Teheran." The shooting down of an Iranian civilian airliner by the U.S. guided-missile cruiser *Vincennes* was the final blow, the culmination of Washington's "diplomatic, military and economic campaign" in support of Saddam, Hiro writes. Washington's support for Saddam reached so far as to tolerate an Iraqi attack on a U.S. destroyer, killing 37 personnel. Only Israel had previously been accorded such latitude, in 1967.

Destruction of a prospering society in the world's second largest oil producer should be of little concern to the West. The optimal oil producer, after all, is one that does not waste profits on domestic development instead of directing them to Western energy corporations, U.S. treasury certificates, and Western weapons manufacturers. In their day in the sun, internal documents reveal, the British sought to arrange for the Arab oil producers to be managed by an "Arab facade" of weak and pliable governments, while Britain ruled in the background behind various "constitutional fictions." The conception did not change materially as the U.S. took charge after World War II. Iraq's military coup in 1958 was the first serious break in this system, arousing serious concern in Washington and London. Kuwait was granted nominal independence to prevent the spread of independent nationalism, though with a secret British decision "ruthlessly to intervene, whoever it is has caused the trouble," if Britain's effective rule were threatened. Washington acquiesced, assuming the same rights in the richer oil producing regions nearby. Formal takeover of oil production by Saudi Arabia and the Gulf emirates left the basic structure of the system more or less intact, though not without potential conflict.

Sooner or later, Iraq will be restored to the system, but only when the U.S. and its British junior partner decide to allow it, presumably after ensuring that they will once again have the inside track, displacing France and Russia. A prediction as to when that day will come was offered by James Akins, former U.S. Ambassador to Saudi Arabia, who has long experience in the region with the State Department and the oil industry. Asked about U.S. policy towards Iraq after the Clinton-Blair bombing in December 1998, he quipped that when the price of oil reaches $30 a barrel, "we will then discover that Saddam is not the new Hitler — but the new Mother Teresa." As the price of oil reached that level a year later, Washington initiated a Security Council Resolution to permit Iraq to import $1.2 billion to reconstruct its half-destroyed oil industry. The reason was "so that more oil can be pumped efficiently and safely to pay for civilian goods and public service projects," *New York Times* UN correspondent Barbara Crossette reported; the immediate effect, however, was to warn Gulf oil producers to produce more oil to lower the price to a range that Washington considers acceptable.

The conjunction was so hard to miss that it was necessary to issue denials. "Western diplomats said there was no direct connection" between the move to upgrade Iraq's oil industry and pressure on "other oil-producing states to raise output," Crossette reported, "because upgrading Iraq's oil industry has been an issue for many months." Not overly compelling.

Crossette also reported Iraq's position that even with added money, "it cannot upgrade its oil industry effectively as long as the United States and, to a lesser extent, Britain, block critical contracts for spare parts or related oil equipment in the Security Council sanctions committee." The punishing iron grip remains, while the Gulf producers receive the message. Saudi Arabia quickly announced a significant increase in production, violating an OPEC decision; price per barrel fell sharply.

And the grip is intended to punish. Chlorine for purifying water is banned, John Pilger reports; one effect is that "in 1990, an Iraqi infant with dysentery stood a one in 600 chance of dying. This is now one in 50." Vaccines to protect children against diphtheria and yellow fever were banned "because they are capable of being used in weapons of mass destruction," a Minister of the British government explained, stoutly upholding New Labour's "ethical foreign policy." The U.S. and U.K. governments claim that medicines are available but withheld by Saddam. "If Saddam Hussein believed he could draw an advantage from obstructing humanitarian aid, he would no doubt do so," Pilger observes. But von Sponeck, who ran the Oil for Food program until his resignation in protest, says that "The goods that come into this country are distributed to where they belong. Our most recent stock analysis shows that 88.8% of all humanitarian supplies have been distributed." His observation is confirmed by representatives of UNICEF, the World Food Programme, and the Food and Agricultural Organisation, which also reported that Iraq's rationing system "provides basic foods at 1990 prices, which means they are now virtually free," a "life-saving nutritional benefit [that] has prevented catastrophe for the Iraqi people."

More than half the people in the world are subject to unilateral U.S. sanctions, even without including UN sanctions under U.S. pressure, as in the case of Iraq. In some cases the sanctions are cruel and vindictive, without any remotely credible motive, notably the case of Cuba, where even food and medicine have been barred. Washington has made it clear that it will keep the stranglehold on Cuba's economy as long as it chooses, unconcerned by the severe human costs and the overwhelming international opposition that reaches as far as judgements by the normally compliant Organization of American States that the sanctions violate international law.

In 1997, the UN General Assembly condemned "unilateral coercive economic measures against developing countries that were not authorised by relevant organs of the UN or were inconsistent with the principles of international law,... and that contravened the basic principles of the multilateral trading system." Two years later, the UN Commission on Human Rights added its condemnation. The European Union as well condemned "unilateral coercive economic measures that violate international law." In response, the U.S. agreed that multilateral sanctions are preferable, but reserved for itself the right "to act unilaterally if important national interests or core values are at issue," as in the punishment of the people of Cuba for refusing to bend to Washington's will. The U.S. also made it clear that it would disregard World Trade Organization rulings in the case of Cuba if the EU persisted in seeking them.

In April 2000, the South Summit, accounting for 80% of the world's population, met in Havana in an unusually important meeting, the first meeting of G77 (now 133 nations) at the level of heads of state. It issued a Declaration stating that:

> We firmly reject the imposition of laws and regulations with extraterritorial impact and all other forms of coercive economic measures, including unilateral sanctions against developing countries, and reiterate the urgent need to eliminate them immediately. We emphasise that such actions not only undermine the principles enshrined in the Charter of the United Nations and international law, but also severely threaten the freedom of trade and investment. We therefore call on the international community neither to recognise these measures nor apply them.

The Declaration, taking strong stands in opposition to U.S. policy in many other crucial respects, received no mainstream coverage in the United States, as is the norm.

When he resigned from his position as UN Humanitarian Coordinator for Iraq in February 2000, Hans von Sponeck asked "how long [can] the civilian population be exposed to such punishment for something that they have never done?" The answer is: as long as we allow it to happen, either by direct support or silent acquiescence. The answer to this question will also provide a partial, but significant, response to the hope of the Gulf Peace Team that their efforts have contributed to "the ongoing evolution of a more peaceful planet."

The Enemy is a Friend

The immediate object of nonviolent interposition is to make it more difficult for the soldier to kill, for the politician to give the order to kill, and for the public to support or allow the killing. War is possible due largely to the dehumanising of the act of killing. Soldiers and the public are distanced from the people they are killing. They are told that they are "eliminating targets" or "undertaking an operation", or "fulfilling a mission". In closer combat where "the enemies" are visible, they are perceived as threatening, evil or subhuman. In the Gulf crisis, the Iraqis were classed together as being a singular evil person, Saddam Hussein, rather than the multitude of individuals they are. The killing was perceived as "kicking Saddam's arse."
If the soldiers, the politicians and the public instead perceived that they were killing fellow human beings; people who are intelligent, loving, scared, caring and brave like us, people who share pain and joy, poetry and music like us, it would be much more difficult to kill, for it would be like killing their own kind, which is what it is. What's more, if there develops a relationship between those of opposing sides, it would be even more difficult to kill, because that would then be like killing their own friends and family.

Alyn Ware

Introduction

Introduction

Bela Bhatia and Jean Drèze

"It is reported that two kingdoms were on the verge of war for the possession of a certain embankment which was disputed by them." Thus begins one account of an early act of nonviolent interposition, by Gautama Buddha in the sixth century B.C.[1] Buddha is said to have prevented the war by placing himself between the standing armies and pacifying their leaders. There have been many other events of this kind over the centuries – most recently in 1990-1, when a similar dispute "for the possession of a certain embankment" led hundreds of peace-minded people from around the world to unite in another attempt at nonviolent interposition. This one took the form of setting up an international peace camp on the border between Iraq and Saudi Arabia, between the opposing armies, shortly before the Gulf war began.

Unlike Buddha, the Gulf Peace Team did not succeed in its basic purpose of preventing a war. Yet it did achieve much that is worthwhile, and even in what it did *not* achieve, this experience is full of interesting lessons for the future. That is why we have thought it useful to present in this book a candid account of the team's travails.

The book is divided into four parts. Part one (*The Peace Camp*) is the story of the peace camp, as seen through the diaries and notes of members of the Gulf Peace Team. The second part (*The War and After*) consists of first-hand testimonies on the impact of war and sanctions on the people of Iraq. Part three (*Viewpoints*) presents some reflective comments on the work of the Gulf Peace Team and the future of nonviolent interposition. The fourth part (*In Memoriam*) is a short tribute to three deceased members of the team. We shall return to the content of the book at the end of this introduction, but before that, a brief overview of the work of the Gulf Peace Team is in order.

Early Days of the Gulf Peace Team

First Steps

Futile attempts have been made to identify the "date of birth" of the Gulf Peace Team. In fact, the project evolved gradually, as part of an or-

---

[1] Paul Carus (1894), *The Gospel of Buddha* (Open Court Publishing, reprinted 1990), p.197.

ganic process of search for an adequate response to war preparations in the Gulf. This process spanned many countries, though much of the early action took place in Britain, with peace groups in other countries ultimately rallying behind the British proposal of a peace camp on the Iraq-Saudi border.

The roots of the Gulf Peace Team go back to other actions that had occurred previously in relation to the "Gulf crisis". As early as 2 August 1990, when Iraq invaded Kuwait, some members of the future Gulf Peace Team were arrested in London for nonviolent protests at the Iraqi Embassy. Limited as it was, this action has some political significance as an early expression of our opposition to the invasion of Kuwait, considering that the Gulf Peace Team has sometimes been accused of "siding" with the Iraqi government.

The following months were a period of intensive military build-up in the Gulf and growing momentum towards war. In contrast, efforts to oppose the war looked relatively feeble. It is worth remembering that those were days of widespread fear that the approaching war might escalate beyond control, perhaps even all the way to nuclear war. Against this background, the response of mainstream peace organisations (e.g. sporadic demonstrations and vigils) appeared rather inadequate. In London, for instance, these organisations barely managed to sustain a weekly one-hour vigil at Trafalgar Square. In Britain and elsewhere, committed peace activists were searching for a more radical response. Many of the proposals that were floated at that time involved going to the war zone, e.g. to take the place of Saddam Hussein's then hostages, form human shields against possible bombings, incite Iraqi soldiers in Kuwait to desertion, or engage in various forms of nonviolent interposition. Many of these proposals stretched the limits of credibility, but a few did see the light of day.

In London, this search crystallised around the idea of a nonviolent presence in or near the war zone. On 1 October 1990, a meeting convened by Pat Arrowsmith and David Polden led to the following letter being sent to various dailies for publication:[2]

---

[2] The signatories were Pat Arrowsmith, Mark Chapman, Richard Crump, Jean Drèze, Tishi Kohli, Milan Rai and John Steel. The office of the Peace Pledge Union in London was given as a contact address.

We are a group of people seriously concerned at the prospect of war in the Gulf. We wish to act for peace by going to the conflict area and setting up a peace camp there or having some other form of non-violent presence. By doing so we hope to make a small contribution to the worldwide efforts of ordinary people to prevent war. We should like to hear immediately from anyone willing to support or join this project.

The letter was published (with minor editorial changes) in *The Guardian* on 15 October. It evoked a good response, and from then on, regular meetings were held to pursue this plan under the banner of the "Gulf Peace Team"

The problem remained that we did not have the faintest idea as to how to translate the idea of a nonviolent presence in the war zone into reality. Looking back at the minutes of some of these early meetings, one does not know what to make of proposals to (say) ride camels to the frontline through the Saudi desert, or row across to Kuwait from Abadan. Initially, the idea of going to Iraq with the permission of the Iraqi government had been ruled out, to avoid manipulation.

The next spell of progress occurred in the context of a brief and uncomfortable association with Yusuf Islam (formerly Cat Stevens). Yusuf had been working on a related project, which involved sending thousands of unarmed "peace guards" to Kuwait.[3] He contacted us after seeing our letter in *The Guardian*, and expressed interest in supporting our efforts to set up a peace camp in or near the conflict zone. Yusuf came across as a peace-minded person, and the prestige he enjoyed in the Muslim world promised to be a major asset for the project. But there were fundamental incompatibilities between Yusuf Islam and the Gulf Peace Team, which threatened to sink the whole project. As it turned out, Yusuf withdrew after a little while for his own reasons (to this day we remember him as something of an enigma). Meanwhile, this brief association had raised the public profile of the Gulf Peace Team and also opened many new doors. The possi-

---

[3] According to our notes, the proposed role of the peace guards was not only to prevent further violence but also to facilitate a peaceful withdrawal of Iraq from Kuwait.

bility emerged, in particular, of negotiating an acceptable agreement with the Iraqi government for setting up a peace camp on the border between Iraq and Saudi Arabia.

Two clarifications are due. First, we wanted a camp on *both* sides of the border, and accordingly, a similar agreement was sought with Saudi Arabia. Our appeals to the Saudi government, however, fell on deaf ears. Second, we did not want to be on the border between *Kuwait* (as opposed to Iraq) and Saudi Arabia, even though that might have seemed closer to the objective of "interposition between the standing armies". This is because interposition on the Kuwait-Saudi border would have looked like an attempt to protect the Iraqi take-over of Kuwait. Our wish was to be as close as possible to Kuwait on the Iraq-Saudi border, preferably in the "no person's land" separating the two countries.

The London Days

Our contacts with the Iraqi government were aimed at securing not only the permission to set up a peace camp but also some specific assurances of transparency and independence. The ambassador of Iraq in London was very encouraging and responsive, but it soon became clear that the required assurances could be obtained only in Baghdad. Preparations were made to send a delegation there.

Meanwhile, the Gulf Peace Team consolidated itself, more as a network than as a well-defined organisation. The cornerstone of this network was the Gulf Peace Team's "policy statement" (see below), written on 8 November 1990 and endorsed in due course by a large number of personalities worldwide, from Noam Chomsky to Mother Teresa. This statement clarified the team's intention to "withstand non-violently any armed aggression by any party to the present Gulf dispute", and also affirmed its independence from all the parties to the conflict, none of whom were considered blameless. Based on this statement, like-minded peace activists who had been thinking along similar lines in other countries (especially Australia, Canada, Germany, Italy, the Netherlands and the United States – and later on India and Japan as well) established "branches" of the Gulf Peace Team world-wide in the following weeks, and started mobilising volunteers for the future peace camp. The response was very encouraging in many countries. It is another matter that only a minority of persons who had expressed interest in joining the camp eventually reached it.

> ### The Gulf Peace Team's "Policy Statement"
>
> *We are an international multi-cultural team working for peace and opposing any form of armed aggression, past, present or future, by any party in the Gulf. We are going to the area with the aim of setting up one or more international peace camps between the opposing armed forces. Our object will be to withstand non-violently any armed aggression by any party to the present Gulf dispute.*
>
> *We aim to have peace camps on both sides of the frontier in the war zone and have accordingly made representations to the Saudi, Iraqi and Kuwaiti authorities.*
>
> *We as a team do not take sides in this dispute and we distance ourselves from all the parties involved, none of whom we consider blameless. As peace-minded people, we deplore any human rights violations that have already occurred in the area and urge that they cease forthwith.*
>
> *We recognise the intense suffering, death and environmental devastation that would occur in the area (and beyond) were the war to escalate, and we consider any non-violent action to prevent such a catastrophe to be of paramount importance.*
>
> *The Gulf Peace Team is an entirely independent body of individuals sponsored by no organisation and looking for support from any source provided no political strings are attached.*

Central to this whole effort was the London base of the Gulf Peace Team, consisting of a "coordinating committee" as well as a small office ably coordinated by Ginnie Landon, initially with Mohamed Sidek Ahmad (who belonged to Muslim Aid, headed by Yusuf Islam). Later on, tensions developed between the London office and the peace camp, because the former felt responsible for the latter while the peace camp felt no need for external directives. "On the ground" (in Baghdad, at the peace camp, and later in Amman), the Gulf Peace Team volunteers took their own decisions and paid little attention to the London "HQ", but the latter did play a crucial supporting role throughout and deserves much credit for it.

On 12 November 1990, there was a stormy meeting with Yusuf Islam, which ushered the decline of our association with him.[4] This is an instruc-

---

[4] At one point during this meeting, Yusuf called Richard Branson and asked him whether he would charter a plane to Amman for Gulf Peace Team volunteers, free of charge. Branson politely declined. We mention this anecdote as an example of the dreamland atmosphere in which much of this initial work took place. Few of us believed in our heart of hearts that the peace camp would ever see the light of day.

tive but murky episode, a detailed account of which is beyond the scope of this introduction. Briefly, a gulf emerged between us on the question of what volunteers at the peace camp should do in the event where war did break out. Yusuf argued that they had a right, indeed a duty, to defend themselves, but others felt that this was incompatible with our "policy statement" as well as with the spirit of the project. To his credit, Yusuf remained forthright and constructive in his dealings with the Gulf Peace Team even after fundamental differences had emerged. The end of our association had one major drawback: Muslim involvement in the Gulf Peace Team has been much smaller than it might have been otherwise.

On 16 November 1990, an "advance party" of seven was despatched to Baghdad. Its mission was (1) to agree on a "protocol" for the peace camp with the Government of Iraq, (2) to find a suitable site, and (3) to position a few volunteers at the site (to remain there until other volunteers joined them).

The Advance Party

In Baghdad, the advance party's negotiations focused on three crucial demands. First, we wanted our "policy statement" to be published in the Iraqi press. Second, the peace camp had to be on the Iraq-Saudi border (or at least very close to the border, ahead of the Iraqi army). Third, we wanted assurances of autonomy and independence, both in terms of the internal management of the camp and in terms of logistics. Initially, these demands were conveyed to the Iraqi government in a series of meetings at successively higher layers of the hierarchy. This was followed by a frustrating period of silence, during which various alternatives were considered, some of them rather unrealistic (e.g. a unilateral march towards the border).

During this period the advance party, like all foreign delegations, was the guest of the Organisation for Friendship, Peace and Solidarity (OFPS). This involved staying at the OFPS-run "peace village" in Baghdad, not to be confused with the border peace camp. The OFPS was, of course, a wing of the Iraqi government, and it operated within the framework of official policy and ideology. Yet it also appeared to have some degree of independence. Our relations with OFPS officials were very cordial, and it is possible that their sympathetic understanding of our project had an influence on the way the Iraqi government dealt with it. The Iraqi government's handling of the Gulf Peace Team has been surprisingly forthright on the whole, and one would like to think that this was not just shrewd calculation on its part.

Finally, on 6 December 1990, we were informed that the Gulf Peace Team would be allowed to set up a peace camp at the Iraq-Saudi border near Judayyidat Ar'ar, on a compound normally used as a resting place for pilgrims on their way to Mecca. The location of this site appeared to meet our requirements. Our policy statement was also published in the Iraqi press, and though the editors dropped a few sensitive words, enough remained to give the Iraqi people an accurate idea of what the Gulf Peace Team stood for. As for our demand of autonomy and independence, it was only partially met. The Iraqi government did not interfere with the internal management of the peace camp, but we had to make compromises on the question of logistic self-sufficiency. We shall return to this point below.

The peace camp was set up on 24 December 1990, with an initial contingent of 25 volunteers or so. These included not only the advance party, but also other peace activists who had come to Baghdad on similar missions and had decided to support the peace camp. From then on, the size of the camp grew rapidly: within three weeks, 85 volunteers had joined the camp from all over the world. We were very hopeful, in those days, that the camp would live to attract hundreds more over the following weeks or months, and perhaps become a significant factor in the politics of the Gulf crisis. As the 15 January "deadline" approached, however, it became clear that war was imminent. A few volunteers left the camp before Iraq's borders were sealed, preferring to use their experience in Iraq for more effective campaigning at home. Seventy-three others decided to stay and put nonviolent interposition into practice.

The Peace Camp

We have dwelt on the "early days" of the Gulf Peace Team because that part of the team's history is not so well known, even among those who joined the peace camp. What happened from then on is clearer, and is narrated from different perspectives in various chapters of this book. The following account is relatively brief, and interested readers are referred to the rest of the book for further details.

Calm Before the Storm

The peace camp was situated on a large compound (about 400 metres long and 200 metres wide) adjacent to the Iraqi border post on the road to Mecca. We were not quite in the "no person's land" between the borders, as we would have wished, but we were certainly between the opposing armies.

A small contingent of Iraqi soldiers occupied the border post (civilians had left the area). They rarely entered the camp, and were not encouraged to do so, but one or two of them always stood guard at the entrance, much to our irritation.[5] A liaison officer ("minder") of the Organisation for Friendship, Peace and Solidarity stayed nearby and visited us from time to time, though his visits were discrete and unobtrusive. The compound included a few basic structures: corrugated iron roofs under which we pitched large tents, an empty shed soon turned into a kitchen, and simple toilets and showers. We cooked our food (bought mainly in Kerbala) using portable gas stoves and an improvised oven.

Glimpses of life at the peace camp *before* the outbreak of war can be found in some of the diaries in Part I of this book. Many of us have fond memories of those early days, despite the physical discomfort (especially the blistering cold). As Hasan Kilgour puts it, this was a time when "camp life had settled into a gentle routine". The atmosphere at the camp was very "peaceful", not only in terms of interpersonal relations, but also in the sense that most of us appeared to feel an unusual inner peace. Speaking for ourselves, this serenity arose from a feeling that we had reached our destination, and that the rest was not in our hands. Whatever the dangers involved, it was right to be there. Also, because what needed to be done had been done, it remained for us to focus on refreshingly simple activities such as cooking, cleaning, singing, making banners, and holding amicable group discussions. One reason for highlighting this early harmony is that the tensions and animosities that developed later on (after the war started) command much more attention in this book. Here again, it is worth noting that things might have turned out quite differently had the peace camp been allowed to find its feet over an extended period, instead of being quickly disrupted by the outbreak of war.

On 12 January, we were informed that our last chance had come to leave Iraq before the country's borders were sealed. A few volunteers departed, the rest decided to stay. The "stay" group took this opportunity to send a press release to Baghdad, explaining this decision. Appended to the press release was a series of "personal statements" clarifying our reasons for not leaving the camp; a sample of these statements is reproduced below, to give the reader an idea of the diverse motivations of Gulf Peace Team volunteers.

---

[5] To be fair to them, camp members could hardly be allowed to wander around the surrounding area as parts of it were mined.

Personal Statements
of Gulf Peace Team Volunteers

On 12 January 1991, as Iraq's borders were about to be sealed, the Gulf Peace Team issued a press release clarifying its intention to continue camping at the border. A sample of the "personal statements" attached to this press release is reproduced below.

"My physical presence here on the Iraqi/Saudi border is a statement of my refusal to accept war without resisting in every way possible for me." (Jerry Smith)

"I will not sit idly by and be a guilty spectator of this gross act of humiliation and degradation. By resisting this war I refuse to be humiliated and degraded." (Steve Blair)

"I will remain at the Gulf Peace Camp and will choose not to be evacuated because I am a Christian and pacifist and want my life to declare as clearly as possible: "NO WAR - NO DEATH." (Kathy Boylan)*

"This hostility will not be done in my name, I will oppose it with every non-violent means." (Bob Bossie)

"I hope to remain in solidarity with the first victims of war, the children and their mothers cannot leave the combat zone." (Anne Montgomery)

"We must end as a culture the dehumanising attitude which is prevalent, and realise that all humans everywhere experience joy and suffering on a par with each of us. Peace and understanding is the answer." (Michael Crouse)

"It is my intention to non-violently resist evacuation from the peace camp should this be attempted, using the Gandhian spirit of satyagaraha (literally "firmly grasping the truth") to pit unarmed against the armed might of injustice and oppression inherent in the Gulf crisis on all sides." (Mark Chapman)

"Called by the spirit to face ourselves with countless brothers and sisters who have no choice, between opposing armies, we offer a sign of a world free from a war giving death, destruction, suffering and injustice. As pilgrims we choose a new way, that of love, hope, faith and reason." (Jerry Hartigan)

"I believe the time will come when all the world will see war solves nothing. By remaining at the camp I hope to reduce that time." (Clifford Twiddy)

"As a Christian I am committed to peace, reconciliation and dialogue. Experience in South Africa, Vietnam and Molesworth has helped me to make the decision to be on the border between the two opposing armies." (Peggie Preston)

"If my country contemplates or goes to war I am at least partially responsible. Therefore I feel I must do all I can to either support or oppose my country's decision. This is part of my reason for coming to the peace camp and why I must stay

> *even if the war does commence. Together we can create peace, love and hope." (Kevin Hemsley)*
>
> *"Surely no one need question why people should risk their lives, as we possibly are, in order to prevent the deaths of many others, especially children. What I question is why soldiers are prepared to risk their lives in order to kill strangers." (Jimmy Johns)*
>
> *"I refuse to be evacuated. I do not wish to endanger anyone." (Kharun Khan)*
>
> *"Having been among those people on whom our missiles and bombs are targeted I feel I must stay here. I believe that if all those who advocate the war could be here there would be no war." (Sylvia Boyce)*
>
> *"War is insane, useless, cruel and above all iniquitous. If we approve of war it means we are brutalised, dehumanised - no longer human beings." (Jenny Hales)*

Nonviolent Interposition

Around 3.00 a.m. on 17 January, we woke up to the ominous sound of hundreds of bombers flying north. Soon we heard distant explosions, and saw huge red flashes on the horizon. Unreal as it all seemed, we had to accept the dismal truth: the Gulf war had started, right there, in front of us.

The days that followed were a difficult period for the peace camp. We had virtually no contact with the outside world (except for the visit of an OFPS emissary on 22 January). Most of our time was spent in endless "meetings" about our new predicament. Irreconcilable differences emerged, especially on two related issues: whether the camp should continue, and how to handle a possible "evacuation".[6] For instance, some argued that an evacuation should be resisted (nonviolently of course), others that resisting an evacuation would endanger the lives of those who had a legitimate wish to go. Byzantine arguments were spun on all sides, virtually paralysing the camp. Tempers rose, all the more so as the pangs of hunger began to make themselves felt (food was severely rationed, in anticipation of a long haul).

A week or so after the outbreak of war, things began to improve again as the camp adapted to a new physical and psychological environment. Futile discussions were shunned, decision-making procedures were improved, and energy was redeployed in more creative directions such as political education, Arabic classes and cultural activities.

---

[6] We anticipated evacuation from *either* side. Unconfirmed reports had been received that in the event of a ground assault on Iraq the camp would be forcibly evacuated by coalition forces.

The Evacuation

This revival, unfortunately, came to an abrupt end on 27 January 1991, when the camp was evacuated by the Iraqi authorities. According to Iraqi officials, we were being evacuated for our own safety. No doubt sceptical readers will smile at this touching display of concern on the part of a regime not known for its humanitarianism. Yet the chances are that this was indeed the reason for our evacuation. In cold tactical terms, the Iraqi government stood to gain from leaving the camp in place in the hope that it would be bombed (presumably by mistake), causing much embarrassment to US military commanders and boosting worldwide opposition to the war. If the camp was evacuated instead, it is likely to be due to the influence of highly-placed members of the Organisation for Friendship, Peace and Solidarity. We have every reason to believe that some of them at least had genuine sympathy for our project and felt responsible for our lives.

The final evacuation was preceded by an ill-fated act of nonviolent resistance on the part of a small group of Gulf Peace Team members who did not wish to leave the camp. This is the most controversial episode in the brief history of the Gulf Peace Team. Alternative accounts and interpretations of it can be found in the chapters that follow, especially those by Martin Thomas, Detlef Enge-Bastien, Jerry Hartigan and Jack Lomax. We leave it to the reader to form his or her opinion on this sensitive matter.

The next three days were spent in Baghdad, where we had an opportunity to witness the devastating effects of war and sanctions on the civilian population, as well as to experience coalition bombings first-hand. Some Gulf Peace Team members wished to stay in Iraq and work in hospitals, or help the victims of war in other ways. Initially, we were told that this would be possible, and instructed to prepare a list of volunteers. Two days later, however, the Iraqi government changed its mind, and informed us that everyone would have to leave immediately. Rumour has it that this U-turn was caused by the suspicious wanderings of two Gulf Peace Team members and a Russian journalist, who had made an impromptu visit to the presidential palace in Baghdad.

We were taken to the Jordanian border on 31 January. This day-long bus drive was by far the scariest episode of our sojourn in Iraq, as the road was a regular target of coalition bombings. Taxi drivers, we were told, charged US$ 5,000 (a huge amount in terms of local currency) for the journey. Pulverised trucks and other vehicles, mainly civilian, littered the side of the road. This experience later inspired the idea of escorting relief convoys to Iraq, on the assumption that our presence would give them some protection from bombings – the spirit of nonviolent interposition was alive and well.

After the War

From Amman, most Gulf Peace Team volunteers proceeded to their respective countries, where their experience in Iraq gave them rich opportunities to contribute to the peace movement and anti-sanctions campaigns. Others decided to remain as close as possible to the war zone. They formed a new base in Amman and continued working from there, with the support of Gulf Peace Team branches in various countries (mainly Britain, Canada, Australia and the United States). Humanitarian convoys soon became the main focus of this work. During the war, escorting convoys was undertaken in the spirit of nonviolent interposition, to protect them from coalition bombings. Later on, humanitarian convoys to Iraq were organised in response to the catastrophic effects of continuing sanctions on the civilian population – effects that have been aptly described as "biological warfare" and "psychological terrorism".

During this period, some ambiguity developed as to whether specific activities could be appropriately taken up under the "Gulf Peace Team" banner. The platform that united us, the "policy statement" (see p. 5), had lost its relevance, and the Gulf Peace Team had no other agreed basis as an organisation. This issue became more and more complex as Gulf Peace Team members in Amman started getting involved not only in post-war relief work in Iraq but also in activities (e.g. peace walks) related to the Israeli-Palestinian conflict. While this conflict had obvious connections with the Gulf war (and the broader issue of peace and justice in west Asia), it did not belong to the original focus of the Gulf Peace Team. Gradually, the Gulf Peace Team banner wore out and the work continued under different auspices.[7] By the end of 1991, the Gulf Peace Team had effectively ceased to exist as an organisation, though it continued to live as a network of kindred spirits.

Nonviolent Interposition in Retrospect

We now turn to some key questions arising from the Gulf Peace Team experience. Alternative assessments may be found in other parts of this

---

[7] An offshoot of the Gulf Peace Team, for instance, organised the Walk for a Peaceful Future in the Middle East (Atlit to Jerusalem) in June 1992, to mark the 25th anniversary of the Occupation.

book, especially Part III.

The Question of "Independence"

As the Gulf Peace Team's "policy statement" makes clear, independence from all parties to the conflict was paramount to the entire project. Our act of nonviolent interposition was intended as an appeal to *both sides* of the conflict. Yet the credibility of this two-sided appeal was compromised by the physical dependence of the peace camp on the Iraqi government. This was perhaps the most important limitation of the project.

As stated earlier, the initial plan was to have peace camps on both sides of the Iraq-Saudi border, but appeals for permission to set up a camp on the Saudi side did not bear fruit. So there was a single camp, on the Iraqi side. There was no access to the camp other than through Baghdad, and from Baghdad with transport (usually a bus or van) arranged by the Iraqi government. At the camp itself, despite our efforts to achieve logistic self-sufficiency, some physical dependence on the Iraqi government remained, e.g. for access to water and electricity. Further, the Iraqi government had the power to evacuate the camp at any time.

The camp's position was also far from symmetric in political terms, despite our "policy statement". The project was obviously advantageous to the Iraqi government. It can be argued that since the peace camp effectively represented an "obstacle" for one side only, we were inevitably partisan.

Needless to say, these and related arguments were handsomely used by the mainstream press in western countries to "rubbish" the Gulf Peace Team as a pawn of Saddam Hussein. They were also the subject of protracted debate at the peace camp. A sample of viewpoints on the question of independence can be found in different chapters of this book, including those authored by Martin Thomas, Pat Arrowsmith, Ulli Laubenthal, and Robert Burrowes. For our part, we see several possible responses to the accusation of effective one-sidedness. First, in the absence of any alternative, it seemed preferable to seek the best possible arrangement with the Iraqi government rather than not to have a peace camp at all. Indeed, the Iraqi government had its own reasons to respect our independence, as it did to a much larger extent than many of us had anticipated. Second, while the project was no doubt advantageous to the Iraqi government (at least initially), by the same token it gave us some potential bargaining power. This bargaining power was used to obtain the assurances we needed to proceed with the peace camp, and it might have been used again in different circumstances. The idea of sending a fact-finding team to Kuwait, for instance, was discussed at the camp, and could have been pursued had the war not started so early. Third, there was the possibility of resisting evacuation, as an affirmation of our independence from the Iraqi authorities.[8] It is precisely from that point of view that this act of resistance, however unlikely to succeed, appeared to us to have much political importance. It is another matter that our attempt to resist evacuation turned into a farce due to lack of support from the camp as a whole (and lack of unity and preparation on the part of the resisting group). Fourth, while the camp was probably a one-sided obstacle *before* the war started, it may have had some two-sided interposition value during the war itself; we shall return to this point below. Also, the peace camp came very close to being "cut off" after the war started, as roads and bridges were gradually blown to pieces by coalition bombings. Had the camp been cut off, our much-sought independence would have been finally achieved, if only at the cost of extreme physical vulnerability.

Group Processes

One recurrent theme of this book is the draining and ineffective nature of decision-making processes at the camp. Given the cultural and ideological diversity of the team, the anxieties of living in a war zone, and the nature of some of the decisions we had to face, it is not surprising that effective decision-making structures were hard to devise. Even after taking into account these special circumstances, the Gulf Peace Team did not do well in this respect. It is not clear, for instance, why seventy-three people should fail to reach an amicable agreement on whether the kitchen door should be locked at night, or why these and other simple decisions should require long plenary discussions.

The root of the problem seemed to be a contradiction between (1) insistence on highly participatory decision-making procedures such as consensus, and (2) lack of the spirit of compromise and tolerance that makes such procedures viable. It is not that most members of the Gulf Peace Team lacked this spirit – far from it. In fact, the general pattern was one of tolerance and good will, and some members had exceptional skills for facilitating meetings, resolving conflicts and promoting participation. However,

---

[8] Another possible affirmation of independence would have been to leave the prescribed compound without permission and set up an entirely self-sufficient peace camp in the wilderness of the desert. This idea was seriously considered by a small group at the peace camp. As Jack Lomax points out, however, this proposal had "almost the same degree of improbability as would any proposal to build a rocket from the rusty tanks around the camp and set up a base on the moon".

it does not take many loose cannons to rock the boat.

The practice of democracy involves a good deal of "learning by doing", and future projects of a similar inspiration will hopefully do better than the Gulf Peace Team in this respect. One condition for this is further progress in developing a democratic culture in the peace movement. As Agnes Bauerlein and others point out in this book, if we are unable to resolve conflicts peacefully and democratically among ourselves, who are we to castigate authoritarianism and violence? In addition, there may be a need for greater flexibility in decision-making procedures, taking into account the prevailing shortage of democratic spirit. Some Gulf Peace Team members considered anything short of consensus decision-making (e.g. majority voting) as a form of authoritarianism. Yet, consensus decisions give tremendous veto powers to those who are unwilling to compromise, and in that sense they sometimes end up being rather undemocratic, if not "a fascistic form of prevention from reaching decisions", as Martin Thomas notes in his diary.

On a more positive note, our decision-making processes were steadily improving towards the end of the peace camp, partly based on a "fishbowl" system whereby all important matters were first discussed in affinity groups and then resolved in a steering committee consisting of one rotating member of each group. Had the camp lasted longer, viable decision-making structures might have been achieved.

Seventy-three Flowers Bloom

The camp's 73 volunteers (45 men and 28 women from fifteen countries, aged 22 to 76) came from highly diverse backgrounds. They included a train driver, a restaurant owner, a Buddhist monk, a cartoonist, two economists, and a sprinkle of priests and nuns, to mention a few of the professions that were represented. As various contributions to this book (e.g. those of Peggie Preston and Ivy Phillips) testify, these 73 volunteers possessed an extraordinary range of talents and qualities. We remember many of them as some of the most wonderful people we have ever met.

The camp also had its share of difficult personalities. Why a project of this kind attracts more than a fair share of persons with special psychological needs is itself an interesting question. Perhaps such persons fit comfortably in the peace movement's fairly tolerant and non-conformist environment. On a more positive note, those who are already on the margin of society may find it easier to take positions of dissent, such as opposing a widely-supported war. The fact remains that several members of the Gulf Peace Team suffered from varying degrees of inner confusion or agitation. It is perhaps to the credit of the team that it gave space to such people. Yet their presence represented a heavy moral responsibility for the peace camp. It also made group processes very difficult (two examples are described in Jack Lomax's contribution to this book). An extreme case of disruptive behaviour pertained to an individual named "Baba", who developed a habit of standing aside during camp meetings and showering the audience with colourful invectives ("cockroaches" was one of his favourites). He upheld that habit at our first press conference in Amman after the Gulf war, making us a laughing stock of the world media. This was one of the lowest points of the Gulf Peace Team.

One answer to this problem, in principle, is better "screening" of volunteers prior to joining the camp. Screening and training procedures were, in fact, used in several countries, but their practical effectiveness was far from clear. Baba himself passed a long interview in London with flying colours. On the other hand, Muriel Sibley (who had a highly constructive influence at the camp and made a big impact in Canada) was nearly turned down by the US branch of the Gulf Peace Team. Screening procedures also ran the risk of undermining the democratic spirit of the project, one distinction of which was its openness to ordinary people of all backgrounds. As Jack Lomax points out in this book, "our presence at the frontier camp exploded the myth that only heroes can involve themselves in ventures such as this."

Paying for Peace

Many of the volunteers who came to the peace camp were either self-financed or supported by friends and peace groups at home. Some, notably the Indian contingent, had joined the camp with support from the Gulf Peace Team's fund-raising efforts in other countries, mainly Britain. As for the "overhead" expenses of the team (e.g. the costs of sustaining the advance party in Baghdad, setting up the camp, and providing basic amenities), they were met from four main sources. First, a few members of the Gulf Peace Team made substantial donations or loans to the organisation. Second, branches of the Gulf Peace Team in various countries raised money from the public, not only to fund their own campaigning activities but also, in some cases, to support the peace camp. Third, the Gulf Peace Team received a fair amount of help "in kind" from various sources. For instance, the Indian members of the Gulf Peace Team were repatriated without charge by Air India after the war. Finally, there was a good deal of "deficit financing", as the London office of the Gulf Peace Team accumulated debts on many fronts (e.g. to British Telecom, travel agents and various suppliers) both to finance its own activities and to support the camp. The deficit-financing approach, combined with severe financial mismanagment, led to ballooning debts, which appeared to have little chance of being repaid as the Gulf Peace Team gradually dispersed after the Gulf war. According to our records, the Gulf Peace Team in London still owed £ 27,811 to private businesses in December 1991.

The Gulf Peace Team was heavily criticised at that time for this deficit-financing approach. It looked like the team was bound to default on most of its debts, and this financial irresponsibility threatened to undermine the credibility of the entire effort. However, it is not clear how else the team could have succeeded in mounting such a major operation in a very short time (especially in the absence of much active support from established peace organisations). Here again, it is worth remembering that in late 1990 many of us anticipated the outbreak of a major war, possibly involving weapons of mass destruction. In these circumstances, the sin of deficit financing to the tune of £30,000 or so seemed relatively minor in comparison with the moral imperative of resisting the war in every possible way. While some consistency of means and ends remained important, a few short-cuts were clearly justified in light of the stakes involved.

Also, in late 1990 and early 1991 the prospects of being able to repay our debts in due course were not as bleak as they appeared a few months later, when the deficit became the object of widespread criticism. Indeed, the fund-raising efforts of the Gulf Peace Team office in London were quite successful at that time. According to John Steel's records, public donations to the Gulf Peace Team (UK) rose steadily between November 1990 and January 1991, when £ 14,500 were received from 321 donors. It is the sudden outbreak of war (much sooner than had been anticipated), followed by the early evacuation of the camp, which throttled the flow of donations and caused a large deficit. While it is easy to criticise the deficit *ex post*, the situation might have turned out quite differently had the camp lasted and grown, as we were all hoping at that time.

Last but not least, we are happy to report, ten years on, that most of the debts were eventually repaid (or dealt with through amicable settlements with the creditors), contrary to all expectations. This achievement is due to the patient efforts of John Steel, a man of exemplary honesty and optimism who continued raising funds for the Gulf Peace Team over the years. We are hoping that a similar miracle will follow the publication of this book, also made possible by deficit financing.

The Gulf Peace Team, the Media and the Public

The Gulf Peace Team received a fair amount of media coverage. The extent and nature of the media coverage, however, varied a great deal. The mainstream press mainly ignored the project, or treated it with condescension ("Peace Campers in Middle of Nowhere," *The Independent*, 4 January 1991) if not contempt ("Peaceniks Hypocrites," *The Age*, 11 January 1991). Sympathetic coverage in the mainstream press focused mainly on the more endearing members of the Gulf Peace Team, especially grandmothers (as in "Peaceful Grannies Ready for War Zone", a New Zealand headline). After the war started, mainstream media coverage became mostly hostile, as propaganda and hysteria took over.

The Gulf Peace Team received a much fairer hearing not only in the "alternative" media (e.g. peace magazines and the radical press), but also in local newspapers published in the areas of residence of members of the team. This is because the Gulf Peace Team, in such cases, was associated with a local resident, often known for his or her integrity or commitment. The fact that many readers were friends, relatives or acquaintances of the team member made it harder to misrepresent his or her motives or actions. Quite often, local press coverage was overwhelmingly sympathetic, if not to the project then at least to the person. Several members of the Gulf Peace Team had a strong influence on public perceptions of the Gulf war in their locality. In a few cases, the personal touch reached much wider. In Canada, for instance, Muriel Sibley – a mother of five with a good support group – became a celebrity of sorts.

We are not mentioning this to beat the drum of our fellow team members, but to underline the value of personal testimonies in influencing public attitudes. Gulf Peace Team members received an even more sympathetic hearing in face-to-face interactions, e.g. during speaking tours in their respective countries after they returned from Iraq. As Kathy Kelly's second contribution to this book illustrates, listening to someone who had firsthand experience of war and sanctions in Iraq is often an eye-opening experience for western citizens fed on mainstream media. The public response to these personal testimonies has been, in Kathy's and many other cases, overwhelming. As Eileen Storey, another member of the Gulf Peace Team, writes: "I welcomed every invitation to speak. Engaging in face-to-face dialogues at town meetings, with college and high school groups, I saw much more promise for the future."[9]

```
                                                                1991 01 20

     Dear Mum,

          My best wishes, love and hopes to you. How are things holding up? The
     stereotypes seem to be getting reversed here; here I am worrying about whether
     you have warm clothes and are getting enough to eat. We've heard from the
     Peace Team offices in Toronto and Vermont that no fighting had broken out in
     the vicinity of the camp; I can only hope with all my heart that this is true.
     Let me say once again how much I admire you for this. It's an inspiration for
     all of us. Everyone we know seems to be enormously impressed, and they have
     been unbelievably supportive. So far we have had two full meals and a number
     of desserts given to us by a number of people from Meeting, and of course
     the phone is ringing off the hook most of the time with messages of support
     for you from all and sundry.
          The press has not been leaving us alone, either. So far, we've had
     another Chek-6 appearance, and one on the National. We've had interviews on
     CBC radio, too. The CBC-TV interview was a little trying, I'm afraid to say.
     These national TV reporters really seem to enjoy their power, or something:
     after being helicoptered (excuse the verb) over here from Vancouver, and then
     losing their way on Durrance Rd., they insisted on staying for two hours and
     filming us eating dinner! Emmy had one moment of panic when she was talking
     about her day and school: she said casually, "Mr. Halroyd is really weird,"
     and then realized that her remark might be broadcast all over Canada. It
     wasn't, of course, and I think she was a bit disappointed.
          The protests here against the war are enormous. We had about 3000 peo-
     ple down at the Cenotaph with candles, and in Vancouver there was a march
     that blocked main roads and bridges for hours. I've heard there was a protest
     in San Francisco by 30 000.
          But of course all of our hopes and thoughts are with you. Please hurry
     home as soon as it is safe to do so - someone has to cope with the expected
     boom for Winter Creek Pottery. With all my love.
                                                                Nick

     Dear Mum,
          Hi!! Having a good time? (Ha Ha) I really miss you. A few days ago some
     reporters came and asked me some really screwy questions. I really, really,
     really, really, really, really,really love you!!!!! Emily

     Dear Muriel,
          Hi! I'm fine. I hope you are to. I miss you very. We were on T.V.
     again eating spageti. It was hard not to slurp. Suta

     Dear Mum,
          Miss you very much! So far everything is okay. Devon and I are expecting
     exams in one week. I will be giving a speech in assembly tomorrow about the
     Peace Camp. I'm feeling extremely panicky. All my teachers and friends have
     been extremely supportive and wonderful. I can't wait for you to get back. I
     love you very much and admire what you are doing. B

          (A note from Jean Hoffman: she sends her prayers to you and her respect
     for what you are doing.)
          (Marguerite and Bruce send hugs and best wishes.)
```

Letter to Muriel Sibley from her children. Gulf Peace Team members with good support groups at home were able to reach out, through them, to the public.

[9] Eileen Storey (1991), *The Victory of Grass* (New York: Aletheia School of Prayer), page 4.

Was it "Interposition"?

There are two ways of viewing nonviolent interposition. One is as an act of concrete physical interference with military action or combat preparations. Another is as a "symbolic" act, meant to inspire other forms of resistance to war elsewhere. Though different emphases can be placed on each interpretation, the two are obviously related. If there is no physical interference at all, nonviolent interposition also loses much of its symbolic value.[10] On the other hand, if nonviolent interposition is de-linked from the wider movement against war, the power of physical obstruction is greatly reduced.

This raises the question of whether the peace camp did constitute a physical obstacle to the armed forces on either side, and if so in what way. Before addressing this question it should be recalled once again that the camp was, in a sense, killed in the bud by the early outbreak of war. Had it been able to grow over several months as anticipated, perhaps reaching a strength of several hundred by (say) early March, its interposition value – both symbolic and physical – might have been much greater. Even our small contingent of seventy-three, however, may have achieved something by way of physical interposition.

Before the outbreak of war, the peace camp was clearly no obstacle to military operations on the Iraqi side, since the Iraqi government had effective control over the camp. But then there was little likelihood of hostilities being initiated from that side in any case. On the other side, the possibility that the peace camp interfered with military planning by the US-led coalition forces is remote, but it should not be completely dismissed. Given the deep aversion of the western public to war casualties among its own citizens, it is hard to believe that military planners could have been indifferent to the prospect of overrunning the peace camp. This is not to say that the peace camp was a serious obstacle to Desert Storm; yet its presence may have made it just a little more difficult to treat the whole of Iraq as "fair game". We were never under any illusion that a single peace camp could stop the war; but we wanted to contribute to worldwide efforts to stop it, and there is no reason to think that we have failed in that purpose.

---

[10] This is one reason why Ulli Laubenthal, in this book, questions the rationale of the peace camp. Since the impending attack on Iraq was bound to consist primarily of bombings inside Iraq, the camp – she argues – was no obstacle at all. As an alternative, Ulli advocates a presence in Baghdad, in solidarity with the victims of aerial bombings.

As a footnote, we learn with interest that one of the strategic plans initially considered by the US top brass involved "making a ground assault into Iraq somewhere far west along the Saudi-Iraq border, 300-400 miles from Kuwait."[11] This would have taken the coalition forces right through the area where our peace camp was situated. It would be naïve to think that our presence played a part in the rejection of that early plan (indeed the plan was rejected before the camp was set up). The fact remains that, *had that plan been adopted*, the camp would have been a thorn in the flesh of military planners. The peace camp was, thus, far from irrelevant as a potential if not actual physical obstacle.

The interposition value of the peace camp changed after the outbreak of war. At that time, some members of the Gulf Peace Team took the view that, war having started, the peace camp was futile. They advocated leaving the camp at the earliest and working for peace in other ways, e.g. by serving in Iraqi hospitals or campaigning against war in our respective countries. Others felt that the outbreak of war had not made the peace camp redundant, and that a role remained for nonviolent interposition.

One plausible role of interposition in wartime was to dissuade the coalition forces from bombing the area. There is no doubt that military commanders knew exactly where we were. Whether our presence was the reason why the area was not bombed, or whether there were other reasons, we do not know. The fact remains that our presence, by itself, made such bombings extremely unlikely. How far this "safe haven" (if any) extended is anyone's guess. But even if our presence protected no-one else than the people living in the immediate vicinity, it was worthwhile.[12]

Did the camp also stand in the way of military operations initiated on the Iraqi side? This is less likely, though not impossible, since the Iraqi government lost immediate control of the camp after the war started (due to the breakdown of transport and communications within Iraq). One of the many "theories" that enlivened our endless discussions at the camp was that our presence made it more difficult for the Iraqi army to retaliate. One member of the team (who felt that the outbreak of war had made nonsense of any "neutrality" and that Iraq had clearly become the victim) even argued

[11] Bob Woodward (1991), *The Commanders* (New York: Simon & Schuster), page 309.

[12] By that time most of these people were soldiers, rather than civilians (the latter having fled for safer areas, before the camp was set up). These "soldiers", however, were hardly distinguishable from civilians, since they had no capacity to fight and were really sitting ducks for coalition bombings.

that this made our presence immoral, as it forced the Iraqi army to "fight with one hand tied behind its back". This theory, however, was a trifle far-fetched, and its real purpose was perhaps to add to other arguments to the effect that we should leave the area.

Finally, one has to consider the uncomfortable possibility that the peace camp might have *facilitated* military operations of one sort or another. According to one rumour, the evacuation of the camp by the Iraqi government was followed by a skirmish in the area, initiated from the Iraqi side.[13] It is conceivable that this "surprise attack" (if there was one) was coordinated with the evacuation of the camp, on the assumption that our presence had made the area a "soft spot". But here we are delving deeper and deeper into the realm of imagination. Even more imaginative is Martin Thomas' hypothesis that the air space above the camp was used as a "safe passage" by coalition forces (see p. 51).

Of all these conjectures, the notion that the peace camp created a local "safe haven" around it during the war appears to be the most plausible.

What Happened to Ar'ar?

Many of us have been eager to know what eventually happened to the site of our peace camp. Here again, we have only fragments of evidence. A few months after the end of the Gulf war, Agnes Bauerlein sent us a photograph of the Pax Christi banner she had hung at the camp, with the following words: "The Pax Christi banner was the only one left after the evacuation. We learned later that the ground war came right through the camp and I was glad I'd left it hanging there." Another clue comes from Hasan Kilgour's diary: "... a few months later we heard that the camp had been bombed, shortly after evacuation by the Gulf Peace Team, with many casualties". There are other fragments of evidence to the effect that the site of the camp was destroyed by the coalition forces very soon after it was evacuated.

This is a sad postscript to our brief presence at Ar'ar. On a positive note, this anecdote is consistent with the notion that the camp did have some interposition value. Without the peace camp, the site might have been destroyed earlier. Also, had the camp not been evacuated (either due to the

---

[13] This rumour, mentioned in the diaries of several Gulf Peace Team members, appears to be based on unverified press releases from the Iraqi government, where the skirmish is described as a "glorious push" into Saudi Arabia. We also read that CNN and the BBC reported an Iraqi raid into Saudi Arabia immediately after the evacuation of the peace camp, at an unspecified location.

breakdown of transport facilities in Iraq, or to successful resistance on our part), we would have been in the way of the coalition forces.

Was it Worthwhile?

Wide-ranging views about the Gulf Peace Team's achievements and failures are presented in different chapters of this book. Some of them are far from positive. The team's lack of unity, especially, is a bitter memory for many of us. Yet there is one point on which everyone seems to agree – at the end of the day, the Gulf Peace Team was a worthwhile experience. As Ivy Phillips wrote to us on 27 September 1991: "Of one thing I am sure, that whatever the outcome, we were right to go."

Indeed, the Gulf Peace Team made many valuable contributions to the cause of peace, in the Gulf and beyond. First, the team achieved its purpose of nonviolent interposition, partially at least – we have already covered that ground. Second, the peace camp gave inspiration to the anti-war movement worldwide. Here again, it was only a partial success, and much more could have been achieved. The inspirational purpose of the peace camp was compromised by its disunity and ineptitude, rumours of which were often relayed far and wide. By and large, the "peace bureaucracy" (i.e. the mainstream peace organisations worldwide) maintained a polite distance from the Gulf Peace Team, which did not fit into the established structures. Biased media coverage also reduced the peace camp's impact on the public. Even then, the Gulf Peace Team's witness galvanised many people into action, and lifted the anti-war movement to a higher level of commitment.

Third, the Gulf Peace Team became a source of uniquely authentic testimonies about the ground situation in Iraq during and after the war. A few of these testimonies are included in this book, especially Part II, but there were many more in 1991, when Gulf Peace Team returnees had plenty of opportunities to speak and write about what they had seen. Ten years on, the western public has an idea of the catastrophic effects of war and sanctions on the people of Iraq, thanks to high-profile voices such as those of Denis Halliday, John Pilger and Hans von Sponeck. In those days, however, few were able or willing to speak out on this issue, and the Gulf Peace Team played a major part in breaking the silence.

Fourth, the Gulf Peace Team had many creative offshoots after the war. These included humanitarian convoys to Iraq, investigative reports on the consequences of war, and facilitating the work of other fact-finding teams. Detlef Enge-Bastien worked as a doctor in Kerbala hospital. Eric

Hoskins coordinated the International Study Team's mortality survey in mid-1991, which demonstrated that war and sanctions had led to a massive increase in child mortality in Iraq. Peggie Preston tirelessly visited Iraqi hospitals and gave a voice to Iraqi women and children in Britain. Kathy Kelly continued visiting Iraq over the years and co-founded "Voices in the Wilderness" (with Bob Bossie, Jim Douglass and others), the radical wing of the anti-sanctions movement in the United States. Many other team members continued working for peace and justice in the Middle East in various ways, especially by using their experience in Iraq as a basis for more effective campaigning at home. Some also initiated new experiences of nonviolent interposition, notably in former Yugoslavia. Most of these activities did not take place under the Gulf Peace Team banner, but they had firm roots in Ar'ar. In retrospect, it is after being "disbanded" that the Gulf Peace Team finally flourished.

Last but not least, the Gulf Peace Team created human bonds across the battle lines ("the most valuable aspect of all our activity," according to Caroline Dobson). This brings us to one of the most moving memories we all have from our experience in Iraq: the extraordinary warmth of the Iraqi people. As almost every chapter of this book testifies, members of the Gulf Peace Team were received with the greatest kindness everywhere they went. None of us remember any gesture of animosity, let alone violence or hatred, towards any member of the team. Cynics might argue that the Gulf Peace Team was bound to receive a warm reception from the Iraqi people, since our peace efforts worked to their advantage. What is profoundly moving, however, is that the kindness and hospitality of the Iraqi people continued *after* the war, when they could no longer expect any protection from us. Their friendliness towards American members of the Gulf Peace Team (and indeed other American visitors as well) was particularly admirable, given the role of the United States in leading the merciless destruction of their beautiful and prosperous country. As Bob Bossie, Jenny Hales, Andrew Jones, Sunil Arora and others observe in this book, the Iraqi people never allowed the deeds of the US government to make them lose sight of the goodwill of many American citizens. Eileen Storey, who travelled extensively in Iraq after the war, goes further:

> ... one thing became clear as we moved from city to city, from village to village, from street to street: Iraqis do not blame the American people for the decisions of the American government. Their own political helpless-

ness makes them too lenient with us, too willing to believe there was nothing we could do to prevent that final decision of the President to pound their highly developed infrastructure to the dust.[14]

Perhaps the most humbling testimonies of this goodwill towards US
citizens come from visits of Gulf Peace Team members to the Ameriyeh
neighbourhood in Baghdad, where they were received with love by Iraqi
women and men who had lost all their children in the bombing of a civilian
shelter on 13 February 1991.[15] In these human encounters, the Iraqi people
taught us more about nonviolence than we were ever able to practice in our
own "peace camp."

These human bonds across the battle lines have many ramifications.
For the Iraqi people, we believe that the Gulf Peace Team was a sign of
hope. It was important for them to know that citizens of the countries that
had destroyed Iraq had opposed the war (and, today, oppose the sanctions
that continue to devastate the country). For us, this sojourn in Iraq has been
a time of deep personal transformation. Further, these human encounters
have given a much sharper edge to the testimonies of Gulf Peace Team
members at home. If Detlef Enge-Bastien, Kathy Kelly, Peggie Preston,
Eileen Storey, Muriel Sibley and many others have been able to speak with
such power to western audiences, it is because they have witnessed first-
hand the agony of the Iraqi people. Ten years on, these authentic testimonies (along with those of others who have visited Iraq over the years) have
defeated the relentless but superficial propaganda relayed by the mainstream
media.

Outline of the Book

The remainder of this book is divided into four parts. The first part
consists of first-hand accounts of the peace camp by members of the Gulf
Peace Team. The lead chapter is a brief overview by Richard Crump, a member of the "advance party" of seven volunteers who set up the peace camp.
This is followed by long excerpts from Martin Thomas' diary (chapter 2);
the intention here is to give the reader a chance to follow one Gulf Peace
Team member's entire journey, from the decision to join the team to the end
of the Gulf war. Other chapters in this part of the book consist of shorter

[14] Eileen Storey (1991), *The Victory of Grass* (New York: Aletheia School of Prayer), page 49.

[15] See particularly the chapters by Jim Douglass, Jill Castek and Louise Cainkar.

excerpts from diaries and other notes written by Gulf Peace Team members in 1991. A certain amount of repetition is inevitably involved, but there is much to learn from complementary accounts of the same events. For instance, alternative perspectives on the final evacuation of the camp in different chapters provide much food for thought.

The second part of the book focuses on the humanitarian situation in Iraq immediately after the war. Throughout 1991, members and associates of the Gulf Peace Team continued visiting Iraq with relief convoys and fact-finding missions. A selection of their testimonies has been included here, in rough chronological order. The last two chapters were written in 1996 and 1997, respectively.

Other than what has already been discussed earlier in this introduction, two points emerge forcefully from these testimonies. First, the devastating effects of war and sanctions on the civilian population, widely understood today, were already clear in 1991 to all those who had visited Iraq.[16] Second, it is only by being kept unaware of these facts through relentless propaganda that the western public has been led to accept the continuation of monstrous sanctions on Iraq over the years. The concluding chapter by Kathy Kelly is particularly telling in this respect.

Some readers may wonder how these post-war testimonies fit with the Gulf Peace Team's "policy statement", in particular its policy of non-partisanship. One answer is that these revisits to Iraq were made by Gulf Peace Team members in their personal capacity. Another is that, whatever the merits of non-partisanship before the war, any peace-minded person who has witnessed the devastation inflicted on Iraq by war and sanctions is bound to take the side of the victims. This does not, of course, mean supporting the present Iraqi regime. Finally, as the policy statement makes clear, the Gulf Peace Team has always condemned human rights violations, of which economic sanctions on Iraq are an extreme example.

Part III consists of four retrospective evaluations of the work of the Gulf Peace Team. Robert Burrowes, the peace camp's resident "peace scholar", presents a balanced assessment of the team's achievements and shortcomings, which complements this introduction. Ulli Laubenthal, a member of the Initiative Freiden am Golf (a German peace group of simi-

[16] On this see also Bela Bhatia, Mary Kawar and Mariam Shahin (1992), *Unheard Voices: Iraqi Women on War and Sanctions* (London: Change), and Jean Drèze and Haris Gazdar (1992), "Hunger and Poverty in Iraq, 1991", *World Development*, 20.

lar inspiration), explains why she decided *not* to join the peace camp. In a moving counterpoint, Jerry Hartigan argues that "the value of the peace camp lay in its simplicity which made its message clear to all." Alyn Ware, who represented the Gulf Peace Team at the United Nations in 1990-1, puts the team's work in historical perspective and shares his own thoughts on the "effectiveness" of the project.

Finally, in Part IV, we have included brief tributes to three members of the Gulf Peace Team who are no longer with us. Aside from wishing to remember these dear friends, we thought that these glimpses of their unusual lives would give the reader an idea of the diverse backgrounds of members of the Gulf Peace Team.

Part 1

The Peace Camp

"My own feeling is that the value of the peace camp lay in its simplicity which made its message so clear to all. Of course one does not need to go to the Arabian Desert to reject a punitive and genocidal war; but the symbolism of being there is certainly very striking, something that is actual and real, like the hammering of the controls of an F-111 by those who beat swords into plough-shares. It makes a powerful symbol recognizable as such and unmistakable for all."

Jerry Hartigan, Gulf Peace Team

Memories of the Gulf Peace Team

Richard Crump

This is a personal account of my service as a member of the Gulf Peace Team, culled from journals and memories.

The seven-strong "advance party" consisted of: (1) Pat Arrowsmith, the veteran peace campaigner aged 60, and enthusiastic co-initiatior of this project; (2) Jean Drèze, a Belgian lecturer at the London School of Economics and exponent of nonviolent direct action; (3) Bela Bhatia, a sensitive young Indian lady who had been politically active in her own country, especially in trade union and women's pressure groups; (4) Bassam, a British national of Ghanaian origin, in the full vigour of life, charming and diplomatic, a speaker of Arabic who was aware of the importance of protocol; (5) Sadallah, a British national of Nigerian origin, with Algerian desert experience, who had the vital task of interpreting when the advance party were received by high-ranking Iraqi officials to discuss the peace camp. During these discussions we realised that we were under close scrutiny and that both we and our ideas were being assessed, concerning the practical and political value of establishing an international desert camp close to the Saudi Arabia border. Sadallah became known as "Mr. Fix-it". His qualities shone in the practicalities and he found the interminable discussions, which were necessary, a wearisome chore.

The sixth member was John Steel, aged 76, a fellow member of Ex-Services CND, a friend and mentor during several years' campaigning. John, a man of extraordinary patience, courtesy and modesty, had been a teacher with good organising ability. As for myself, Richard Crump, the seventh member of the team, the discreet veil is indicated. Like Pat, I have been known to write verse of questionable worth. My particular and unique qualifications were (a) a vague knowledge of climatic conditions in the Gulf region gained from war-time service on oil tankers plying up and down the Persian Gulf; (b) peace camp experience, painfully acquired at the Molesworth cruise missile base in 1988, and at Upper Heyford in early 1990. I am 67.

Publicity about the aims of the team resulted in considerable public support so that we were able to acquire an administrative base in London (coordinated by Ginnie Landon and Mohamed Sidek Ahmad) from which negotiations with various authorities began. An approach made to the Saudi Arabia government evoked only a cool response so in the end discussions were held with Iraqi officials, who were more responsive. As a result the advance party were able to fly to Baghdad where we landed on 18 November, 1990. We were then installed in a bungalow within the Iraqi government-sponsored "International Peace and Friendship Village" at Al Arras, several miles out of the city.

My initial fears and suspicions concerning our possible treatment at the hands of what, in Britain, had been portrayed as a vicious and ruthless regime, were gradually allayed. We never did know whether our conversations were overheard through hidden microphones. Obviously the Iraqi authorities were presenting their most benevolent face, with the aim of countering the negative image portrayed by much of the British media. It was after some unaccompanied shopping expeditions into town with one or other of the two Arabic speakers of our party that I formed a more reasonable and favourable regard for the people who were playing host to us, and the various delegates and other individuals from many countries who were enjoying the comforts and amenities of the international "peace village" at Al Arras.

Obviously, without a knowledge of the language and having only superficial dealing with the local population it was impossible to ascertain whether there were "nasty" undertones or criticisms of the regime, but my impression of the attitudes of people thronging the busy streets was of general vigour, industry, optimism and a remarkable degree of honesty. I reminded myself that here was a country not long relieved from a state of war with Iran, and apparently showing few outward scars. This revived memories of the increase in community spirit and the reduction in frivolous pursuits in war-time Britain. There appeared to be little vandalism, general thuggery and the loutish behaviour that one endures in present-time "merry" England.

An event which influenced me profoundly for the good was the arrival in Baghdad of a monk of the Nipponsan Myohoji Buddhist Order. His name is Junsei Terasawa, aged 40, and he stayed at the International Peace and Friendship Village at Al Arras. He came out from England from the Buddhist community at Milton Keynes, directly after the adoption of the United Nations resolution authorising military action against Iraq after 15 January 1991, unless certain conditions were met. I was overjoyed when I chanced to see his robed figure on the very evening of his arrival. Many times over past years, at different places where there have been protest marches and rallies against nuclear weapons particularly, monks and nuns of this Japanese Buddhist Order have been present. Their custom of making public witness for peace and harmony is by beating rhythmically on a hand-held drum and chanting the mantra Na-Mu-Myo-Ho-Ren-Ge-Kyo for periods of hours on end. I made myself known to this remarkable man, who spoke excellent English, as a solitary Buddhist of the Friends of the Western Buddhist Order. He told me that his plan was to fast for one week, beginning next day, as a mark of the tremendous gravity of the situation. During the week he witnessed publicly at different venues in Baghdad, where large numbers of people would see and hear his chanting and drumming. I often joined him at his morning prayers, and also on the first day of his public witness in Baghdad, when we fasted and chanted at the martyrs' memorial. This experience was one of the most remarkable and memorable I have ever known, with physical and spiritual aspects.

When Junsei Terasawa had completed his fast and public witness for a week, he spent the next few days walking around in the busy city and meeting as many ordinary people as possible. Then he left to visit capital cities in Europe and the Soviet Union, trying to bring influence to bear in favour of a negotiated settlement instead of military intervention. I believe his journeys eventually took him to Japan. Before he left, he declared his intention of joining us at the desert camp for which we were negotiating before the expiry of the 15 January deadline.

Junsei Terasawa did come to the desert camp around 13 January, when a good number of other volunteers also arrived. From then on until the evacuation, the monk faithfully took up his position at sunrise and at sunset, and his rhythmic drumming could be heard in the distance in all parts of the camp. I found it too cold to leave my sleeping bag until the sun was well up (there were some cloudy days and occasional rainstorms). But in the evenings I would join him regularly, as did some others, particularly Jerry Hartigan, an old friend in the peace movement, who is a Buddhist supporter although primarily a Roman Catholic. Junsei had a steadying influence on many, and his well-informed views carried weight. He also played an impressive game of football, as was noted later in the course of a remarkable and highly acclaimed impromptu football match between peace campers and Iraqi border guards from their post nearby, which took place *after* hostilities had begun.

The aim and object of the advance party was to persuade the Iraqi authorities that it would be politically worthwhile to assist us to set up a peace camp as near as possible to the border with Saudi Arabia, symbolically interposed between the opposing armed forces. In this we succeeded, but only after weeks of frustrating negotiations during which tempers within our, by now enlarged and diverse, group had frayed and sometimes emotion would displace rational judgement. Eventually, on 24 December 1990, we arrived at our desert goal, 2½ km. inside the Iraq/Saudi Arabia border. There-after, the number of those staying at the camp steadily increased day after day.

I have vivid memories of 17 January when hostilities began. At about 2.40 a.m. a small group of us heard the distant but unmistakable sounds of exploding bombs. Because of the general feeling of tension and unreality following the expiry of the United Nations deadline on 15 January we had stayed up late playing "crazy" Scrabble (a mixture of Greek and English original words). We could discern the sounds of aircraft flying at great altitude, and then across the hundreds of miles of flat desert we could hear (within the communal tent) those ominous thuds. I remember that we looked at each other aghast, unbelieving, despite the forewarning of previous months. It was as though the clock of civilised progress had been viciously turned back and the scene set for God knew what death and destruction.

It was a strange period, for in the border camp we became used to living in a state of suspended animation, apparently safe from the risk of sudden death or injury. British and American airmen (and women?) flew periodi-cally at great height to deliver hate and ignorance to selected targets - inevi-tably killing civilian men, women and children. In order not to offend the delicate feelings of TV audiences and radio addicts, this mass criminality is enclosed in its plastic wrapper labelled "collateral damage". I do seem to get myself a little "worked up", but surely where a scandal is concerned that is no bad thing. By writing, rhyming, thinking up slogans and sometimes talk-ing to people, I manage to both unwind and to campaign. Sadly, when talking to people, particularly those who are not sympathetic, I find myself becoming emotional, probably obnoxious and regretful of involving myself in a fruitless exercise.

Well, there we were, 73 people of diverse backgrounds and cultures from a number of different countries, including representatives from first, second, and third worlds. We had become isolated, because no-one could join us and none could leave. We were cut off by the military situation. I believe that had anybody become seriously ill, the Iraqi authorities would have provided transport out, for their previous attitude had been marked by a responsible and practical concern for our safety and welfare. But the perimeter fence of the large compound (about the size of six football fields) was the limit of our world and only the occasional official car from Baghdad brought news to our beleaguered garrison. However, we did have at least two portable shortwave radio sets, around which addicts huddled for long periods, listening for what passed as "news".

How did we behave in this situation? Neither exceptionally well nor badly. We had no elected, accepted or imposed leader. As one might expect, greedy individuals or small groups acted in character, often by appropriating for their present or future use quantities of the more tasty food items (tinned stuff, coffee, sweets, etc.). I suppose it was inevitable that those who acted most unfairly in this way were those from countries with high living standards (and maybe with the lowest morals). In microcosm, we were still in a world in which the wealthy grab ever more, and are prepared to use all means to uphold the status quo. Politically-minded people would probably identify the darker side of the capitalist system.

Possibly, some in the camp would have wished to suppress such information. Those who would not wish it to be known that un-peace-like action took place, probably felt that it would detract from our image as mature and responsible campaigners. That is a quite valid attitude because many people who oppose our actions are glad of opportunities to discredit us. The hostile press, for instance, would have been delighted to make the most of dissension in our ranks. However, I am curious about such reasoning. Nobody likes being cheated or wants to admit to outsiders that they have been continuously cheated, yet were able to do almost nothing about it. To be fair to myself, I should diagnose an ambivalence in attitude. My better self (or maybe timidity) would wish to be law-abiding, approving fair shares etc., and my middle-class background reinforces the respectable conformist; but tucked away is the more primitive animal, which, not completely stifled, applauds piracy, and envies gypsies and law-breakers who flout rules. Still on a personal level, there was resentment (and envy) of the "wise guys". Why could I not be more like them? More honest, ruthless; less furtive about my vices. Yes, I both admired and hated hedonistic villains. We in Britain are conditioned by a society in which privilege and unfairness of distribution are the norm. "Britain still enjoys Norman rule" (E.P. Thompson).

Each day there were meetings of various kinds. Affinity groups of a manageable size (around 15) would gather outside, if the weather was fine, or in a tent. All sorts of topics were discussed, and ideas and decisions agreed to were carried back to a meeting of representatives. Some meetings were so unproductive, rancorous, etc., that certain people, including me, would absent themselves upon occasion. Some of these were anarchists, others had a conscientious objection. There were of course other activities of a more practical and creative nature, e.g. cooking, which had to be done for a large number, by using temperamental paraffin stoves bought in Baghdad. Some energies were applied to making banners with a sewing machine provided by an Indian lady who also brought quantities of various coloured materials. Slogans were painted on roofs and asphalted areas, for the benefit of airforce pilots. Educational and Arabic classes were organised, as were other recreational activities. All these were additional to the more formal gatherings. The inevitable chores were performed by those who placed their names on a list.

There was much speculation about our possible fate. Evacuation? But by whom? However, on 27 January the matter was decided for us, when two coaches and an open lorry drove into the compound at 3.00 a.m. There was no sleep from then on, as the camp gradually roused. We were told to pack and make preparation for an early start after daybreak. A mighty breakfast was prepared by a noble Scottish lady assisted by a few others. When it was time to leave, with personal effects stowed on the coaches and food, cooking equipment, blankets, etc., loaded into the lorry, a group which had been planning to make this gesture for many days refused to leave, in Gandhi style, and made a symbolic seated protest. But the larger number in the camp did not agree, so that on this morning of our departure, irritation and hostility were exhibited by those who were being delayed. The few Iraqi officials to whom this behaviour was inexplicable, dealt with the situation with admirable patience and tact.

There is not a great deal to say about our journey to Baghdad, which we reached at dusk. The results of Allied bombing were in evidence. Smoke was still drifting from the distant outskirts of the city, doubtless from fuel stores, factories, power stations and railways. Upon arrival, we all helped to unload the assorted contents of the lorry. These were placed in the now unoccupied Al Arras friendship village. Lastly we removed our personal belongings to the inside of the gloomy, unlit foyer of the Al Rasheed Hotel.

I shared a well-appointed room with John Steel, where we had two divinely comfortable beds. Water flowed only for an hour in the mornings and evenings, and there was no room lighting and of course no heating. Yet it was a supreme luxury to sleep in blissful comfort, on sprung mattresses after many weeks on padded concrete. That first night of sound, undisturbed slumber ranks high on the list of high spots in my life. We learned from others, the next morning, that there had been air raid warnings and the sound of falling bombs of which John and I had been blissfully unaware. The plate-glass windows deadened all sounds.

When requested to do so by staff, we descended to the purpose-built shelter. But air raids were not the only occasions on which I used the shelter; it was a good place to use for reading or writing in the evening. Also, it was a good place to meet and talk with both old or new-found friends. Those who spent most time and almost lived in this shelter, were mainly Iraqi family groups having children of various ages; hotel staff and their families; professional people and officials who, no doubt, had priority. On one occasion a very personable, attractive young Iraqi woman of 18 or so spoke to me, thus starting a friendship which encompassed Rand herself, her more retiring sister Reem, and her mother and father, and which I valued greatly. I looked forward to the evening conversations I had with Rand and her family. We all found ourselves in strange circumstances with an uncertain, possibly dangerous, future and sudden death an everyday occurrence. What happened to these good people later, when physical conditions deteriorated and the doomed city was plunged into chaos, I shudder to think.

Much of what I describe in this account may appear to be of a rather trivial nature, but remains in the memory, and I have not dwelt on my feelings which would take greater literary gifts than I have to commit to paper. I tried to convey something of these through verse that I composed during this time. However, I recall one remarkable and dramatic event. This was a semi-formal occasion when an important and impressive government minister, Mr. Dawood, announced that he would be addressing us, following the evening of our arrival.

Members of the advance party had previously met Mr. Dawood who had gained our warm regard and respect. Mr. Dawood began his address - which was part complimentary (he told us we were heroes and heroines, which although not justified in all cases, fell pleasantly on our ears) and part reprimand. Some of us had squirmed under his headmasterly strictures on previous occasions. He asked us to complete two lists: one giving names of those who wished to leave the country and one giving details of those who had some useful skill and wished to stay. As I have some nursing experience and wished to stay, my name was entered on the latter. The proceedings were considerably protracted and I began to feel drowsy, when a sudden crash and blast of bombs exploding nearby roused me, and it became clear that the meeting was over. Cool and well-disciplined Iraqis led us to the shelters. These bombs were the closest I had heard.

The bombing was intermittent, taking place mainly at night, but on one occasion in daylight I spotted vapour trails at immense height and looking like a shoal of minnows. There were also trails of what I guessed were defensive fighter aircraft, but the planes themselves were invisible. At night we could see the explosive flashes of ground to air missiles. The sound-proofing effect of our plate-glass windows gave an illusion of unreality to these scenes.

During our stay at the Al Rasheed Hotel and before supplies of fuel ran out, we were taken on a number of "educational" tours. These included visits to hospitals where we were shown patients injured by bombs, and emphasis was placed on shortages and disruption caused firstly by the UN blockade and later by bombing. We were also shown the celebrated bombed baby-milk factory 20-30 miles out of the city. En route in the city we saw a many-storied modern building (a government ministry of some kind), the ruins of which made a spectacular sight. The steel girders were still stand-ing, but partitions, window frames, concrete cladding etc., were shattered and hanging or scattered around. Private dwellings close by appeared to be undamaged. At that time I had not heard of the laser-guided missiles. This surrealist spectacle was a sample of the effectiveness of these weapons.

On 30 January all foreign nationals, with the exception of press repre-sentatives, were informed of an important meeting. We assembled in the hotel garden that sunny afternoon, and an unsmiling official announced that *all* of us must be packed ready to leave by coach for Jordan by 7 a.m. the next morning. There was a numb feeling inside me. Pain mixed with relief at the peremptory end of my idea to stay and serve. Perhaps I am alive today as a result?

I must mention that the Gulf Peace Team members were well thought of not only by Iraqi officials but also by the public, in recognition of our willingness to face some hardship and danger in our efforts to prevent hostilities. I felt certain that others like myself in Britain and America would have been bitterly ashamed and guilty about what was being done by our fellow countrymen. I felt a misery and frustration in being prevented from giving service to these wronged people. It was a difficult mental state with which to cope. I endeavoured to express my feelings about the whole situation in letters to those who I know care for me, especially those in the local CND group at home.

I think too of the various individuals with whom I was able to make good contact. For instance, El Haadi, a gardener in the "peace and friendship village" at Al Arras who was a native of Somalia and a Muslim, with whom I had several friendly conversations. Then there was the Iraqi doctor based at the nearby border post who attended me very professionally, when for several days I was quite unwell and demoralised during a bout of diarrhoea and vomiting. There were the several liaison officers ("minders") we got to know and trust. I remember too, the doorkeeper and Arabic coffee dispenser at Al Arras and one of the mini-bus drivers who transported us on "cultural" tours, whom my fractured Arabic reduced to mirth. But it was of course my warm friendship with Rand and her family that I would miss most.

The next morning, breakfast was served at 5.30 a.m. The bright lights of a TV camera were shining on us while we were having our breakfast. It was CNN, whose considerable equipment - generators, lorry cables, satellite dish etc. - had been littering the environs and disturbing the peace earlier on. My thermos flask was filled after breakfast by a kind and helpful member of staff and I shook hands with this waiter. I think he was an Indian chap and I thanked him for all the kindness we had been shown and wished him "safe". The waiter raised his hands in a simple gesture as a prayer and spoke of a God that would protect them. I felt very choked; in fact I was tearful, but the lights were so subdued that I was spared any embarrassment as I went away, leaving all these people.

Engulfed

Martin Thomas

A Very Personal Battle

Sanity, the CND magazine, carried a letter in late 1990 which caught my eye. It spoke of a Gulf Peace Camp and asked for volunteers to form a team in support of the camp. I wrote offering help with leafleting and so on. This I intended to be my only involvement. I was busy at the time with sabotaging local fox hunts and many other activities. One Saturday morning, I arose to find a letter inviting me to a meeting that evening in London; fortunately I had swapped rest days from my work as a train crew on London Underground and my evening was free.

The meeting was not massively informative, but I came away with the strong conviction that I personally could not simply support the effort for I would feel uncomfortable sending other people off. It was a case of Go or No, I felt. I went back to my one room apartment and began a very personal study of the expected war. My opposition to Saddam was known. I · had commemorated Halabja by letting off smoke bombs, writing letters etc. Yet my opposition to Syria was hardly less and what little I knew of the Al Sabba regime would hardly qualify them for my Christmas card list. I formulated the notion that this was to be the first modern resource war and would thus set a precedent for others if it were allowed to happen. Surely, I mused, if it were about borders Syria would be under pressure first; if it were about human rights, the UN resolutions regarding Palestinians would have been enforced against Israel; if it were about democracy, Kuwait could hardly be supported. So what was the vital factor? Oil, I said. Not just Kuwaiti and Iraqi, but Saudi too. Hence the excuse for Desert Shield which fooled nobody.

I began to read back into the history of Iraq and its formation by the Western powers; into the Baathist movement and the rise of Saddam; into current affairs such as the arms sales and export licences to Iraq, the trial and surprising execution of *Observer* journalist Farzad Bazoft which told the West something was not right, the rush to get tapering oil pipes through Turkey before it was "discovered" that they had gun-barrel specifications. As I read between the lines avidly at what was not being said I was reminded always of the war satire "Catch 22".

The political left were split between their continued loathing of the West-tolerated Saddam regime and their dislike of a war by proxy in the Middle East. They had also failed to anticipate Gorbachev's pragmatic line within the UN. I began to feel that any political solution would need a kickstart from a moral highpoint such as the peace camp.

I had to question the strategic value of the camp, based undoubtedly I felt near a minefield and only supplied from within Iraqi territory. There had been plans for a camp near the "neutral zone" close to Kuwait, but there were political problems with this for we would be seen as protecting the invasion, and there were time and diplomatic problems with the Saudis who would not reply to requests for recognition and the Kuwaiti government-in-exile who would not wish to get involved. The camp was undoubtedly strengthened with the involvement of human rights advocates within it, and any calls for peace always carried a criticism of the original invasion and the rumoured rights violations which I'm happy to say later turned out to be greatly exaggerated, though still harrowing where they did take place.

My first reaction had been to become a voluntary human shield, perverting Saddam's intentions and perhaps allowing the release of one or more foreign "guests" in return for being a sitting duck.[17] However, protecting a hospital was one thing, shielding a site of German gas or British anthrax was quite another. Suddenly the peace camp and the tactic of interposition between land forces seemed not only more romantic, but also more practical, and I resolved to listen to one of the peace campers when he visited Britain.

Jean Drèze spoke to a meeting of very quiet peaceniks as the preparations for the war picked up. I attended in full uniform during my lunchbreak and was immediately nicknamed "The Postman" because I looked like one. With my experience of strongwilled and argumentative pacifists, I was amazed at how passive everyone seemed.

I was given an application to become a volunteer and put my skills down as driver with the intention of driving a supply truck. Had it been possible to predict Cruise missiles being programmed to follow the highways I would have also quite happily tracked, nudged and diverted them! The application involved endorsing the peace camp's strict "code of conduct", including consensus decision-making which I misinterpreted to mean general agree-

[17] *Editors*: In those days some peace activists had offered to take the place of western "hostages" held by the Iraqi government.

ment, but actually turned out to be what I regarded as a more fascistic form of prevention from reaching decisions. Had I known that one person would be able to block the consensus of the majority I would have had to abort my plans, as a democrat, so perhaps it is as well that I did not understand this interpretation.[18]

One night, after work, I had to face up to my fears. Not of going, of kidnap, injury, torture or death, but of telling my family of my plans. In my culture, charity begins at home and world events happen to other people; this view is reinforced powerfully by informal education and, most potently, ridicule of any alien influence. Thus in the working class of Britain fear of physical pain is very small and fear of ridicule is paramount. It is easy to send men of my age and class to war. In some ways I had overcome this when I became a vegan, but always it has to be faced again over a new issue. I felt I could not do it. I would have to do something else. With a heavy heart I wrote a letter to the Gulf Peace Team saying that I had reconsidered and enclosing a cheque for £120 as I had previously sold my car.

As the days went by and politicians shuttled about I began to question what my life was worth if I could not back my own convictions. Ludicrously, I tossed a coin saying if it was heads I would go; it was tails. Best of three I thought; it was tails again. After a sleepless night I decided I wasn't superstitious after all and resolved to go.

Linda at the Gulf Peace Team gave me a thorough grilling to assess just how committed I was, but I must have said something right over the two hour interview at Cazenove Road. My departure date was set for 12 January – three days before the UN deadline. I told my family: some tried to talk me out of it, some ignored me and some tried to understand me. My mother chose to support me, though not my actions, and perhaps she more than most could understand my philosophy - she grew up through the London blitz and was bombed out of every home and school she had then.

My philosophy was as follows: I am a pacifist, not an apathist, though I respect all peace-lovers. I reserve the right to act on instinct, but I shall not carry arms, nor pre-meditate violence, nor pay war tax or support terrorism

---

[18] *Editors*: The peace camp's "code of conduct" actually made room not only for consensus but also for majority voting, as well as for various decision-making structures such as a general assembly and a coordinating committee. It is true, however, that some members insisted on consensus decisions when it suited them to have veto power. Besides, the code of conduct ended up being treated as little more than a sort of reference point, especially after the outbreak of war, when it no longer seemed adequate for the situation.

in any way. War is perpetrated against the innocent before it reaches the guilty; the purpose of modern warriors is to avoid each other whilst killing each other's civilian populations. War means martial law and unjust courts. Civilians will go hungry before armies. In seeing an act of torture or rape I would interpose myself between aggressor and victim, particularly if there was more than one aggressor where this would be the only effective action anyway. I had learnt from hunt sabotage the danger of confrontation with numbers; some deal with you while others get on with the original victim. Only by forgetting one's own fear, loathing and thoughts of revenge can one keep the mind on the victim and protect them. I had no objection to judo, using an aggressor's momentum to bring them to the ground harmlessly, nor to aikido, blocks and holds.

None of this would protect anyone from bullets or bombs or gas or germs. So I read my brother's *New Scientist* to see just what the threats were. Gas, it seemed, would not be much use in the open desert, blowing away quickly, and germs were more of a threat to static large populations such as Baghdad. In fact the measures against them, such as chemical warfare suits, were a bigger threat to life in the daytime desert temperatures, and some of the last resort vaccines could induce a heart attack! It was the more conventional weaponry which I perceived as a threat. I had been shot at before, whilst sabotaging a grouse shoot, but to be shot at indiscriminately by someone who had no argument with me was a totally new concept, should it happen. I also had to face a very real fear of kidnap and this probably overrode all else. I completely misunderstood the Arab attitude towards invited guests and my fears were groundless.

As a relief aid worker and with the help of the BBC who were filming me, I jumped the bureaucratic queue at Petty France to pick up my passport on the day of departure. I had jabs the day before. All the rush saved me from thinking too much. At Heathrow I was reunited with slight acquaintances from the team – Penny, Tim and Miller as well as many new faces, including a very individual figure in beaver hat and brandishing a cricket bat, Edward Poore. I had to convince my family once again that I was with a very capable band of individuals mentioning one or two former desert rats and doctors etc. However, the chaos of our departure amongst three film crews and lugging large amounts of food and medicine with us left everybody in some doubt!

If Heathrow had been chaos, then the airport at Amman was a disaster that night (if Hell exists I think it resembles an airport lounge). Not only did we have our own problems marshalling all the cargo with the team, but the duty customs and other authorities gave us as hard a time as they could in marked contrast to all other Jordanians who made us as welcome as possible. Here I held up the team, refusing to go anywhere until my baggage was positively identified at the retrieval point - I had a ready made survival kit, compass, map, etc., in case I ever had to leave the camp, and I did not want to go without them. Being pacifists everyone smiled sweetly though there must have been a few choice words spoken out of earshot.

We piled aboard the buses to our brief stay hotel in Amman. It was quite a long journey and people began to open up and talk. Edward started to play "It's A Long Way To Tipperary" - the war song - on harmonica, a choice which earned him a stiff rebuke from Miller. The two later became good friends in Baghdad. I began to marvel that I had gotten this far - against my own fears, my culture and my government. Did I really want to go further? Only time and continued reappraisals would tell. From here at least we all had to face our own very personal battles, but being social animals we all looked to each other for example, advice and support. Without a role model, I found myself in my accustomed position of loner, but not lonely as since Heathrow I had struck up a good friendship with my now roommate Giovanni.

Suddenly things were deadly serious. Yet also absurd. There were many examples of this and I shall concentrate on mine. As we reappraised as individuals whether or not to go to the camp or stay and help in Amman, someone told me in a meeting that the London office of the Gulf Peace Team had accepted various forms of aid from the Muslim League in London. As a member of the Peace Pledge Union, I was aware of this group and their support of Ayatollah Khomeini's *fatwa* against Salman Rushdie. The Gulf Peace Team had always said it would accept funds from any source if no strings were attached, but this snippet suggested a deeper involvement. As an individual I could not afford to be involved with League personnel and for a moment my world turned upside down. Others could not fathom my objection and a number felt that I had already decided to stay in Amman and was simply attempting to rationalise my change of heart through this new information. In fact I was not entirely sure that this was wrong and so I excused myself from the meeting, saying "I need twenty minutes to myself" in order to hold an internal dialogue and test my motivations.

Now, I was never a role model: everyone else was bigger, older and more experienced than me, but as a result of my abrupt departure everyone's uncertainties came out into the open. Robbie was now not going, neither were Giovanni or Sally and Tim was saying that he wasn't. Keith did not know what to make of it all. Everyone, seeing my slightly tear-stained face peep round the door, clearly expected me to be staying to help in Amman, but I had a proposal to make. I said that if this rumour were true - and there was no way of verifying it then, though Ginnie later vigorously denied it - then I no longer wanted to be a Gulf Peace Team member or associate. However, I had identified my motivation as interposition (initially as a human shield, then with the camp) and as far as I was concerned nothing had changed regarding the camp. So if I declared myself independent, could I travel on with them as an independent pacifist as if they had picked me up on the way; then play it by ear at the camp, perhaps going off on my own? Clearly there was an element here of eating my cake and still having it to look at, but I felt that it was a good compromise in the circumstances. It emphasised the fact that I trusted everyone around me with my life.

Flight Into The Unknown

We left for the airport soon after. I gave strict instructions to Sally as to what I would want done in the event of being held hostage, my xenophobia not improved. Among these details was the fact that I was registered with the PPU as a peaceful protestor and I hoped that this would give my case a headstart with Amnesty International investigators for prisoner of conscience status. Interestingly, I had disagreements with many Amnesty policy decisions, particularly the fact that they would not adopt PoCs amongst those thousands of lesbians and gays who were imprisoned for practising this right with consenting adults where it was illegal. My membership had lapsed years before, but I was not so principled that I was not prepared to use their expertise if necessary. This expertise, however, was called into question after the war when it became apparent that the file which they produced on the invasion of Kuwait, published before the deadline and with accounts unchecked of necessity, was extremely inaccurate and prejudicial. The rapes of foreign nurses and close down of baby incubators were being refuted right from the start - Kuwait had no record of owning that many incubators in the whole country - but it made superb propaganda for the crusader-type image of the Western coalition forces. Undoubtedly, human rights violations had occurred including, I had no doubt, torture, but using secondary sources of information and publishing in a panic only helped to sell the image in the West of Saddam as a Hitler figure, which was extremely insulting to all those Europeans and particularly the Jews who had suffered under a genuine Hitler and his orchestrated attempt to wipe out a race. I personally saw Saddam as more of a Stalin figure, thriving on power for its own sake rather than any sense of destiny. As such he could have been handled, but the inertia was now towards war and both sides were waiting for the other to blink. From Amnesty's point of view they were simply producing another in a long line of files, but it was rather simple-minded to imagine that this one, in view of the climate, would be covered by the media only as much as their file on Syria, Israel, Turkey and others. It was bound to be taken out of context. This file broke the limited left and liberal opposition to war and left peace activists rather stranded the world over.

Nevertheless, I was still counting on Amnesty for long term protection. I then told Sally to inform my parents where my will was kept at home, a singularly unthoughtful act which she decided to hold back on. I had always maintained in Britain that when I died anything which could be used for the living should be; not just heart, eyes, spleen etc., but also using the body as a cadaver or even a practice model for training surgeons - rather than practising on live pigs and other animals which is all too often the case and must mislead medical science no end. Being always "the runt of the litter" and small compared to my peers it would be particularly rewarding to know that my body would be used to continue producing Human Growth Hormone for the treatment of stunted growth. It was, therefore, sobering to realise that if I died in this venture, there would be none of that, no tree planted in my name, not even a body-bag. Still, c'est la mort, I thought!

In Baghdad airport, Tony Lawrence was being interviewed by a film crew and talking about his two sons who would be serving in the American forces not far from our camp and how they had joined years before to protect their country, not get involved in proxy wars. It would have been very poor secret services indeed who would have failed to get at least one passive observer into a group of nearly a hundred, but I felt that Tony - being Washington-based - was too obvious a choice. He was a valuable asset to the camp not only in that the American public could easily identify with his slightly conservative image, but also because he was one of the few campers prepared to use the press. At this stage publicity was still our biggest weapon, and we were worryingly under-exposed.

As we emerged into a sort of hall we were enveloped by a cacophony of bugles and drums as a militia, mainly of young women in fatigues, held up signs partially in English welcoming peace-makers. The pilot of our aircraft had announced a welcome both to the Gulf Peace Team and to a British Green Party delegation which was going to meet Saddam to urge a withdrawal for environmental reasons. I hoped that this welcome was for them and not us for I feared a propaganda coup was in the offing, rather like the Viet Cong's use of peace activists who had gone to North Vietnam during that infamous conflict. I kept my head down and pushed my trolley by quickly. In fact the welcome was actually for the crew of a sanctions-busting vessel which had been turned away for carrying salt amongst its medicinal cargo. The Greens and the Gulf Peace Team were virtually ignored compared to this crew which I think showed a proper sense of priorities in sanctions-hit Iraq.

A Dream in the Midst of a Nightmare

My personal tactics had been simple: firstly, as a British passport holder I hoped through my presence to buy time for a diplomatic solution to be found, such as partial withdrawal. Any postponement of military action could lead to a normalisation in relations or at least put off war until after the desert summer months, perhaps allowing some civilians an exodus to Jordan or elsewhere first. This tactic was somewhat diminished when the authority to control UN forces was delegated to the USA. Perhaps I should have anticipated this, but in view of the past history and the fact that Muslim forces achieved unilateral responsibility the surprise was justified. Secondly, I had managed to achieve widespread coverage in various media for an alternative point of view which I would not have access to if not for my commitment to see my task through. Thirdly, in the event of war, I was prepared to experiment with interposition between military forces. Fourthly, apart from ourselves the area was entirely cleared of independent witnesses including journalists and non-government aid workers; this made our presence vital. Fifthly, with doctors, nurses and medicines we could provide limited assistance to victims. Sixthly, I was personally equally prepared to offer food and hiding to any deserting soldiers and convey a positive image of pacifism to the rest; this would naturally require the accommodation of the rest of the camp, but that was an argument which might be worked through provided there was not too much dependence on the military at the peace camp. Other long term possibilities might have presented themselves such as marrying into a refugee family to lend them some national status.

I saw the camp as a practical tool rather than a symbolic one. Quite properly this was not everyone's point of view. Some saw military action as inevitable, but would not have it done in their name and so were demonstrating against this in the most extreme way available. Others saw it as having a potent spiritual dimension worth more than the sum of it parts. Many saw it as a publicity exercise thus having little further relevance should war break out. A number of the originators saw it as a physical obstacle. Each of us was assessing our motivations as we came towards the camp for those motives would affect our relationships, philosophy and action.

The coaches moved off the main road and down toward the gate of the camp. Here I was disappointed but not entirely surprised to see soldiers around a fire, keeping watch. Unlike the soldiers we had seen on the road, who had waved back at us in a bemused fashion, these were clearly used to Westerners and had been here some time. In Britain I had been assured and reassured that the Iraqi border guard had been confronted with a "Go or we go" ultimatum and had backed down to the extent of not patrolling the perimeter etc. Now here were the military warming their hands and guns at a kerosene-fed fire. They had been well established for a long time. Naturally there was a real sense of betrayal here, but at least I had got to the camp and all my mixed feelings were swamped beneath the surface of a wave of relief. I even found myself smiling!

From this time on the timeless constancy of the camp had its effect on me - we should have called the place Rivendell - and so, whilst I describe further events in chronological order, I cannot place dates and times to them until the Iraqis came for us on 27 January.

The next morning dawned pale with a slight haze and as I lay getting my bearings and feeling my usual morning inertia I could hear a rhythmic drumming which I had first become aware of in my sleep; my brain telling me to wake up and check on what subconsciously it had assumed was a very irregular heartbeat. It turned out to be Junsei Terasawa's Buddhist welcome to the day. Junsei spoke perfect English and he had been based in the UK for many years helping to set up the peace pagodas in Battersea and Milton Keynes. In Japan, as a student, he had gone through the conventional training and familial discipline until he had satisfied his parents that he had a trade to fall back on. Having thus reassured them, he took up practising the Buddhism he had been studying for many years. Though very spiritual, his feet were firmly planted in the physical world and he was always looking for practical applications for his beliefs. His influence was one of several which ensured that we were, as we boasted, a non-sectarian, multi-cultural and multi-ethnic camp. Being from a western pagan nature religion background through choice myself, I also appreciated his representation of an ancient eastern pagan faith, and his chanting was that of an order of monks several hundred years old. Set against a backdrop of the campsite which was an old resting-place for a traditional Muslim pilgrimage the image was very potent, this was simply a place of reflection with a sense of peace, or the possibility of it, hanging in the air.

The camp enclosure was set in the depth of a slight, human-made depression, from the roadway on one side to the raised earth on the other. We could nevertheless look out at the sun rising and setting across a sparse land pockmarked with clumps of vegetation. On occasion, one or other of the border guards would pick some of this and chew on it, pulling a sour face. This expression and the secretiveness with which they did it told me that this was no herbal delicacy, like dandelion, but simply grass. Sanctions were biting hard by mid-January, if even the military were not marching on full stomachs, yet clearly that was the case and I wondered how the peasant folk outside cities were surviving.

The camp was partially bisected by a structure of sloping corrugated iron roofs, held aloft by a metallic framework, under which our canvass tents were pitched. The tent openings all faced out towards a concrete parade ground and beyond this a number of small, young trees were installed at a uniform distance apart rather like a file of sentries. Further still were two barnlike structures housing small basic and unused toilet cubicles connected to a disused cesspit. Following the line of the rear of the tents would take you towards a building designated for the storing and cooking of food. All around the fence large water tanks were sited and just off the parade ground two demountable sheds served as gents and ladies toilets and washing points. That basically was it; functional and tidy. A more human face was added gradually with the addition of cosmetic slogans and banners. The dream became reality.

Many Meetings

Back in Britain I had been told that there would be just one general meeting per week. From here on, however, due to events there was to be a general meeting every day and the resulting clashes and arguments were to sap the morale of the whole camp. I was upset to discover in the first meeting that drinking water was brought in by an Iraqi state business and that Sadallah was only handling the buying and transport of food from a local market.

The meeting was useful in introducing me to some of the originators of the camp. Sadallah Attrib was, it emerged, a former British tank soldier during the Falklands/Malvinas conflict. His Arabic heritage and grasp of the language made him an ideal choice as go-getter for the camp, but he had a wealth of experience from other conflicts in which he had attempted various forms of peace-activism - not all of them pacifist. I should explain that within the broad boundaries of pacifism there are many schools of thought; pacifism by itself being simply opposition to organised warfare between nation states. Anti-militarists do not rule out the use of assassination. Meanwhile apathists follow the New Testament path of turning the other cheek, whilst the Asian path tends to aim for dynamic harmlessness. We had all agreed however that the camp was to remain a non-violent space in the war zone and generally this was adhered to. Well aware of his own take-charge attitude, Sadallah was attempting to adapt it to allow delegation and teamwork, but was severely hampered by his inherent lack of confidence in pacifists. His own attempts to accommodate others against his natural inclinations made him short-tempered on occasion, humorous and a real magic-worker.

Pat Arrowsmith has a reputation within the British peace movement for being hard to work with. This is because of her painful honesty and tendency to tackle problems head-on, like a bull at a gate. She also commands tremendous respect from those who know her well. Before I was born she was already carving a niche for herself in the peace, women's and human rights movements and was a valuable rallying point for all three. Her constant reference to Gandhi's *satyagraha* and the tactic of interposition did not endear her to those who had gone to the camp with a different purpose than physical action, and even those who were there with such a purpose were apprehensive of her talk of "sitting in front of tanks, if necessary." Nobody, however, was in any doubt that here was an activist who would do exactly what she said. Inevitably, Sadallah and Pat enjoyed some spectacular disagreements.

The arbitrators between these two were Jean Drèze and Bela Bhatia.

Though no less determined, this couple also recognised the value of diplomacy and achieving a position through step-by-step argument and the agreement of all. Despite the obvious drawbacks of this in a war situation, they nevertheless managed to begin to build and adapt a system which, given time, would have worked and it is one of the bittersweet ironies of the camp that just as we had begun to work through our differences, the camp was uprooted. Yet Jean and Bela did not see themselves as great architects of social invention and most of the time did not even realise that they were in a creative process.

Richard Crump rarely seemed to enter into deep philosophical debates yet he missed nothing, though with his humour, his memorable long laugh and his ability to lighten an atmosphere, he was invaluable to the camp at this stage. Many a gathering was preceded by his singing at the top of his voice "let's have a meeting" until it became an unofficial anthem among the Brits who appreciated the absurd. His serious side often manifested itself in the well-crafted poetry which he produced from time to time and in his Buddhism which was less demonstrative than Junsei's, but clearly personally rewarding. He had been active in ex-services CND for many years since retirement. Also active in that vital organisation was John Steel, who joined us from Baghdad shortly before the war. His very precise military manner at first hid a generous and remarkable nature in that he was so well-adjusted to seemingly any situation. Here was a man who would do all in his power to achieve what he felt was right, but was also strong enough to accept the inevitable. Rather than present ideas, John preferred to be given a task which he could then pursue to the n'th degree.

If there is such a thing as general national qualities, the Germans at the camp were also like this and took pride in their organisational abilities, but I suppose it was more to do with the comparative ages rather than cultures. The Brits, in general, were rather more argumentative, requiring a philosophy to back any action, and as there were a great many philosophies represented at the camp this led to a good deal of internal wrangling to be worked through. This may, though, have been simply due to a greater confidence in the common language and the resulting sense of power. The Australians saw themselves initially as the facilitators here, but slowly began to give up the ghost of the battle for a unified camp philosophy which was a hopeless task.

My own philosophy towards the future of the camp was guided by the fact that I had signed the Gulf Peace Team constitution, with its rigid guide-lines against alcohol etc., thus endorsing a code of conduct and stating an intention to interpose myself between forces. It appeared to me that many others had not seen or signed this and so were at a loss as to what they were doing there and what action to take in the event of war. As a result many meetings were taken up with this subject and slowly I realised the fatal flaw in the consensus process. Here we had seventy-three individuals each strong-minded enough to overcome the difficulties of getting to the camp. This melting-pot supported at least five mutually exclusive philosophies. Con-sensus, under such circumstances, was clearly a sham. I would personally have preferred a majoritarian voting allowing unilateral action for the camp whilst giving individuals a liberal freedom of action. It might have required a new form of democracy, but we had the right people and the right extreme circumstances to make it work. Unfortunately, the start of war was always going to entrench attitudes and highlight differences and so by mid-January it was far too late to overhaul the establishment - even supposing that those already established had been willing. Later in the campaign, the situation crystallised into three distinct groups, but at this stage there were just two evident: the "go" advocates and the "stay if we can" group.

The nuts and bolts of the first meeting I attended were about the work at the camp, hygiene, warnings about animals particularly cats, etc. Inter-jecting at almost every stage was a colourful new arrival who had travelled independently, calling himself "Baba." Baba felt that the whole ambience of the place was too authoritarian and he set out with anarchist zeal not to avoid meetings, but to attend and disrupt them thus stamping his perfectly fair and in some cases justified point of view unfairly on others. His inabil-ity to recognize the pros and cons of his own argument made most of us reject his points out of hand when in fact some things had a ring of truth about them. Baba betrayed his deep loathing and disrespect for those who did not subscribe to his point of view by referring to them as "chickens without heads" or "poisoned cockroaches" and he felt that some of us exhibited signs of both types of unfortunate creatures.

The End of the World... And a New Beginning

Apart from the general meeting, the last day of peace was spent in reflection, religious ceremony, humdrum chores and the general activity which characterised life at the camp. Underlying this I detected a charged atmos-phere of expectation. I found myself sitting at the treeline at one stage singing to myself - in various stages of fervour and emotion - the harmonic variations of John Lennon's "Give Peace A Chance" treating it very much as if it were a Buddhist mantra with mystic powers. Indeed what else did I have now as a tool for peace?

By now we all knew from our short-wave radios that the UN Secretary General had failed to persuade Saddam to withdraw his forces from Kuwait. We also knew that the Pope had called for peace, that there had been massive demonstrations in European and American cities for peace and that Bush had overcome Powell's objections to immediate military action. The Catch 22 absurdity of the war was reflected in Saddam's pronouncement that military action against Iraqi forces would result in Scud attacks on Israel.

We were joined by one last bunch of recruits, and from this day on, anyone else travelling to the camp would be stopped in Baghdad. This last group was Dutch or perhaps I should say Netherlands-based and, due to two significant events over the day and night, they were to remain almost an exclusive sub-group for most of the life of the camp. They consisted of Carol, of British descent but very Dutch-orientated; Kees, a gentle giant who it emerged had managed to sabotage military hardware in the past and been imprisoned for his pains; Vivian, who removed my status as the "babe" of the camp by virtue of being born several months before me; and Gerrit, who was the best equipped for argument and debate. Almost upon their arrival they were involved in controversy as several had left the camp perimeter, presumably by scaling the fence, and were brought back like errant children by border guard conscripts encamped and patrolling nearby. Such action was apparently against agreements reached with the local military commander, but it was surely inevitable that someone out of 73 pacifists, many of them used to confrontations with the military, would try this if only as a political statement of independence. Somebody amongst the established campers must have spoken to the Netherlands group for they kept very much to themselves for the rest of the day.

In the "War of the Worlds" H.G. Wells writes something like: "It seems extraordinary to me now that we spent this day (before the Martian invasion) just like any other." Yet despite the record amounts of TNT that were about to be unleashed that night I found myself helping Janet Cameron bury food waste at the perimeter fence in an attempt to avoid burning it, wasting kerosene and adding to global warming whilst attempting to fertilize the soil for when it rained. At the same time there was a constant nagging litany at the back of my mind for emergency procedure: "In an air raid go to the sand, keep your water bottle in your coat, compass, knife, roll sleeping bag and move fast, no lights…." We had decided to adopt a buddy system as our one concession to Vietnam and my buddy was Keith. Theoretically we were supposed to know where each other was at all times, but as no one was going anywhere we gave it a fairly liberal interpretation. If the camp was to be a first casualty of war, fighter-bombers were expected to aim for the tents and so Sadallah advised everyone to spread out widely so that if we were hit by strays we might not all go together. Basically as the Iraqis soon discovered there is no protection from air attack anywhere in the world. We had the closest thing to protection, neutrality, but we also had a military encampment for neighbour and the certainty of so-called collateral damage if they were a target.

So here we were relying on two things: a) that the military knew we were there and would be under some political pressure not to hit us, and b) that neither tried to take advantage of our presence. For example, it would have been easy for the coalition to use our non-violent space as an opportunity to hit the border guard without being retaliated against. Conversely, the Iraqis could have installed attack batteries nearby, under camouflage netting, and picked off stray aircraft. They could even have moved us altogether and the West would not know immediately. Neither of these possibilities occurred, but there is an area of great controversy where I feel that the coalition tried to use us to advantage, though it is worth pointing out that I was the only camper to hold this view: from the second night of war onwards the airspace above us seemed deliberately targeted as an area to safely marshal flights of bombers. Several events involving a spy plane and a low-flying aircraft led me to this conclusion.

For now, however, it is important to consider just what the peace camp represented to various sides in the conflict. My ideal was of a peace embassy and a non-violent space and for me that territory included the airspace directly above us. For diplomatic or other reasons the Iraqis respected this for the most part; though it would have been easy for them to install Frog or Scud offensive systems nearby thus threatening Saudi oil wells and forcing the coalition to realign along a wider front so delaying the ground advance. In fact they limited the military presence to border guards, lightly armed. Throughout the London representations to the Saudi embassy, the Saudis had procrastinated in recognising our presence on the border, thus leaving us in an effective limbo. This unsatisfactory state of affairs left the coalition military to make up their own minds about us which was very awkward for everyone concerned.

Through a paternal instinct it was not beyond the realms that they might launch a risky mission to remove us, causing bloodshed in the process. Alternatively it seemed conceivable that they could want to remove witnesses from the area by directly targeting us. Whilst we were not near Kuwait we all knew that the war could escalate to border incursions as was later proved in the opposite direction at the site of Hafji. As the only independents in Iraq we were treading a very thin tightrope - the journalists in Baghdad were no longer being treated as independent. In this respect a satellite telephone would have been invaluable to us at this stage and should be considered a prerequisite for any future ventures whilst actual UN recognition of a presence would also be desirable as a way of circumventing national prejudices.

A gentle shaking brought me to consciousness and I was immediately aware of an atmospheric heaviness in the air and a droning in the very lowest audible register. Andrew said: "Martin, keep calm. The war has started. Help wake people and get them out." Following his example I flashed my torch so that people could see who was talking to them. Various persons were going round the tent and it was not long before George was filming for posterity. I recently went to his studios and watched a tape of me believing I might die and yet still checking that I had the straps for my sleeping bag in my pocket - it's an unreal experience. I was still among the first out whilst Gerhart was alarmed at this turn of events and announced he intended to stay. I talked to this handsome German for a while and he clearly disliked not being with a crowd, but was adamant that he would not be moved which I respected. I suspect that several others in different tents also took this line, but I found myself with the more pragmatic majority shivering on the uneven terrain at the camp perimeter and gazing up at the truly apocalyptic scene as bombers and cruise missiles traversed the sky in wide formation.

Guiltily I remembered Keith and called out to him - it was impossible to see your hand in front of your face in some places - he answered. Gradually tactics were forgotten and people were drawn by the cold, awe and an indescribable emotion closer together. Somebody brought spare blankets from the big tent and I cursed myself for not having thought of it. I began to move around, keeping busy. An Iraqi driver who had left his seven children in Baghdad to bring us our food supply for the week was sobbing as he watched vast payloads of death pass overhead towards Baghdad and Kerbala. In view of my own willingness to have done this I found the scene unbearable. Soon we had more light than we needed as Kerbala glowed on our horizon whenever it was hit. Strong vibrations could also be felt in the ground and the air all around and the only sense which hinted to the distances involved was smell, for there was no hint yet of cordite or fuel in the air.

Everyone was huddling into smaller and smaller groups until most had formed one to one companionships and unspoken contracts to last the life of the camp. Stumbling across Sadallah, his fiancée Irmgard and Melissa I did at first settle with them, looking up at the red landing lights which had puzzlingly become evident in the sky. These obviously sub-sonic craft were weaving a precarious path around the bombers going to and fro around them and had left their lights on in the hope that fly-by-wire technology could help avoid a collision. Either these were civilian airliners caught out or they were Iraqi craft disguising themselves for a suicide mission or in order to defect.

I was starting to get a stiff neck from gazing upwards, but as I looked around Sadallah was hugging Irmgard on one side and Melissa on the other and repeating a litany without conviction that everything would be alright. Realizing that this made him feel better the two women were generously tolerating this. Feeling very much an outsider I left them draped in blankets in a picture the envy of macho men everywhere. Though I could have used some comfort myself a part of me would have prevented me from accepting it, so I wandered to the fence where I could be alone and looked back at the camp with this unique band of pilgrims in the foreground. The scene would have made a great painting, but sadly words are all I have.

The second night of bombing saw aircraft crossing the desert in much tighter, less widespread formation directly above us before splitting to go after different targets. After this, I saw them going singly to raids still using "our" airspace. They could afford single sorties as by that time nearly all of Saddam's airforce was either safely tucked away in Iran or destroyed in bunkers. As with the infantry at Ar'ar, the fighters heading for Iran had not fired back, even in the process of being shot down. I began to wonder whether the Iraqis actually had any ammunition, but was to discover with a shock at the camp and later in Baghdad that they had. The second day of war brought a shock much closer to home.

Emotional Dynamics

Keith and I were standing fairly isolated and having a chat when a woman walked up and asked for a word with me. Her demeanour was not distressed in the usual sense, but she was certainly pensive and confused, so I did not doubt what she told me. The previous night when everyone had felt drawn together under the doomsday scenes enacted above us like some perverse planetarium show, she had found herself huddled with a man who it seemed wanted more than comfort and she had been left quietly struggling against these advances all night long. She was not offering the name of the culprit. It seemed clear that she did not want an issue made of this, but also needed to be sure that it would not happen to her again. I was uncertain of this for who knew at this stage how many similar nights we had to endure and it could happen to someone else unless it was nipped in the bud. It was not my right however to raise the point and I made clear that she had my full support whatever she decided. What, though, did "support" mean. If I had known who it was I could have cautioned them and made them aware they were being watched, but I did not. The best I could offer was to invite her in future scenarios to join Keith and myself - he being very much in control of his own libido and I being smaller than her and less of a threat. I did also half jokingly offer some advice on the best parts of the male anatomy to hold in check when in a desperate situation, but this was rejected perhaps because it sounded violent or just plain disgusting. Keith, who had overheard, regarded me as if I were a madman.

Although she seemed satisfied at this stage, she later went to another man for advice and he suggested to her that he had been getting up to the same sort of thing on that night and that it simply showed the gulf of difference between what the two genders expect from closeness. This actually consoled her far more than my advice, though we still shared comforting moments together. Sure enough, in times after this when we were close I found myself becoming aroused yet knowing that I must do nothing to betray her trust in me which was a really awful situation. Though I was past the libidinous peak of my male teenage years, which Dudley Moore has referred to as "spermatozoa city", it was still a painful ordeal, more physically than emotionally. Gradually I knew I had to distance myself from this sweet torture but without distancing myself from her as a friend. In fact, as she got more into camp life and organizing, I became an irrelevance in every sense which I recognized with a mix of loss and relief.

On the more general subject of sex; it did occur at the camp, but less than most would think and more towards the end rather than the beginning. It has been suggested that people in radical, youth-based movements of the past such as peace and animal liberation do so either to work away sexual tensions or to connect with sexual partners. In some cases this may be true, particularly where youth will confuse its own motivations in that jumble of emotions characteristic of the age, but I have always viewed this argument as putting the cart before the horse. People decide first what is right and then try and find a way to live and love within those parameters; they do not seek love and then adapt themselves to it. Certainly the massive majority at the camp were celibate and happy to be so. There was, however, one night late in the campaign when I stumbled into the darkened big tent and kept stumbling as several bedding spaces had moved and several couples were quietly making love. I had not even realized until Keith, pining for his girl-friend and disgusted to be caught between two scenes, made his opinions known and then stormed out.

The realities of war were coming closer to us by now. One night we dozed in the big tent just as an aircraft flying impossibly low, which I thought I recognized as sounding like a British Tornado, from the sound they make low-flying in Cumbria, passed over the camp and then hit us with a sonic boom. Either he was scouting around lost and suddenly got his bearings or he knew exactly where he was and just wanted to keep us on our toes. Either way I felt with certainty now that we were viewed as a safe passage for aircraft. At first I mistook the boom for a bomb impacting, waiting a mo-ment in the tense silence and then yelled, "Na na, you missed us!", which elicited some laughter from the others.

Several nights on I was in no mood for joking when small arms fire started on the border and I thought that the land offensive was beginning at Ar'ar. Militarily it would have made perfect sense to ignore Iraq's sover-eignty and sweep round to Kuwait through the weak point in the Republic's armour.[19] At first I was confused, and then a certainty hit me and I said to myself that this moment was what I was here for and no matter what hap-pened now I had done my best. Comforted by such thoughts I went and joined a group in the kitchen that night, singing by candlelight and awaiting the bullets. So we sat in a biblically-lit scene, baking bread and Kathy Kelly sang with an American twang and the sweet innocence of an angel.

[19] *Editors*: As mentioned in the introduction, this option was indeed seriously considered by US military commanders.

Mistrust and Mayhem

Somebody was using lights for their own separate agenda. On one of my periodic walks with Prabha we both happened to be looking across the parade grounds towards the barns when a reddish light aimed at the aircraft passing overhead lit up and flashed several times in a lazy fashion, too slow to be Morse dots and dashes. We looked at each other. I said "Keep talking as if I'm still with you," and then set off across the parade ground. Getting that far quietly was easy, but as soon as I hit the stone and sand I had to go down on all fours which rather impeded my progress. Realizing I was making too much noise to be a surprise I leapt up and charged headlong, but too late. By the time I got around the barn there were several people milling about. I was convinced that this was not an agent - to be caught out so easily - but either an idiot having fun at everyone's expense or a deeply troubled personality in dire need of help from some quarter. I kept quiet about who I had seen at the perimeter, and we saw no point in raising the issue with the rest of the camp. I suggested it might be someone testing a torch, but it was not. This was a light deliberately aimed into the sky at a moment when aircraft were directly overhead and the red tinge was caused by the light passing through a hand masking it from the ground level.

After this incident, I put my name down on the duties roster every day for the nightwatch duty which had continued in the main tent as a habit even after the last coaches of volunteers had arrived. Nightwatch consisted simply of keeping kerosene burners going, ready for the breakfast crew to warm their hands on, keeping water boiling, etc., as well as wandering round the camp on occasion to ensure that no lights were visible and nothing untoward was happening. It also gave me the perfect excuse to avoid people in the mornings and I began to construct an emotional shell around myself, wanting to be entirely separate but lacking the nerve just yet to walk out of the gate which was left enticingly unmanned for part of the early hours. I felt that I would gradually find the motivation for this and kept my survival kit prepared.

The committed activist self-image I had was crumbling away and I was ageing like that picture of Dorian Grey. By this stage I was listless, uncommunicative, sullen and seeking to isolate myself, to have responsibility just for me. We were down to one main meal per day plus a small breakfast which I frequently avoided. Various people offered their own characteristic solutions to my deliberate isolation: ever practical Tim Barker asked me to help build the oven, take out lights, etc.; sporting and extrovert Ruhe wanted me in a volleyball team; Susan tried to console whilst Muriel was prepared to listen. I asked Muriel to pass around that I would be fine if left to my own devices. Such devices though basically consisted of me arranging my own escape. Slowly at first I got the Iraqis used to seeing me walk the perimeter of the camp until I knew every inch of the fence - where the dogs dug under, where a water tank could be scaled and the fence leapt over, the area behind the kitchen where conscripts congregated to beg for food and the blind spots. I had been gratified to see after a superheated, dusty desert wind that whereas our banners still flapped defiantly at their posts, some of the barbed wire had come down. This had a symbolic significance for me.

I knew now that I needed a confrontation and some small sense of personal empowerment even if it might lead to my death, but I was not ready to endanger other lives. Thus I sought a confrontation other than escape. I put up a notice in the communal tent to the effect that I was actively seeking to experiment with empowerment and welcomed ideas, discussions, workshops, etc. To this end I was fasting from solids as a test to discover my personal value to the Iraqis and with the stated purpose of having an agreed statement read on Baghdad Radio without censure. This notice was undersigned by Junsei who I think was also fasting and by Keith who had fasted for separate reasons, but who signed more out of loyalty to his increasingly unpopular ex-buddy. There was a valid point underlying this that we were no longer as a camp testing our value and forcing the pace. In many ways my fasting was irrelevant as my body had already begun to cannibalise on itself, so I was simply adding a political aspect to the inevitable. Without scales or mirrors at the camp I did not realise until much later how much I was reduced, but I hid my sunken eyes behind sunglasses and wore several layers of clothing which hid the fact that I had fallen from 8½ stone in weight to about 6. This was mainly due to nervous tension from meetings. Anyone who tries to claim that "names can never hurt you" is lying. In debate a verbal attack has the same physiological effect as a punch to the stomach. Thus I now stayed away from meetings on the whole.

Our removal now seemed inevitable and the Iraqis seemed to be just awaiting a lull in the air war to get us to Baghdad. This left Sadallah falling between two stools as he tried to negotiate for the camp and put the Iraqi military commander's point of view to us. Sadallah wanted to leave and was under pressure from Irmgard to do so, but his own machismo and commitment led to a feeling of responsibility for everyone. I felt that this was unfair both to him and ourselves and we began to plan for his departure with Aisha Khan, a London-based Indian woman acting as interpreter for another negotiator. The popular choice for negotiator was Jean, but Pat exercised her single veto to block the consensus and that was the end of that.

We split between those who felt that removal would be an evacuation and a small though significant minority who would consider it an eviction and wished to resist it. So the challenge we had to rise to as a camp was to accommodate and represent both views in the mayhem of a removal. At one meeting I suggested that we offer to take in Iraqi civilians who had been bombed, offer them shelter, food, medical assistance and status and that this action could pre-empt our removal and make the military commander's decision more difficult - Saddam having handed over unilateral responsibility to each military commander in anticipation of his command and control centre being bombed. The camp humoured me as a favourite family eccentric by listening quietly and then ignored the suggestion.

Before anything else could be dealt with, however, there was the question of who was taking food from the kitchen between meals. As someone who had managed and cooked in restaurants in the past I knew that I should generally avoid kitchen duties as my temptation was always to "pig out" on the food I was preparing. This, though, was something very different as people had actually been seen just blithely walking in and out with packages of stuff. The views on this ranged from: "people should be allowed to take what they want, when they want, otherwise it will add to resentment and mistrust"; to the view that we should be strictly rationed and the kitchen locked. As I was fasting, I stayed out of it, but it is certain that the politics of food is the hardest to reconcile. My fast did not last much beyond this as the final major event of the camp left me with an uncertain future, though in retrospect I think for this reason I should have continued it.

I was on nightwatch at 3 a.m. when the coaches turned up on 27 Jannuary. Baba was the first to hear them, indeed he seemed to be expecting them, and leapt up to make his own arrangements and associations. I called Sadallah from sleep and people began to rouse and find out what the engine revs were all about. I am sorry to say that this was the stage that I freaked out as the expectation of some action came over me like a tidal wave of relief, having been bottled up for so long, and I was racing up and down the camp yelling out each tiny new development like a town crier when all most people wanted to do was finish their sleep for the ordeal that lay ahead. I knew now what I wanted to do when they tried to remove us in the morning: I would attempt to stay. As soon as the drivers had gone off to sleep - they chose their coaches as they saw me hovering round them ominously - I began to separate my essentials and put them in my coat of many pockets which filled out until I looked like a Michelin Man. This effect was enhanced by the fact that I had "padded up" in expectation of a violent reaction from the bemused authorities so that my knees and elbows had extra protection.

Meanwhile there was a meeting going on! Around the kerosene stoves people voiced their fears and hopes for the day ahead and we concocted a plan which might yet create unity within our now unique culture and give us the authority to say that we separated with mutual respect and hope for each other's futures. The plan was that those intending to stay would form a circle while those leaving would form an outer circle, symbolically protective of us. We would sing an anthem and then it would be farewell to the leavers and they would get on the coaches. Faced with such a fait accompli there was an outside chance that the Iraqis would take the leavers and postpone removing the remainder. This would be in their pragmatic nature if faced with such finality.

Some of those who had intended to stay could now see a hopeless situation because a military reason for removal had been given and also we did not have consensus support. We made placards explaining our action. These placards were in English and Arabic script and said simply, "We choose to stay. Peace be with you." Some attempt was made at the double circle thanks to Susan, Muriel and many others as they accepted that we were entitled to try and stay. On the other hand, Baba between yelling at us about headless chickens was busily loading the coaches with our packs and the inner circle suffered watching everything they now had in the world going to Baghdad, where hopefully it would at least be put to good use by the leavers. Meanwhile we were singing We Shall Overcome in bravura fashion with additional verses of Gay and Straight Together and We Don't Want This War in case anyone was left in any doubt!

I had assumed that the Iraqis behind me were soldiers as Sadallah had promised, but have since been told that they were only drivers and the soldiers never entered the enclosure, though they were gathered around the fence to watch this spectacle. The credit for this has to go to Tariq who was handling our removal. He was quite simply brilliant and should teach some western agencies how to handle crowds: staring up at the sky at imaginary bombers behind us, tapping his watch self-consciously, pleading, cajoling, laughing, threatening, all in the space of about an hour. At one stage he went round kissing us all, to which Pat puzzled him by saying, " You might have some hope if you were a woman!" Finally he appeared to give up and the coaches were closed and began moving out towards the road, their occupants (some of whom I am sorry to say were laughing at us) waved, still perhaps unaware that they had our packs with them; I prefer to think so anyway. I did some mental calculations with my supplies and felt that with luck and good judgement we would be ok for several days on my rations alone. I fully expected John Steel at least would have something up his sleeves too as he never seemed unprepared for anything. The coaches stopped opposite us and then I knew that there was to be no reprieve. Tariq now tried a new approach. He wanted our fellow campers to lift us aboard the coaches. To their credit they refused as a whole though some did agree to come and talk to friends saying that we had made our point and it would be better for all concerned to go to Baghdad now, etc. It was a fraught time for all.

With the halting of the coaches the incredible mixed emotion of final farewells which had welled up inside me evaporated and with a deep sense of anti-climax I knew that they were not going to give up on us. Many were finally persuaded to get up and climb aboard the coaches. There was a good bonhomie among the remainder and Pat started to lead us in a vigorous song to rally the nerves as my stomach tightened in its customary knot and I awaited the first signs of violent impatience as I stared steadfastly ahead. For their part the Iraqis could not understand why we wanted to stay and were terrified of being caught on the road due to the delay which was my last forlorn hope that they might leave us if only in military custody at Ar'ar. To achieve this we would have to spin it out as long as possible.

It was an emotionally charged occasion as we were finally disempowered by the Iraqis, still showing our independence from the state to the last. My private hell is not physical pain, but ridicule and as I was picked up, slipped from their grasp, picked up again, I was being laughed at on one coach, the faces ingrained on my memory. Perhaps it was relief or being separate from the charged environment; it probably did not look much like a big deal, being reduced to going limp in someone else's control as a last effort to achieve your goal. All I can say is it took all of my reserves to do it and I am proud that I stood up to it for a while. However, my spirit was broken as I had glimpsed perhaps the worst side of the camp which had come to mean so much to me: I felt betrayed. Some of my companion stayers, such as Liz and Steve from Australia were also in an emotional state as we awaited the final removal of Pat which would signify the last death rattle of a peace presence in the Gulf. I feel that they should be remembered for posterity, but suspect that I have forgotten many of the stayers, though I do recall Liz, Steve, Jean, Bela, both Kathys, Detlef, Pat, Mark, John, Sylvia and Carol. I am proud to have been one of this "inner circle." As I stood beside them Pat was giving the Iraqis, not predisposed towards handling women at the best of times, social and personality problems for the rest of their lives as she out-stared them, grunted and moaned at them in an alarming fashion and generally shifted her weight so that they could not manoeuvre her up the coach steps. Eventually though she was pushed on board and the camp was suddenly an irrelevance. I picked up my pack and carried it aboard and it was goodbye to this empty space in the desert. Any chance of carrying the camp with us in a spiritual or metaphoric sense had withered away with our disunity and we were now just a bunch of individuals. If I had known the outcome in advance I think it likely that I would have followed my natural inclination to escape days earlier, but hope is a cruel deceiver who fools us all sometimes and I had borrowed life from hope for too long.

I am sorry to say that what I wanted as we sped along the deserted roadways to Baghdad was to be hit by a passing aircraft and all go up together, cleansing our presence from the area - such was my state of mind.

Epilogue

It sounds strange, but the journey back to London was probably the high point of my tortuous life. I was returning to my family in one piece; I had a job to go back to; my ambition as a writer was about to be fulfilled; I had "proved" myself as a pacifist, etc. Gradually over the weeks and months I saw these illusions disappear. Mistakenly I had based my writing relationship with Sally on an exclusive friendship. When I next spoke to her and she had got a friend to act as agent I felt a confidence had been betrayed and I could not trust her. This, coupled with the loss of funds through the theft of my credit card, made our project untenable. Articles I sent off were mainly returned with reject slips and I was badly treated by *New Statesman* magazine in particular; it seems that no one wanted peace news at the time. Rather than censor interviews the media tended to put them in afternoon slots and then leave them out for the all important evening programmes.

I began to receive hate mail and telephone calls, probably from a Nazi group I had infiltrated years before. My activism fell away to nothing and I had to question all my values. Friends would not talk to me. The personnel at work had changed and nobody knew me. Even the weather got me down. Then I had to face two bombshells. In May my father was diagnosed with a terminal cancer and given a year to live. Then one day I was picking up and reading newspapers on my train when I read this headline in *The Sun*: "Zany Ed killed by Giant Rat!".

Edward Poore, a fellow Gulf Peace Team member, had gone to Israel where he had been offered a job as a child physiotherapist. Always dogged by the salmonella he had picked up on his travels, he had an operation to remove it from his bowel. Whilst recuperating a cat in the house had brought a rat in and Ed tried to separate the two; whichever bit him, he went down with blood-poisoning. He turned down medical help and died in hospital a week later. If I had not read the paper I would never have known. Ed and I would probably have never seen each other again anyway, but it would have been nice to know he was spreading his humour elsewhere. Having made contact with his family I gave details of his memorial service to John Steel and he, Marnie, myself, Jerry and Julie Hampshire all managed to get there and mix with the great and the good. The Edward Poore Memorial Cup was set up by the squash world in his memory, as he was Britain's greatest coach of junior squash players. He now lies at Coddington church in the beautiful Malvern hills near his beloved Coddington Court. An Englishmen Abroad, as they say, he managed to represent all that is good in Englishmen without any of the bad attributes. I loved him dearly.

Now I have to face up to the future and I guess I am writing this as therapy. It has not all been bad. I was honoured to give a speech at Fairford airbase alongside the Right Honourable Tony Benn, MP and (the equally honourable) Bruce Kent. I am still trying to get my "Gulf medal" as I refer to those talismans from Mother Teresa.[20] I have met Miller, George, Jimmy, Carol, Richard and others since leaving Amman.

Whatever awaits us now we can be proud that we stood up for what we believe in and created a little piece of history in a dusty patch of land with the ridiculous name of Ar'ar. Peace be with us.

---

[20] *Editors*: This is a reference to the medals sent by Mother Teresa to the Gulf Peace Team, as a token of support.

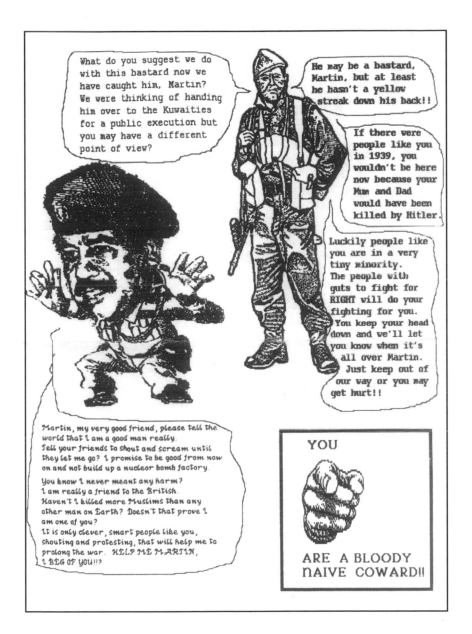

A sample of the hate mail that Martin received after returning to London.

Calm before the storm

Hasan Kilgour

After the bustle and confusion of London it was a relief to be in Jordan at last. Amman felt friendly, peaceful and immediately comfortable. I was travelling with Mark Chapman, an Irish "trainee anarcho-pacifist-green-veggie-internationalist-traveller". We stayed a night at the Ammon Hotel, later to become the Gulf Peace Team's Jordan HQ, but at that time almost deserted. I awoke at dawn, to the sound of a particularly beautiful call-to-prayer, which bounced its multiple echoes around the seven hills that Amman is built upon.

The next day we flew to Baghdad, where we were met by an official from the Organisation for Friendship, Peace and Solidarity. We were driven to the hastily renamed Peace and Friendship Village outside Baghdad, which had previously been a holiday resort for weddings, honeymoons and family weekends away; now it was home to a variety of peace missions and delegations, with food and accommodation laid on for free. We had a bungalow to ourselves, with central heating and plenty of hot water, which were very welcome, as the weather was chilly and damp. We met Ulli, from Germany, who was to stay in Baghdad and act as a link for the Gulf Peace Team. She had built a lovely little crib in her bungalow, using clay and rushes from the banks of the river Tigris, which flowed past the camp. Seeing the crib, I realised it was Christmas Eve

Christmas Day was bright and warm. It was good to be hundreds of miles from seasonal TV jingles and drunks falling over on the underground. Instead, we were sitting in the sun by the green banks of the river, seeing some blue sky for a change and heading for the desert. In the afternoon a minibus arrived from the peace camp and we met up with Jean, Bela, Pat and Sadallah. Bela was off to India, but the rest of us boarded the bus late in the evening and set off for the camp. A stop at a roadside teashop on the outskirts of Baghdad was followed by four hours of looking at nothing in particular and half-dozing till we reached our destination at two o'clock in the morning.

What a vividly awful first impression - cold, dark, wet, windy, flooded in places after a rainstorm, hard white aro-lights glinting on the perimeter fence, a wide expanse of dark asphalt inside the fence, wild dogs howling dementedly in the distance, an enormous metal shelter, reminiscent of a cattle enclosure, with big square tents underneath it and a floor of concrete. It soon became more humanised as Richard woke up and greeted us with cheery tales of rainwater flooding into the tent and forming rivers, necessitating speedy relocation of beds. Then off to a drier tent, and peaceful slumber, with earplugs to cover bouts of dog-noise.

Boxing Day dawned cold and grey, but was soon enlivened by introductions to fellow occupants, over tea in tiny plastic mugs with Iraqi bread and Scottish marmalade. I took a liking to that bread, which was like layers of light, thin chapatis. Breakfast was followed by a meeting, during which we decided to clean up the camp. I spent the morning clearing up litter which had been blown by the prevailing winds against the nearest section of the fence. Unearthing ancient Turkish cigarette packets and Syrian sweet-wrappers, I mused about litter problems on the road to Mecca.

We had lunch in the tent that had been designated as the main communal room, which had been transformed and beautified during the morning. I don't remember anything else about that day, and indeed the next few days swam together in such a way as to make it difficult to order events. The idea of keeping a diary slipped away, as did the one about sitting alone on a big dune under the moonlight, having mystical experiences. For a start, it wasn't possible to see much of the outside world at all. The camp was predominantly a social event. I remember fascinating discussions, interesting ideas from unusual individuals whose characters became more well-shaded and likeable as the days wore on.

From Boxing Day to New Year's Eve the same twenty people were living in the camp. Jean spent a day or two in Baghdad and Sadallah took a daytrip to Kerbala to buy supplies, but otherwise we were in our own world. We were a wide variety of people with little in common except an aversion to war, yet we did manage to live together in a very amicable way. At the camp at the same time as me were: Pat Arrowsmith, Britain; Irmgard Ehrenberg, Austria; Annelise Gehring, Germany; Trace Hodgson, New Zealand; Kees Koning, Holland; Monika Krohns, Germany; Doris Kurz, Austria; John Livesey, New Zealand; Marylene Schultz, France; Gisela Smolik, Germany; John Steel, Britain; Maurizio Torti, Italy; Francesco Tullio, Italy;

Hans Uwland, Holland.

Some days were sunny and dry, but few were warm. Nights always freezing. Sometimes a hot shower helped, though too many for too long assisted the dry desert air in cracking skin and lips. Breakfast was taken outside, standing around a laden bench. At first it was situated on the shaded, windy side of the tents, until we twigged and moved to the sheltered side, where the weak sun crawled slowly above a line of trees, the only ones in the area. Those still in sleeping bags knew that breakfast was afoot when they heard the whistlings and deep "On-pabom-pabom" humming of Kees, who only ever whistled and hummed at breakfast time. A morning meeting followed, to discuss the day's practicalities. Cooking rotas were filled, rubbish pits dug - having an Iraqi rubbish truck remove it was voted ideologically unsound and burning it ecologically so. Some people took on the task of painting and decorating the camp - new ideas arose at each meeting.

It was usually fairly warm and sunny by the middle of each day, so we took our mats and chairs and had lunch outside, with a dish each for carnivores and vegetarians. Before supper the evening meeting was held, usually of a more philosophical or ideological nature than the morning's. At this stage in the group's history, meetings weren't the ordeal that they often later became, when the mere word could reduce grown men to shivering wrecks. At the time there were less people, so it was easier for everyone to participate. The meetings were conducted in English, necessitating slow clear speech by native speakers, particularly when excited and anxious to make a point. Gisela knew no English, but had the salient points whispered to her in German.

We decided that it wasn't appropriate to encourage much of an Iraqi presence in the camp, the guards being dissuaded from entering the compound. We were aware of the danger of being compromised; after all, the Saudis hadn't allowed us to set up a camp on their side of the border, but the Iraqis had welcomed us and were looking after us very well. It was no trouble for our salivating home media to portray us as Saddam's stooges, all-purpose traitors and twits. Amir, our young Iraqi liaison, was likeable enough but was generally kept at something of a distance, albeit friendly. He was the only Iraqi we saw much of, apart from the genial camp doctor, who was always around when needed. A few of the team were struck down by stomach ailments and the like. Richard was out of action for a few days and Trace had a nasty bout of something-or-other.

Midway through the week we played football against the Iraqi Army - well six of them anyway. Sadallah, Mauricio, Trace, Mark, Francesco, Bruce and myself played for the peace camp. The Iraqi soldiers drew well ahead at the beginning of the match, so gave us a chance by putting the camp doctor in their team - I was relieved that his doctoring wasn't like his football. It was a hard, energetic game that left me aching for a day or two. We fought back bravely, but lost 10-7. After the game we limped and staggered our way to the tea and biscuits, which the soldiers politely declined, quickly disappearing, obviously not comfortable about too much fraternisation. A few months later we heard that the camp had been bombed shortly after evacuation of the Gulf Peace Team, with many casualties. I wonder how many of their team survived?

Later in the week we started to make plans for an event on New Year's Eve. A variety of visitors, bigwigs, media people and international peacepersons were due to visit for a celebration. Doris was the main initiator of artistic events, teaching songs, circle dances and games to anyone who could be pulled in them. By this time, camp life had settled into a gentle routine, and we were more or less cut off from the world. We'd heard nothing from the London office of the Gulf Peace Team, or anywhere else for that matter, and our only source of outside information was Mark's short-wave radio. But whatever grim portents crackled out from the world service, life was enjoyable in the camp.

New Year's Eve brought a change of mood. Suddenly, loads of people were walking through the gates - they seemed to be everywhere, some bristling with cameras, lights and microphones. After songs of welcome, handshakes and embracings, a press conference was held in the packed main tent. Some of the camp occupants had prepared food and drink (non-alcoholic, in compliance with the camp regulations) and officials from the Organisation for Friendship, Peace and Solidarity had also brought some. So we all set about it and made merry. But this wasn't any old New Year's Eve. So the occasion became more quiet and thoughtful towards midnight as we focussed on where we were and why we were there - the bloody new year crept quietly in.

The intimate atmosphere that had prevailed in the camp had now passed. Half the group was leaving for Baghdad the next day, so it felt like the right time to go. I was due back in London on 7 January and wanted to see more of Baghdad and Amman before leaving. Anyway, I'd had enough of camping. An overnight rainstorm left the camp looking as bedraggled as when I'd arrived, if more lived-in, not only by humans - the camp cats had raided the rubbish bags during the night. After long goodbyes, some tearful (plenty more of those to come), we set off in two minibuses through puddles into the desert.

On 5 January I flew back to Amman, where Trace met me at the airport. Carol, whom I knew from London, was at the Ammon Hotel, having come over to smooth the passage of incoming campers. Over the next few days she, Trace and I worked closely together, organising arrivals and departures, briefing and orientating volunteers (often culture-shocked, jet-lagged or plain nervous), keeping communications open with London, Baghdad and elsewhere and dealing with media attention. Each day a new bunch of volunteers arrived, each with different characteristics that changed the hotel's atmosphere while they were there.

I was supposed to be back in London, but it was difficult to leave Amman - it was such a friendly place, sitting quietly between warring giants. One day there were no arrivals or departures, so Trace, Carol and I decided upon a daytrip to the Dead Sea with Attar the taximan. We didn't reach our destination, as we were arrested in the Jordan Valley and spent half the day being interrogated. They had probably seen me waving a camera around, ignorant of the surrounding hidden military installations. However, it was polite and friendly as interrogations go. Having seen the interiors of two cells, we were finally ushered into big armchairs in the lushly-carpeted office of a head honcho, where coffee was served. After his profuse apologies, accompanied by offers of tea and cocoa, we were released.

Life became hectic at Ammon Hotel. The tension in the air was palpable, each change in the news bringing a change of mood amongst the local population, sending them constantly veering between hope and despair. By the time I left on 14 January I felt as overstimulated and half-mad as an amphetamine user, only to be assaulted by severe culture-shock upon arrival in London. It felt cold and hard after Amman, with a smell of war fever - a huge psychic bow being tightly stretched, tensed for release.

16 January. The phone rang - it was Daniel. "They've gone in" he said. That night, twenty premature babies were born at Alwiya Children's Hospital, Baghdad. Two were alive by the morning. The cost of that first night of war could have sorted out the famine facing twenty-seven African countries. Britain's contribution to the relief of that famine was less than the cost of

one Tornado bomber. Returning to Amman at the end of February, I was next in Baghdad in April, touring children's hospitals with a camera, witnessing the consequences, watching small children dying from starvation and other preventable diseases. So there goes another worse-than-useless war, with the casualties still mounting... and they called the Gulf Peace Team lunatics.

A peace camp between two fronts

Detlef Enge-Bastien

It is 13 January, two days before the expiry of the UN deadline for the withdrawal of Iraqi troops from Kuwait. Press conference and religious service at Frankfurt Airport. Another group of six Germans join the non-violent peace presence in Iraq. We still wish to stop this war. There simply must be a way out. Even before it happens the scenario is easy to see: hundreds of thousands of military and civilian deaths, burning oil wells further damaging this already endangered planet, indigenous peoples driven to war. Now, at a time of disarmament and hope for peace between East and West, the world should not forget we were then on the brink of chemical and nuclear warfare.

Because of these possibilities, our group decided to hold a nonviolent demonstration between the fronts. We trusted one another. We had to stand by each other on this road. But we wouldn't be alone. The next week would bring another peace group to Iraq. We believe both in democracy and our decision to take this risk. We want to call attention to the peace initiative. We want to stir public opinion as we stirred the emotions of our families and friends with our departures for Iraq. But is there enough time left?

On the radio we hear that the US Senate has empowered President Bush to begin hostilities. Short of a miracle, we will be travelling to a war zone. We do not want to turn around. One of the group decides to stay in Germany. He cries. It would be easier for him to go with us. But he is thinking about his mother at home. We all find his decision courageous.

I pray for a miracle and believe that this hope is much more rational than to depend on political diplomacy. Yesterday at a demonstration in Trier I confidently shouted, "We will see each other soon. Ciao!" Now as we go through the airport security controls my knees are wobbly. My face reflects both nervous energy and serious thoughts. Then we are on board and the plane starts. I like the initial thrust of the engines. The pressure on my back tells me: This time I must act! This time say "no" to a war when peace is possible! This time maintain the ideal of disobedience for a greater good! The Scholl siblings had it much harder opposing the Nazis. As young students and members of the "White Rose" faction in 1943 they were quickly arrested and executed for distributing anti-Nazi literature at the University of Munich. But what courage they had in adversity! In the last few days I have thought of them often. With their real bravery, hope, and trust in God they are my inspiration. But the plane has started. The dice are thrown. I relax.

On the plane there are Jordanian families. The children are playful and innocent, the women exude oriental beauty and dignity, the men offer us cigarettes and we talk about the crisis. No one has ever liked Saddam Hussein but now he is a symbol for the self-respect of the Arab world. The industrial nations possess no inherent right to defend "their" oil with weapons of war. I detect no hate in these words. They sound plausible and endlessly sad.

Arabs - what drives us to look down at these educated, friendly and emotional people? I ask myself how many of my own people, who are so sure of their right to the Arabian oil, have ever even spoken to an Arab or visited one of their countries. After this conversation with my fellow travellers I feel I have indeed taken the right journey.

In Amman a reception and connecting flight await us via Tim Barker of the London office of the Gulf Peace Team. He is wearing a T-shirt with the peace team's emblem which embodies this experience for me. He radiates good humour and energy. The other teammates are diverse, men and women of different callings and various political stripes. Even an English Tory is there. All age groups from 20 to 78 are represented. Not just young and healthy types like the American war correspondents. Some of us are even handicapped. From every direction the participants have gathered here: everyone with their own story, no one without deep reflection, many with a profound sense of political commitment. It is a wonderful experience to meet them all.

At the Baghdad airport, there are decked-out soldiers and flashy children's dance groups. Today they display the pasted smiles of a totalitarian regime. Later impressions of the Iraqis will be totally different. Those whom I will eventually meet will be overwhelmingly friendly, caring and humorous. I never saw any who were enthusiastic for war. No flag-waving fundamentalism. My impression is that most Iraqis, even those in the higher echelons of government, don't believe it will come to war despite the official propaganda declaring "the mother of all battles".

At 4 a.m. we arrive at the peace camp, in a biting cold. The tents are laid out on an asphalt field in the middle of an endless desert. This hamlet is a halt for pilgrims on their way to Mecca. We are exhausted but happy to finally reach the destination of our mission.

There are now 73 participants from 15 countries in the peace camp at Ar'ar. In Baghdad there are 11 more people demonstrating by their presence their belief that a peaceful solution is still possible. It is 15 January, the day of the ultimatum. The Ar'ar camp has been there since 24 December. We will soon see what effect our presence has. A communal supper at twilight, group singing, brave jokes. Then to bed on our inflatable mattresses. Our first night's sleep in the desert of Iraq.

On Martin Luther King's birthday some of us pray together for peace. Does President Bush realise that his ultimatum falls on this day? In the evening the group celebrates. Our Buddhist monk pounds on his expressive drums. We practice our meditation stances. And in the evening, under the stars, we have a merry barbecue. It is supposed to be a peace camp, not a depression camp...

It is the evening of 15 January. Tomorrow we will see. Two of our group are on nightwatch. Then suddenly at 2 a.m. we are woken up. "Get up everybody! It's war!" The roaring engines of allied bomber squadrons are above us. Occasionally a dive bomber. Shrill barking from scattered dogs in the desert. They can't stand this strange loud noise. Some of them will bark themselves completely hoarse the whole night.

Bombs don't fall on Ar'ar. The main target of this attack is Baghdad. But as we had practised the evening before we grab our backpacks and sleeping bags and run out of the tents. In small groups we penetrate the surrounding desert and remain there the rest of the night. We feel relatively safe. Then a car comes without lights and drives directly towards us. It stops and stays there, seemingly also happy not to spend the night alone - finding comfort amongst our sleeping bags. True! The Iraqi "minder" assigned to the camp feels safer with us! The next morning he will camouflage his car with loam and, despite continuous bombings, drive to Baghdad to see his wife and children and bring them to the countryside.

The morning dawns. The sky is blood red in the north. Baghdad is burning having been shelled without pause. We think of the people there and our teammates. Some of us cry quietly. We empathize with those being shelled. I myself have no tears, f eel anxious - somehow absurd. I am disappointed and angry. Now we are also in the middle of this war. We failed to prevent it! The bombing even started immediately after the ultimatum was up.

We listen to the BBC on a transistor radio. Again and again we hear President Bush's official reasons for the strike. They sound so hypocritical. None of us has overlooked the Iraqi war policy and the occupation of Kuwait. We carry with us the human rights report from Amnesty International about the Iraqi regime in Kuwait. But this outbreak of war could have been avoided had it been possible for the Iraqis to retreat without being humiliated. The Palestinian question could have been put on the same agenda as the resolution against Iraq. That would not have been a gift but rather realistic politics. But now there is war. Irmgard Krohns will later describe our mood at this point as "our hearts were in the desert".

Now the sounds of missiles and plane shellings on the radio. It seems every military detail is deemed newsworthy for the BBC. However our presence here in the area of conflict is not mentioned by anyone. In November the media noted the release of every individual hostage from Iraq. Now the presence of our camp on the front seems to have been struck from the public consciousness. Without over-estimating the worth of our demonstrations I find this strange and begin to have some doubts about the objectivity of news reports. Only later do I discover that many journalists at home, suffering from heavy military censorship, have the same doubts.

In the following days we discuss how we can work towards an end to the fighting and how, should the situation arise, to prevent an emergency camp evacuation. Considering the great personal risks involved the readiness of our members to take a stand varies widely. Pat Arrowsmith's "rainbow group" plan to wander out into the no-man's land of the deep desert without adequate supplies of water and food frightens me. I think of my daughters at home and don't wish to risk my life unless there is a possibility of achieving our aims.

Finally, we decide on a symbolic form of protest against the now-certain removal of our camp and the imminent outbreak of hostilities in this section of the front. We will demonstrate our objections to evacuation by singing resistance songs in English and Arabic, staging a sit-down and, if necessary, letting ourselves be limply carried off.

In the early morning of 27 January, buses and a military truck drive up. We are informed that because of an impending artillery attack the camp must be evacuated by 2 p.m. Instructions from Baghdad, these agitated officials tell us. Nevertheless they take pains to be friendly.

Around noon, thirteen of our group are still sitting on the ground with their luggage when something amazing happens. One of the Iraqi soldiers, who has absolutely no knowledge of English, comes forward and kisses each of us on the head while saying "Baghdad, Baghdad". He wishes to explain once again that we should not disobey. Without wanting to minimize the gravity of this war or our situation, I must say that this scene deeply touches me and buoys my mood. Do these people seem like the villains who unleashed horror and hate into the world?. The treatment we received at Ar'ar should at least give the world pause to reflect on its negative opinions of Iraq.

The evacuation to the buses follows peacefully. We drive back to Baghdad over a recently bombed road. Soon there will be fighting at Ar'ar. Was our camp a failure? Were we simply used? Or was it a marginal success, a symbolic cry for peace that managed to protect Ar'ar for almost two weeks? The effectiveness of the peace camp is a matter of much debate among us.

We are brought to the dark and ghostly Al Rasheed hotel which is currently used as a base for western journalists. All of Baghdad is without water and electricity. At night I look through the hotel window and watch the shelling of my immediate neighbourhood. Contrary to allied reports there are thousands of civilian casualties in Baghdad. Many of them will have to undergo horrid operations without the benefit of disinfectants or pain-killers.

Nearly all the strategic targets will be hit three or four times over the coming days. Many missiles, however, miss their targets. Instead they land on stores, residences, mosques, the crowded market in Felluja. The baby-milk factory in Abu Gheraib. A petrol service station in Hillah. And finally the civilian bomb shelter in the Ameriyeh residential district of Baghdad, where 386 women and children were killed. Black mourning crepe now carries the names of neighbours who are gone. This quarter of the city will forever remain a testimony to the misery, death and abject cowardice of the politics of war. Did the Kuwait invasion really call for this military solution?

On 31 January, all members of the Gulf Peace Team are driven by bus to Amman, Jordan. Previously refugees and Jordanian truck drivers were bombed on this same road. At home we will plead for an end to this offensive. But the bombings will continue, the ground offensive take place. Our group will later attest to the catastrophic effects of war on the Iraqi infrastructure, and the ghastly contribution of the embargo to civilian deaths.

Members of the Gulf Peace Team will have to undergo dangerous conditions to accompany first-aid shipments to Iraq. We will help in a real and constructive way but still not be able to significantly stem the tide of civilian deaths after the end of the military engagement.

Did we fail? Could we have done anything more during this little slot of history? Were our personal sacrifices and the worries of our families in vain? No! At least there was a "No!", this time, to the historical march of war. Perhaps it was a beginning.

We will see how much strength it takes to establish peace. Many of us are exhausted and sad about the developments of the Gulf war. But we will not give up hope. We were not successful in the sense of hindering the war. But we did all that we could under the circumstances. When the steps others have taken to prevent war have failed, our own steps grow in importance. The quest for effective nonviolent responses to war continues. If we cannot discover the real reasons for this conflict and combat them, then other wars of this sort are bound to happen again.

Letter to the children

Jerry Hartigan

Friday 25 January 1991 (Judayyidat Ar'ar, Iraq)

Dear Rosanna, Martin, Paddy and James,

The sun was shining this morning after wind, rain and invasion of our tent by cats during the night. I was too late to chant with Junsei Terasawa, but in time for breakfast of rice pudding and chapati. After a reasonably short and orderly affinity group meeting I went on my chore of toilet cleaning under instruction from Detlef. The next item on the programme is an Arabic class (my fourth) with Sadallah, but I found that he had gone to Kerbala for provisions.

Everything changed at 3 a.m. on 17 January, when we woke up to hear talk of "five bombs" having been heard. We could then hear aircraft and distant explosions, and see the sky lit up in various areas. All very disturbing and frightening. Since then our Iraqi "minder" keeps reassuring us but, so far, no fresh stores or camper leaving or returning.

There are 73 of us at the camp, divided into five affinity groups. After the war started, we had about four days of constant meetings, thoroughly exhausting and frustrating for everybody - now we consider things in our affinity groups with reps going to the steering committee for implementation. The points at issue were whether, if evacuation came, we would willingly go or attempt to stay (my choice). "Information" suggested the Iraqi military wanted us out of the way. A week later, with no sign of transport, that seems fairly academic. Then there was a proposal, which I supported, that a group, after telling the Iraqi military authorities, would leave the camp with minimal supplies (to be carried by ourselves and with two bicycles and a wheelbarrow) and walk to the "no man's land" between the Iraqi and Saudi border posts to set up a peace camp on genuinely neutral ground. This group was politely known as "the border party", and impolitely referred to as suicidal (it is mainly British and Irish with US and Aussie support). When it became clear that evacuation was not imminent, the idea of the border party was shelved, but the camp is still divided on the priority of (1) maintaining our presence here as a neutral peace camp between two opposing armies, and (2) leaving as soon as possible for Baghdad (or a friendly border). In the latter case, we would disperse to work in Iraqi hospitals, help war refugees in Jordan, or return home to pursue the campaign, all as a development of the peace camp idea.

Monday 28 January (Al Rasheed Hotel, Baghdad)

It seems that 3 a.m. is the significant hour. At that time on Sunday morning, two 45-seater coaches and an articulated lorry arrived to take us and camp equipment away so that the army could have the area clear. Officials from the Organisation for Friendship, Peace and Solidarity had come, i.e. more minders, and they made it clear that they wanted everybody to move. A meeting of 24 who wished to stay and maintain the camp dwindled to 12 of us who sat to "resist" evacuation, e.g. I was carried to the coach by kind and delightful Iraqi officials. Peace camp opponents of anyone staying were by no means so kind nor at all delightful. In fact all 73 left in the two coaches on time at 11 a.m. with the lorry and the equipment destined for a children's hospital.

Once again we had been faced with risking conflict or confrontation with (1) Iraqi officials and (2) peace campers trying to impose their own twisted ideas on us. As usual finding the best course between right and wrong, going for maximum effect with maximum commitment and maximum risk commensurate with sound appreciation of the position and avoidance of unnecessary damage was difficult, like riding a knife edge. "The situation was fraught with difficulties and liable to infinite misconception" as Uncle Hugh used to say. In this sort of situations my policy is to stick to basic principles, not allow myself to be deflected and remember my role.

Wednesday 30 January (Al Rasheed Hotel, Baghdad)

Yesterday we were taken on our coaches to see the bombed milk factory at Abu Gheraib, just outside Baghdad. We approached it via an agricultural area, through a village with a reassuring smell of cattle muck and sight of chickens, sheep, donkeys, etc. The factory was clearly a milk processing plant producing "Alban Milk Powder Sweetened" (for example), said to be the only milk powder for varying ages. It had been hit twice and was a total write off, with sheets of corrugated iron scattered everywhere. We were able to salvage already packaged milk powder, labels, tin tops, etc. The plant was built to a French design and used British skimmed milk, British companies were named and machinery had instructions in English.

We now contemplate the next phase of this adventure, the beginning of our return to the west. Home is the one thing that will be great to see again, but thoughts of our return to accusations of sanctions-busting, or of assisting Iraqi propaganda, or of consorting with the enemy, are depressing. Similar thoughts of having to convince unbelievers that we have been treated as honoured guests by a proud and kindly people, and of using our experience here to generate increased opposition to the war, are somewhat daunting - not to mention returning to the office where life was hairy enough pre-war. Anyway we all seem to have happy memories of Jordan from our journey out and we look forward to renewing our acquaintance with the Jordanian people.

Saturday 2 February (Ammon Training Hotel, Amman)

Today we took a day off meetings and Cliff, Mark and I went to the local *bazaar*, then to a book exhibition. We had lunch in the adjoining hole-in-the-wall café. Recent visitors from Baghdad (especially peace campers) command immediate interest and questions about personal experiences of the situation. A delightful old nun with a rosary round her neck sits down next to us to talk in French and then English. She turns out to be an Arab originally from Palestine, of the Holy Rosary Order from a convent in Amman, and passionately condemns the evils of war brought by the devil, George Bush. All this under wall portraits of King Hussein and Saddam Hussein, whom she referred to as "angels". It was good to hear from her how good relations were between Christians and Muslims in Jordan. It was typical that our snack of eggs, potato, humus and coffee was "on the house". The proprietors of that tiny café would not accept payment.

We all seem to feel very much at home in Jordan. Arab people are so polite, kind, warm and friendly. This of course applies equally in Iraq and, having met people from Algiers, Tunis, etc., one can begin to get impressions and some understanding of an Arab nation. One little incident was so revealing. Our taxi driver lost concentration for an instant and touched a car rushing in from the right. Everybody got out, surveyed the damage (a broken headlight), then hands were shaken all round and cars drove on.

At the moment the first priority is to get home, a frightening prospect. Then I need to find out what has happened and what is needed to pursue the goal of an end to the evils of this war and spare those wonderful people in the Middle East more death and destruction. People in the rest of the world are and will be suffering also. There is also the problem of avoiding the tentacles of the grey people, who might be interested in what I have seen for the wrong reasons, and escaping the line of fire from cameras and newshounds, while at the same time doing my bit for the campaign.

Well, shortly we will be in London in a country which is party to the conflict and I have no doubt it will be easier to see the course that needs to be taken, and to look back at this project with proper detachment. You have to remember that we have all been on a sort of fantasy trip and our various reactions no doubt reveal this. In the course of time we will perhaps resume our normal selves but all of us are indelibly affected by our recent experiences, never to be forgotten.

Sunday 3 February

Now we have come down to earth at Heathrow to a great welcome and lots of hugs, but a reader of *The Sun* has already told us that all the Iraqis are "savages" and this makes me miss the good clean air of the desert. To the last our expedition continued to amaze us with incredible mysteries constantly paraded before our eyes. On the flight home a companion was the American, Ellen Rosser, 17 days into her fast which started at the outbreak of war. She had picketed the US Embassy at Amman and was on her way back to continue in Washington, a truly remarkable woman. Then there were the nine children on their way from Iran to find refuge in Paris, being shepherded through the airports at Amman and Vienna, and off the plane at Orly. It was sad that the adventure was coming to an end but even sadder that we were leaving so many beautiful people behind in such danger in Iraq and Jordan, people who had greeted us with such warmth, kindness and understanding.

So this is just a little bit of my story.

In peace and love,

Jerry

Desert diary

Bob Bossie

Left on Saturday 5 January with Diana. Paul and Rich came to the airport with me. Difficult separation knowing where I'm going and why. Diana's son Evan came also.

Slept well for the first time on an east bound flight. I am particularly calm going into this. I continue to feel right about it. Diana says, no point being anxious. Take it as it comes.

If war breaks out they'll roll over the camp without a thought. All the military will be concentrating on "first blood". A few more civilian casualties can't be a big deal when you're thinking of tens of thousands. Yet, even thinking of this, it seems right to be here. Where and when will the peacemakers stand resolutely against war, violence, oppression? When will they go off to do battle with the same determination as the soldiers? When will families respond to their going in the same way, crying for their young, yet proudly willing to sacrifice? Despite the ambiguities I know deeply that it is "right and just" that we should do this.

On the road to Baghdad, at the border, we talked with a very distinguished Palestinian, who was taking his seven children to Jordan to safety. He spoke to us eloquently, telling us he was driven from Palestine to Jordan, Jordan to Kuwait and now from Kuwait. He would return to Kuwait to defend it against the Americans. "I love the Americans, I know it is the government that does this. I offer my hand in friendship". He shook with Bruce symbolically, "but if you strike my child, I will strike you and your children", he said.

We started passing tanks on carriers as we approached Baghdad, seeing even gun emplacements. Finally we reached the centre of Baghdad at about 11 a.m. Out of nowhere this cabby appeared and took us to the International Peace and Friendship Village for nothing.

Before I go on I want to reflect that for a hundred reasons I should not be here. From the way I came to my decision, the difficulty with the passport, the snow storm in Skokie, my fears at Paul's and Rich's reactions, and so on. All these, to mention a few obstacles, seemed to be signs of Gordan Judd's reflection over our action: "Whenever you set out to do something of serious spiritual consequence, the forces of evil put up obstacles to thwart it."

Thursday 10 January

Word came that the US Embassy was being evacuated. The last group is leaving tomorrow. War seems inevitable. We gathered to discuss our going to the camp or seeking evacuation. Todd will seek evacuation with the Embassy tomorrow. I am having some doubts as we ponder the possibilities of being killed in the war: is this an ego thing or what? Gordan Judd's words come back to me regarding his experience that serious obstacles try to impede serious spiritual positions. The physical obstacle to my coming has become emotional and spiritual, I realize. I pray to God: if this is ego help me to know and return. No clarity comes but still the doubt lingers. I tell God and others I'll go on in trust. I turn to Todd: "Todd, if you get out and I don't, please tell my family I love them." He says he will.

Sunday 13 January

Last night the camp met and discussed, among other things, our staying past the 15th, thus placing ourselves more at risk of life and limb. Carole cried, saying that she was afraid and knew others felt the same way, and that she wanted to be with others for comfort and support.[21]

For some reason I don't feel afraid. Perhaps it is the context, simply a camping experience with mostly agreeable people. What is strange: without the input of impending war, I feel strangely detached from it all. What is real though is the possibility that the US will come to evacuate us at risk of their fighting with the Iraqi border guards stationed here. I want no part of such an effort, however well intentioned. I don't see them as my protectors when they are here to destroy Iraqi soldiers, men, women and children.

What do I think of leaving on the 15th or 16th? I feel I should stay to help maintain the focus of sanity. To return home is tempting, but again, I hear Daniel Berrigan's words, "Are we willing to pay as high a price as those war makers?"

---

[21] *Editors*: Carole's own diary includes an interesting account of this moment: "At one of our many meetings I voiced my personal concern about the mounting tension in the camp. As the mid-January deadline approached, it seemed that many of us, including myself, were internalising our fears, wary of the 'nothing to be afraid of' attitude prevalent in the camp. Many, including the 'brave' ones, sat alone, preoccupied, their faces closed and anxious. I wanted to remind everyone that we were there because wars are a frightening and horrible business, and that the 'stiff upper lip' syndrome helps to create and perpetuate the war ethic. It belonged only in John Wayne movies and certainly had no place in a peace camp. My 'big speech' broke the spell. Several people wept with relief, as I did. A sharing session built up trust and helped us face not the fears themselves, which were often intangible, but the fact that we had them. The arrival of more British and Americans on the 13th, and thirteen Indians the next day, further boosted our flagging morale and lessened that creeping feeling of isolation."

Thursday 17 January

Wakened at 2.45 a.m. by notice that US had been bombing Iraq and Kuwait. We evacuated tents without belongings and hurriedly assembled to stand outside. To the north east (toward Baghdad), we saw glows in the sky. The radio confirmed our worst fears. On a moonless night, immediately after the 15 January "deadline", the US had begun its attack - planned, methodical, persistent. In his address at 3.00 a.m. GMT, President Bush spoke of peace, justice, etc.

While standing in the dark with others between 3 and 5 a.m. I felt great anger and hopelessness. I wanted to give active expression to my feeling: renounce my citizenship, strike back at some facility, etc. The day's meetings went from crazy to crazier, from 10 a.m. to 10 p.m.

Saturday 19 January

John Rogers told me that the bombing kept him awake a lot last night, that he hadn't heard that many flights so far. I heard on radio this morning that the US has flown over 2000 sorties and launched more than a hundred missiles. They are keeping up a 24 hour day bombing of Hussein's elite Republican Guard in southern Iraq, even keeping them from sleeping. They are using cluster bombs there, the news suggest. The evil continues to multiply.

My strong feeling is that I don't want to impede the efforts of the Iraqis to defend themselves against the US aggression by being a hindrance because of their regard for our safety.

Sunday 20 January

Our political meeting went in different directions and I challenged the neutrality of the camp as being perceived as hands off. John reminded me that our "policy statement" condemns both sides. I argued that both sides were not equally responsible, the US being the supplier and supporter of Hussein among other suppliers. Stanley disagreed with my politics and reaffirmed that the neutral posture was necessary to transcend politics and begin to establish a new world order.

Last night Junsei of Japan, Buddhist monk and part of the Indian affinity group, helped us to realise that imperialism reigns here at the camp. He said head leads heart, and that he and others from a non-western culture have to make a greater effort to participate since they don't know the method or rules of the game. He said if purpose is the focus, method will follow. I asked him to help us change our process, to be a facilitator on his terms, perhaps with Bela (of India). He seemed open but reluctant because of the size of the group. This morning Jerry Smith wondered if the affinity group/ steering committee model would be a better model, only using a plenary occasionally. Kathy Kelly thought that the fish bowl method would be a good idea.

Thursday 24 January

Heard Bush's speech to the group of reservists this morning on Voice of America (VOA). He moralized it all to death. Quoted John Major, Britain's new Prime Minister: "Whatever happens to Saddam, I won't mourn him". Bush said: "Saddam started this war on 2 August with his brutal unprovoked attack on Kuwait. On 16 January, we began to stop it. I won't allow another Vietnam, having our troops fight with one hand tied behind their backs." The hypocrisy of it all...

Let's face it. By all accounts that I trust, Saddam Hussein has been a cruel dictator with an intention to expand his power and influence. Whatever his reasons for the Kuwait invasion, this invasion is unwarranted. Having said this, one must not immediately accept the US-led intervention. We need to examine its intent, and whether it will leave the world better or worse off. I have my answer to this.

Friday 25 January

Last night Philip Taylor told me about himself. He went through a PhD in cardiology and then worked for nine years as a virologist. He was interested in nuclear physics in high school but spent 6 hours a day playing table tennis the first year of college and was introduced to more liberal arts and social life, all of which prompted him to change emphasis. Before coming here he quit his job, gave up his apartment and wrote his will. He plans on staying although he is beginning to question the value of doing so.

In a different vein there is Andrew Jones who teaches journalism at Northeastern University in Boston. He brought two video cameras, 80 hours of tapes and his violin which he plays beautifully. He asked his employers for a leave of absence. When they refused, he said how will you feel for firing me if I'm killed or win the Pulitzer prize. They gave him leave. There are many similar stories.

White House admits that war will go on for months with setbacks and losses. The radio (BBC/VOA) seems to be recounting a football game.

Vocabulary even contributes to this: morale, sorties, etc. Nothing regarding ethics, it's all gone with war. I struggle to maintain the belief that this camp is one of the few "visible" counterparts to this insanity. That seems to be our primary mission, along with building our new models of community, the other side of the same coin.

Sunday 27 January

The rain continued hard all day and with cold wind. Everyone made the best of it, but huddled around the heaters with coffee or tea. After sitting around the kerosene stove for a couple of hours, I went to sleep around 9:00 p.m. Around 3:00 a.m. I woke up feeling nervous. Some heavy vehicles were moving nearby but I assumed they were military. A few moments later John Rogers called on me to say our evacuation was to be today.

We met in the main tent going over plans to resist, why we shouldn't, etc. This continued throughout the following hours with myself feeling less and less inclined to stay, physically and psychologically, despite belief that we were a beacon of some kind of sanity.

The divisions in the camp emerged dramatically, with raids on the kitchen, Andrew and others making smart remarks about the food committee, Janet supposedly popping Luke in the nose in the kitchen, Jerry Smith's disowning any connection with those thinking of resisting, Keith's semi-wild behaviour at times (putting everything in the trailer for the hospitals despite the needs of those who might stay), Baba yelling at those who wished to stay, and on and on. It finally came down to some of our own people carrying the stayers onto the buses. An unglorious ending. At 11:03 a.m. we drove away from Ar'ar to the waves of the border guards, some of whom I was told were 14 years old. Would they soon die?

Tuesday 29 January

Around 11:30 a.m. two buses took most of us to tour war damage in and around Baghdad. My image of Iraq was of a simple country with a very basic infrastructure. I'm told the population is about 16 million. I suspect most are poor. Yet, I'm told, there is free education and medical care. I saw no one who appeared to be starving.

About 30-40 minutes outside the city we approached a factory that had been bombed and destroyed. The factory was set far apart from any other structure so it was hit deliberately. We toured the facility, formerly of corrugated steel with a lot of fibre glass insulation lying around. All signs were that the three-storey building was a milk factory: rolls of labels, powdered milk packages, preservatives, the smell of sour milk, milk cans, etc. All of this in various stages of destruction.

Gerhard argued that it seemed unlikely that US forces would travel several hundred kilometres twice to destroy a milk factory. He said that the Germans had been supplying equipment that was drafted - they were told - for chemical weapons use. Charlie said he walked all around the factory and saw a few adjoining buildings that were untouched but easily could have been used for chemical work. He surmised that a milk factory would be a good place to conceal such work. Rorey said that according to US radio chemical work had been going on in some back rooms.

After the morning meeting Steve, Liz and I walked around the hotel grounds. There's shrapnel everywhere, apparently from US missiles. I picked up some twisted parts of metal full of holes, deformed machine parts and an electrical connector. Everything looked terribly familiar, parts that I'd worked with years ago. American made no doubt. Steve and I were sensitive to the genius gone astray, the hungry mouths and the unsheltered persons it represented. Precious machines to be destroyed. Such a misuse of God's gifts, human and material.

Friday 1 February

Early in the morning we came into Amman, it's clean hilly streets and modern homes and buildings. Finally we pulled up to the Ammon hotel to be met by media, welcoming signs, banners. I felt some jealousy that I didn't get interviewed but noticed that the media's main interest was the damage we had witnessed: "The allies say they have only struck military targets and infrastructure - what do you say?" George Rumens responded to a question about our effectiveness in the light of widespread support for the war. His response: we've seen the bodies and the wounds and the destruction, this short-lived euphoria will be replaced by a decade of remorse. Mine: "our" blood has not yet been spilt so it is still at a distance for those in the West.

Saturday 2 February

Up around 10 a.m. feeling very sick again, all day for that matter. Ann Montgomery gave me some Chinese acupuncture medicine which helped a lot. Met with the steering committee and then the affinity group, then the steering committee again.

Kathy Kelly was frequently on the phone with media in the US. She talked with Diana Bean who confirmed that 80% in the US support the war. Diana said that the demos aren't really that effective, though they shut down lake shore and 200 arrests were made. She said grassroots work is the Gulf Peace Team, the hottest thing going. We should get home as soon as possible.

About 2 a.m. Lisa Wagner from the *Chicago Tribune* called my room. Spoke with her for about 30 minutes. Two main points. When she mentioned that the US military had released films of GIs writing sarcastic messages on bombs and missiles, I told her I considered this obscene, that these recipients are real people. I blame the years of propaganda, to the effect that all Arabs are terrorists. She heard me but didn't have much patience with my remarks after a point. She stressed that not much news is coming out, mostly exaggerations: blood running in the river, American pilots being hacked to death.

The second point: I'm not sure to what degree I was used only as her news reporter and to what degree she was interested in things pertinent to our focus. I believe I was successful but her story will tell the story.

I forgot to mention yesterday's press conference, and Baba and John Livesey's outbursts. It was Baba who began the stir with his disparaging comments before Pat Arrowsmith's talk. Then John went into a tirade about our "foolishness" down at the border. He claimed to have persuaded the Iraqis to evacuate us, etc. John's comments were reported back to me by Lisa Wagner of the *Tribune*.

Sometime soon I must try to record my impressions of the internal dynamics of the camp community. It included many strong-willed, even egocentric persons. Eventually the camp split up into those who were method orientated (as Junsei said) and those who seemed more anarchist to use the word descriptively. In the latter group, Baba was certainly the most flamboyant.

Kennedy Airport. Immigration put my passport through their scan computer and waved me through. Not even a question about where I had been, what kind of business I was up to. My statement that I was returning from a peace camp in Iraq went straight over his head.

Upon awakening at Heathrow's Gatwick Stirling Hostel this morning I could hear the faint engine roar of early departures through the sound-proof walls. A sense of anxiety arose in me. An unusual experience. I realised that two weeks in the desert hearing a similar roar through the night had changed the sense of jet planes from one of adventure to that of dread of death from the skies. Now I sense in a small way the recoiling fear of the Salvadoran child or women to such sounds.

This reality looms larger after reading in today's *New York Times* that a heavier tonnage of bombs has already been dropped on Iraq than during the whole of World War II. God have mercy.

Memories of peace and war

Peggie Preston

The Peace Camp

It has always been important to me to actually experience a situation, and this led me to South Africa and Vietnam, to try to "share" (as much as anyone from outside can) the tragedy experienced by the people of those countries. With the peace movement, and for me Molesworth especially, it meant a tragedy faced by the whole world. Whenever possible, I try to "say it with my feet".

Thus, when I heard just four days before their departure that friends of mine were going to try to set up a camp between the two armies, in an attempt to stop the war and untold suffering for people in the countries of the region, I tried hard to tell myself that financial and other responsibilities made it impossible for me to join them – but in the end I knew I had to go!

I feel great nostalgia for the camp at Ar'ar. I know that there were many problems, much heart-searching, but for me it remains a unique experience. At Molesworth I knew it was absolutely right for me to be there, yet I used to count the nights, the cold and discomfort, until I could return to my flat! I never did this at the camp - the discomfort, the problems with my arthritis, never made me feel I wanted to leave. Toward the end I began to worry whether we would ever get away from there, not because I wanted to, but because I realised that lack of food and kerosene could be a problem.

I remember the night we were called to leave. Earlier that day I had gone to bed, aware of the flooding, the drop in temperature - but I thought, "Tomorrow the sun will come out, and it will all be alright again". And then we had to leave. I was very sad.

Before leaving for Iraq I had hoped that a contribution I could perhaps make would be from my experience as an occupational therapist over many years, as a "listener", counsellor, etc. Perhaps I should have made this clear earlier than I did at the camp. I know I enjoyed keeping myself busy, keeping the kettles boiling, etc. – anything where I did not have to do much lifting. Perhaps this particular choice was also subconsciously to provide a welcome, which I always try to do. Also it seemed that people wanted me to become involved with workshops. I realise now that I was not enough aware of the fact that there were people who really did need the expertise I could offer them. Also, I was shy to suggest it, perhaps because I was very aware that there were people in our midst who had done so much more than me to live their commitment against war, often risking imprisonment for their beliefs. Also, at the interminable meetings, I found it difficult to contribute – all the arguments about finer points, about how we should proceed, I sometimes found it incomprehensible that this could be happening at Ar'ar. I realised that there were people at the camp who did not appear to "fit in" – yet they also had taken the unique decision to come there. However different their ideas seemed to be, one could not forget that. And to me one of the miracles of the peace camp, was that it was there, and that it was possible for so many people with such divergent views, lifestyles, and cultures, to come together so quickly at a camp between two armies, 2 km from the frontier! When groups here in Britain ask me to speak about the peace camp, as they still do, I tell them of the miracle of the beginning.

Special memories of the camp include the evening the Indians arrived. They came off the bus and embraced us – they brought a stillness with them, a harmony. I told them I had been born in Assam – and they adopted me as their "mother". It was wonderful! Another special memory is the workshop on "getting to know each other". There were about thirty Gulf Peace Team members present. I asked them to share with us something about themselves, their family, etc. – and then tell us what it was back in their lives that had eventually brought them to the camp. It was a revelation, and extremely moving. For me it would have been tragic not to have known the stories of those wonderful people who were sharing that unique experience with me. Some people had not realized we did not want lengthy life stories, but we bore with them! At the end of several hours we had a wonderful "hug in" - it was a unique moment.

Then there was the friendship of the Iraqi doctor and his nurse. In April, when I returned to Iraq with Sadallah, we went to destroyed Kerbala and found the doctor alive and working in the children's ward. Our joy was great, but no word of the nurse. The terrible tragedy of what has happened since the war to the people of Iraq is another story. I had the privilege of living for a month at the Red Crescent Hospital in Baghdad, and saw some of that tragedy.

I remember so many things at Ar'ar: wonderful friendships; the banner making and the painting on the roof; washing up, cleaning loos, hanging out the washing; starting Tai Chi; the cold in the communal tent on night watch; Anne Montgomery sick and uncomplaining; meal queues; the cultural evening (I was surprised and delighted at the response!); circle dancing; peace vigil at dawn; sand glowing in the sunset; memories too many to mention. And of course that terrible night when the war started.

People said to me I remained so calm – I had been through wars, in Vietnam and during the Second World War – but being suddenly awakened to darkness, told to go over to the sand, my heart was thumping! It was a sudden and terrible awakening. I remember that night I did not return to the tent, I went over to where Penny and others were, and the car from Baghdad arrived the night before. We tried to show our concern to the Iraqis, desperately worried about their families. We watched the skies redden in the direction of Baghdad – it was all so unreal. Every night when the planes flew over us I remembered my time in WAAF during the Second World War, when I was stationed at the Coningsby bomber station in Lincolnshire, working in the control tower as a radio-telephonist. I knew that planes from Coningsby were now bombing Baghdad. I was so sad.

The final journey to Amman, on the bombed road, was the most frightening time, when I felt really vulnerable. We saw many bombed civilian vehicles, some still burning. We were in slow moving buses, which often had to go off the road to get around bomb craters and bombed vehicles. We did not know when the next missile would come and "lock in", perhaps this time to ourselves. Practically the whole way to Amman, I was in real pain with cystitis – I was not the only one as I discovered later.

In Amman, I realised what people were trying to do back home, and what the media were not doing. That's when I changed my mind about working in a Jordanian refugee camp. Having been unable to remain in Baghdad to work in a hospital as six of us had hoped, I decided instead to return to Britain immediately and tell as many as I could the true facts about the war and the suffering.

What happened after my return, the massacre north of Kuwait, the bombing of the Ameriyeh shelter, brought sobs welling from deep inside me. With sounds of "We've won the war! The desert rats are coming home! Let's have a parade!" ringing in my ears I returned to Amman and Iraq – the war was NOT over! For many the worst was yet to come.

Thank you, all of you, for sharing that unique peace camp experience with me and for the wealth of experience, commitment, caring you brought with you to share with us. In our sharing workshop, so many said that coming to the camp was a unique experience - certainly my life will never be the same again.

Back to Iraq[22]

I returned to Baghdad in April 1991, for a month. During this time I went twice to Kerbala (8-12,000 died there), the destroyed Shi'ite town, and heard from others about the same destruction at Najuf and Hilla/Babylon. And of course we know about the terrible destruction of Basra, due to allied bombing as well as civilian destruction. Those towns would not have been destroyed but for the fact that Bush and Major told the people to rise up and overthrow Saddam Hussein, which they did, expecting the allies to help them – but the allies just left them in the lurch. Then the Iraqi army retaliated, perhaps more brutally because of the humiliation they had suffered in a totally one-sided war, in which the allies (America and Britain at least) had obviously "tried out" new and more sophisticated weapons. Strangely, before the war we had seen the stealth bombers having problems on tests - when they were shipped over to the Gulf! Thinking of those deadly weapons unleashing terrible destruction, of the bombing of the fleeing troops, I just cried.

During my April visit to Baghdad, I visited the bombed shelter in Ameriyeh. I spoke to grieving fathers. Every evening around 7.00 p.m. they used to take the children and their mothers down to the shelter – there were bunkbeds for the children, light from generators, and the thick walls meant they did not hear the bombing. Now there is a huge hole in the roof where one of the missiles struck, and inside it is dark, dirty and airless. I found a half-burnt playing card. Many people are still missing. I heard the story of a woman standing near the entrance, who had run out grabbing two children she thought were hers, only to find that one of them was not hers.

I'll never forget the children's hospitals, where hundreds of babies are still dying of nutrition related diseases such as kwashiorkor and marasmus. And also of cholera – in many cities (Baghdad, Basra, Kerbala...) people have to drink polluted water. I saw a photograph of a young boy in Basra

---

[22] *Editors:* This section is based on a letter addressed to the US ambassador in London, also delivered to John Major. An acknowledgment, dated 24 July 1991, was received from John Major, stating that this matter was "receiving attention".

getting water in a tin from a hole dug in the ground, to reach the water table near a septic tank! Many mothers were not able to bring the children in time to the main children's hospital in Baghdad or elsewhere, to get the fluid urgently needed for cholera victims. From my visit to two children's hospitals on 24 April, I learnt that lack of electricity and therefore refrigeration meant that insulin could not be stored. Chemotherapy was also interrupted, resulting in the relapse of a child with cancer of the eye.

I saw the precision-bombed buildings, and how precision bombing destroyed all the communications, sewage, electricity, water purification, etc. Opposite the bombed Justice building was the bombed Local Government building. High up against the remaining outside wall I saw many books - I asked what they were - "All the information for the coming year". The same in Kerbala, where we were told that they had to start again, asking the old people who the residents of Kerbala were, as they would know best. When I left at the beginning of May, there was still no telephone, no postal service. The temperature was 38-40 degrees Celsius. When we visited the children's hospital it was stifling, there were no fans or electricity. In July it will reach 55. I find it incredible that the Iraqis coped in spite of the terrible trauma they had been through.

Reflections

Jenny Hales

Christmas is a strange time to tell your visiting son that you are agonizing over whether to go, in a few days, to camp on the Iraq/Saudi border. His immediate reaction was fierce - but that was only because he hadn't really thought the Gulf crisis through. How painful, at that point, was my own sense of isolation! Three days later, I having decided "Yes" (and facing the huge "How?"), he and I and my other son stood together (*very* together!). "Mum, we understand why you have to go. We want you to know we're behind you. We've written to Mr. Bush and Mr. Major..." (deepening awareness already!). Will said: "You might get killed." "If I do, comfort yourselves that we die once - and old age might have killed me more painfully. Someone with an infinitely more valuable life than mine, at half my age, chose to lay it on the line for the sake of humanity... Ten years ago, when we really thought we were going to lose you with cancer, Will, we talked about the issues of life and death, didn't we?" "Yes," they both said, "and we still believe the same..." "Me, too." Then followed one of those glorious, rare, silent moments, standing together, eyes meeting, feeling our close-twined roots shoot down another 40 fathoms! Bless you, my dear, dear sons!

Many of us found that, having said "Yes!", the tangle of practical difficulties slipped loose. A homeless stranger helped me by feeding the cat and dog - and I gave him a roof and address. The heart-rending prospect of telling my dying friend I was abandoning her in her extremity was cancelled, because she died just before I left.

Those hours in Heathrow: what a sick, weary lot we looked, after a week of frantic activity, missed sleep and meals, and guilt at causing anxiety in our family circles! *But no longer lonely.* Because of our shared concern, which mattered more than anything, we were instantly friends at a deep level. In spite of all our differences of culture, education, age, etc., this pre-eminent passion for averting the violence of war, and its appalling on-going aftermath, bound us together in a way that surmounted all the difficulties and tensions ahead. At the camp, it was a privilege to be among such wonderful people, to hear their "spiels" and share one's own... in groups or in pairs. What did primitive conditions, infrequent meals, and the sheer hard slog of arriving at corporate decisions in a democratic way, matter by comparison? What *did* devastate was the shock, that fateful night, of hearing bombers going continuously overhead to Baghdad. We knew, then, that war had begun, and we knew what was happening to those beneath the exploding evil.

We shall never forget the wonderfully quiet and unembittered fortitude of the ordinary people in Baghdad (nine years of war already behind them) who came up to us as we returned, *knowing* some of us were UK and US citizens, and therefore "part" of the ongoing bombing: "Thank you for coming! We brothers and sisters (pointing to themselves and us). One God (pointing up). We don't want to fight." How heart-warming it was... how humbling!

The road to Jordan, intact when traversed a month before, was now cratered with bombs, and lined with smoking vehicles, and as we reached the Jordanian border, the shivering refugees in the darkness reminded us of all those Pakistanis and Bangladeshis who were waiting in sad conditions to return to their own countries, their jobs gone. We will remember, too, the hospitable and articulate British and American wives of Jordanians, bringing up their families in Amman, with their passionate concern for a solution to the Palestinian sufferings in the Occupied Territories, and their hilarious contempt for the misinformation of the BBC (Biased Boloney Corporation, they called it).

Then the flight back. I was privileged to sit next to Aisha, our serene and wise fellow camper, who knew what it was to have been a refugee her self in past years - and later next to Dr. Ellen Rosser, who had started a water-only fast at the American Embassy in Amman as war began, and was now planning to continue her fast in Washington. (I am glad to say she survived the 33-day fast, broken because of total absence of media coverage, just in time to save her valuable life.) She had done an equally long fast before, in Israel, when incidents in the Occupied Territories were particularly horrendous. And she is still active - a passionate and selfless woman.

On landing, for me, it was the night-coach to Sheffield; in Amman, I had learned that Will was facing major surgery for yet more cancer. (The geneticist thinks his rare, ongoing syndrome could have been caused by radiation from nuclear testing in the South Pacific, near where he was born. But that is another story...) Having spent the day with him, I called, on my way home, on an elderly, courageous, forthright shut-in friend.

"There've *always* been wars," she stated, "there always will be wars!"

"Half-true," I said, "there always have been - but it doesn't have to always be..."

"It's greed! Men have always been greedy. They always will be greedy!"

"Again half-true. Of course it's greed. But we want to change that."

"You can't change human nature!"

"But you can! History is full of it! I hope *I'm* less greedy than 10 years ago!"

How many people, I thought dispiritedly, entering my dark little home, listen to opinions like my friend's, and believe it... and fold their hands, because they are persuaded ordinary folks can do nothing...! The phone rang. It was an Iraqi teacher I'd never met, from the local school. We talked like old buddies. Thank you, Hadi! Nothing could have been better at that point than a voice which *understood*. Baghdad. Where, I wondered, was lovely young Dunga Mikhail, reporter at the *Baghdad Observer,* who gave me a book of her own poetry during our hour-long friendship on the way out to the peace camp? Was she - dead... or worse? I recalled Ivy's quote: "Death's fatal - but it's not serious!" Ivy, 75, with two artificial knees (the only non-genuine things about her). O, I could say *so much* about so many fellow-campers!

A few days later, snow having stopped the buses, I took a taxi, returning from a peace meeting the other side of Sheffield. As we slithered along, the Muslim driver and I talked. You can guess what we talked about! Twenty minutes after I'd paid him, we were still talking in his stationary taxi. He pulled his sleeve and tapped his brown skin. "People here think because of our colour that we support Saddam Hussein. We don't! We brothers and sisters - one God!" We shook hands fervently.

A local, very nice, Canon asked me to write of my experience in the Cathedral newsletter. I knew he was a "Just War" man - and he later confessed to removing a few sentences from the article I had submitted. These turned out to be the ones where I'd illustrated Jesus' "inasmuch as you did it to others, you did it to me" by saying that when we incinerated "enemies", we burnt Christ to death, and when we wrecked their infrastructure, it was Christ who died of cholera and malnutrition. In the event, it wasn't published - because, he said, the war is over. "Over?", I asked him. We talked a long time on the phone. I said I was writing about war in general - and the Christ I follow wouldn't condone *any* war. The Canon did publish another article of mine, no less emphatic, in May.

Then the juxtaposition of Easter and the Kurds. Those two extremes: the willing acceptance by Jesus of suffering, because he taught and lived His "unacceptable" Truth; and the infliction of mass suffering - genocide - by our war machine. Father, forgive us - we *do* know what we're doing... Ronald Sider's *Exploring the Limits of Non-Violence* helped me considerably out of dispiritedness at that point. He cites case after case of *successful* non-violent action - and emphasises that our commitment in time, money and training must be total in this method we rightly believe in.

Earlier this month, on the way back from the Royal Naval Arms Exhibition (where we blockaded the entry road), the coach stopped a while in Oxford. In the square, prominently, a child-height table with guns and a rifle on it, a recruitment display, and three young soldiers in combat uniform. When the children ("Oo! Is it a real gun?" "Yes. Pick it up!") moved off, I asked them what made them choose their career. "Seven months unemployment! Good pay and prospects! See the world!" "And when you're on active service, how will you feel about using these?" I pointed to the guns. "OK! Fine! Do what we're told to! That's what we're paid for, innit? No bother. Obey orders!" Already so conditioned - dehumanized - brutalized (and at an age when independent decision-making is at a peak, normally). So what our peace camp was about, we must live for to our utmost, opposing the heinous genocide of the arms traders in *every way* open to us.

A small beacon of light

Jack Lomax

I first learnt about the Gulf Peace Team when M telephoned me in early December 1990. She said there was a plan afoot to add an Australian contingent to a British-originated peace camp on the Saudi/Iraq border. This camp had not actually happened at that time but M seemed to be pretty sure that the Brits had got Iraqi permission to set it up. I thanked M and said that I did have tentative interest in the proposed venture provided further investigations didn't show it to be too suicidal. I (like her) would register as someone who was interested in receiving further information.

Even though I proceeded with tentative preparations (jabs, visas, etc.), I still felt very uncertain about what I seemed to be getting into, especially when I learned that the "twenty or thirty" interested people had by this time come down to "maybe fifteen, twelve of whom are men". It seemed to me that this was an awfully small number and certainly out of any kind of balance so far as gender was concerned. I worried that this might indicate some weakness in the organisation which I wasn't aware of, but which the hundreds of peace and nonviolent activists who weren't volunteering were.

It was only when I learned that Jerry Smith the Australian organiser had himself decided to go, and that Robert Burrowes of the Melbourne Rainforest Action Group was also going, that I began to firm up on my own resolution. I made my final internal decision one evening soon after and then spent about three hours discussing it with my partner Christine. I went to bed and spent a totally sleepless night during the course of which I had visions of laying in dreary deserts mortally wounded but taking days to die; weeks spent in Baghdad security police cells being interrogated as a suspected allied spy; months or years interned in some desert camp in war-torn Iraq which was growing ever shorter of food and finding less and less to spare for foreigners. My dead and shattered body became quite a familiar sight to me that night, lying where it had fallen after being caught by a bomb or a shell blast in Baghdad, on some snow-covered mountainside or on cold desert sands. After these nightmares (which the bright light of an early morning Tasmanian summer sun melted away) I never felt quite so bad again, although there were lots of times in the weeks to come when I did feel a real fear for my own survival.

The trip from Hobart to Melbourne was really great. We were both wearing "No Gulf War" T-shirts, and this combined with the media presence at the airport had alerted both the passengers and the cabin crew as to who we were and where we were going. During the trip all three of the cabin crew came to us to express support and admiration for what we intended to do. When we got to Melbourne we decided to stay in the plane until the crush had left. This meant that most of the passengers filed past where we were sitting towards the front of the plane. About three quarters of them said things like "Good Luck" or "Good On Yer" as they passed. What a buzz that was!

At Amman airport we were met by Mr. Salleh, the manager of the hotel we were to stay at. This hotel was government run and was known as the "training hotel" because one of its main functions was to train staff in the niceties of the hotel trade. Mr. Salleh himself turned out to be one of the friendliest and most helpful of all the people we were destined to meet on this trip. From him we began to hear a message we would hear repeated by many of the people of Jordan. The message was that the whole of the population of Jordan waited in dread to hear that the Israeli army had crashed its way over the Allenby bridge and had begun to take over the rest of the country.

We spent the next day getting to know the city and doing such things as gathering food supplies for our trip into sanctions-starved Iraq. We got to Baghdad early the following day after a long and pretty uncomfortable overland trip. There we found what was to be our island home for the next few days: a bungalow at the "peace village" managed by the Organisation for Friendship, Peace and Solidarity. This organisation was of course government-funded and as much an arm of government as had been similar organisations I had had dealings with in Beijing and Moscow. Like them it did have some links with common aspirations. Very few people in Iraq actually wanted a war with the US-led coalition. Those few who did, seemed to be mostly members of the fundamentalist Moslem Brotherhood, but I don't think their views were reflected in any but a very small percentage of the Iraqi population at that time.

The staff at the peace village were a long way from the Moslem Brotherhood in their views, and were echoing views we had heard from Palestinians and others in Amman: if the war happened, it would be a disaster both for the country concerned and for the Middle East as a whole. These Iraqis were both helpful and friendly, as were most other Iraqis we met.

The members of the Gulf Peace Team that we then met in the village were also helpful and friendly but, I'm afraid, inaccurate. John Steel was doing most of this coordinating work but due, I suspect, to really inaccurate and misleading tads from London was often (or perhaps even mostly) wrong when he stated "facts" such as "Sixty people are due here from the UK in the next few days, and a plane load of two hundred plus Americans are also on their way."

The peace village turned out to be a real meeting point of ideologies and cultures. The New Zealand team we had been looking forward to meeting turned out to have far more problems than we did. Two of them had gone to the border peace camp, where they rarely spoke to each other. One of these New Zealand men was destined eventually to do more harm to the Gulf Peace Team concept than perhaps any other single person. Those who had stayed in Baghdad consisted of a woman doctor of German origin, N, and two other New Zealand women who, by the time I met them, were refusing to speak to her.

For all of that first day in the peace village and part of the second day, we stayed in our bungalow and thrashed out the difference that had arisen between M and most of the rest of the group. In these early discussions Steve Blair remained largely uncommitted to any particular point of view but he was later to commit himself to the point of view which M was expressing. That view was that as a lone female in a group of seven male activists she was being overridden, suppressed and bludgeoned into accepting a group process with which she fundamentally disagreed.

This whole process was actually more exhausting for me personally than any other I was to experience in the coming weeks. I took the lead in stating the reservations many of us in the group had begun to feel about going to the desert peace camp with one member of the group refusing to accept any of the models of group process which had so far been discussed, and also refusing to suggest any alternative model. It was N's mediation that finally got M to agree (reluctantly, and as it turned out temporarily) to accept the basic group process model which had been suggested by Jerry Smith.

In Baghdad I had learnt that the numbers at the peace camp were sparse - around twelve at that time. The feeling I got was that I was engaged in an action from which the rest of the international activist network were staying away in droves. The impression I got from the camp was not reassuring either. The mood seemed to range from depression to disappointment. Pat Arrowsmith, one of the London organisers, was the *de facto* head of the camp at this time and she called and "chaired" the meetings. After I witnessed one of these I gently told her that I thought she was a great person and a brave woman but by far the worst meeting facilitator I had ever met.

In the next few days the camp population grew until finally there were seventy-three of us as the war started. Many of these people were in the same position as Pat Arrowsmith. That is, they knew roughly what the term consensus refers to but had no idea of group process or group dynamics. Many of them would have felt more at home with majority voting while an all too large section would have felt better without any process whatsoever.

The spokesperson for this latter group was a South American male doctor known as Baba, who thought that he had a spiritual message to give to the listening world. His message (shouted from the edge of every meeting held in the camp) was that meetings were unnecessary and that all events should be organic and spontaneous. He also told us that meditation liberates the body and the mind. He would sometimes be smoking his fortieth cigarette for the day while he was giving this message and this tended to dilute the force of what otherwise might have been a very powerful message.

A couple of days after the war started and we had gotten used to hearing B52s on their way overhead to bomb the civilian population of Iraq, M told us that she was leaving the group and starting an affinity group of one, called the M affinity group. Steve Blair, who had been very supportive of M's position since the heated discussions in Baghdad, stayed with the Australia affinity group but was very withdrawn, and in my opinion often quite negative, although his input into the camp functioning as a whole continued to be strong and positive.

The Australian affinity group had by this time grown into the Australian/American group by reason of a couple of American males having joined it. Earlier N, the New Zealander of German origin, had also been a member, but she left the group after Jerry Smith had stated that if she stayed in the group he would feel it impossible to stay in it himself. I told N that I also thought she should leave the group, since meetings with her presence were just impossible. Everyone usually needs to express themselves at greater or lesser length at affinity group meetings, but N would start to talk and often would not stop until the time allotted for the meeting was over. She, like the South American doctor Baba, was moved by some internal force to spread the word as she saw it. But her contributions were both endless and obscure to all but N; although Dean Jeffries professed to understand her sometimes.

I know that for a group of professed anti-patriarchal males to have succeeded in alienating its only two female members does not look very good. However it is still my firm opinion that both M and N were people who for personality reasons cannot function successfully as part of a group process. Other people both men and women at the camp, in Baghdad and Amman expressed the same reservations about both M and N. Great individuals but definitely not people who could in any successful way function in this sort of a group.

If our affinity group seemed to be hitting a rather rocky patch it was a model of sweet harmony and cooperation contrasted to the camp process as a whole. The reasons for the lack of togetherness in the camp at that time are probably best summed up under three headings.

1. As indicated above there were some people in the camp who had no commitment to group process and whose personal behaviour was often highly idiosyncratic. Perhaps unkindly, our affinity group referred to this sub-group as "the wackers", while others in the camp called them the loose cannons (a rather war-like but apposite description).

2. Another group wanted to cooperate but had all too little idea of how do so in general meetings. This group was balanced to some extent by another of which both our affinity group and the Indian group were prominent members.

3. The war had meant that external conditions such as the possible volatility of the frontier, the impossibility of movement and the growing shortage of food were all factors reducing our attention spans and goodwill at meetings.

Nonetheless the camp did continue to successfully function, especially after a new process based on affinity groups and a rotating steering group emerged to replace the now impossible general meetings.

The period of cold weather and heavy rain which set in towards the end of our stay at the camp, combined with the shortage of food and fuel, were beginning to cause us real worries. But perhaps a bigger worry for many of us was the fact that a significant group were planning to set up an even more forward camp in the desert just ahead of us. It is hard to imagine a more unrealistic proposal than this since the Iraqis had of course firmly ruled it out of any consideration. Nonetheless a group of about ten or twelve people continued to hold meetings and seriously discuss the issue. I began to call them the lunar group since it was clear that their proposal had almost the same degree of improbability as would any proposal to build a rocket from the rusty tanks around the camp and set up a base on the moon.

Many of this group, when the unrealistic nature of the scheme became apparent even to them, decided that they would refuse to leave the camp at all cost.[23] If they could not go forward they were determined not to go back. The Iraqi minders and the local military both gave them the same message: when the time came all of us would be forced to leave the camp and go in the transport provided to Baghdad.

At least when the time came they were realistic enough to have packed up all of their personal gear ready to be put into the transport truck, but they themselves sat in a ritualistic circle and forced the Iraqi people who had come to fetch us to carry them into the waiting buses. Many of the Iraqis had tears streaming down their faces and some were sobbing as this disgraceful action forced them into the role of police with people they had started to think of as close friends. This was the first and only time I felt ashamed of being part of the Gulf Peace Team.

In Baghdad we saw some of the bomb damage and some of the victims. We saw and thoroughly inspected the shattered dried-milk factory which the Americans still claim was really a chemical weapons factory. We also saw shops and houses destroyed by bombing as well as the hospitals treating as best they could the broken and mangled bodies of those caught by this rain of terror from the sky each night. The hospitals were finding it more and more difficult to even relieve pain since the supplies of pain-control medication and anaesthetics were fast running out.

In the hotel at night Tom, M and Steve went to the underground shelter to sleep but the rest of us for the most part stayed on the seventh floor and watched the deadly firework display each night with horror and dismay. We

---

[23] *Editors:* Not all those who wished to stay belonged to the "lunar group".

retreated away from large windows if the bangs got too close and occasionally retreated even further down to the bunker for an hour or so if bombs seemed to be coming really close. A missile had destroyed the hotel's staff quarters before we came back to Baghdad and another had been shot down over the hotel helipad. In spite of this none of us felt much immediate danger, since we were mostly convinced that the Americans would not try to bomb this hotel as it still had a couple of international media people in it.

During a crucial meeting with Mr. Dawood (president of the Organisation for Friendship, Peace and Solidarity), a thousand-pound bomb exploded in a nearby street causing the building to shake and the meeting to end precipitously as we all fled to the bomb shelter. One of the things that Mr. Dawood had agreed to in this meeting was that a certain number of our group who had volunteered to stay back in Baghdad would be given permission to work in the city's hospitals. Not only that, the group had asked not to continue to be billeted in the comparative safety of the Al Rasheed Hotel and Mr. Dawood had agreed that they could live in the bomb-battered suburbs. However, the goodwill which the Iraqi government felt towards us was diluted by an incident in which the Japanese Buddhist monk (Junsei) and two Indians from our group were found in a restricted part of the city very near to the Presidential palace in the company of a Soviet photographer. After some talking by our minders the security police released the three, but at the same time word came down that all members of the Gulf Peace Team would now have to leave Iraq.

In Amman, we were in full range of the international media and the attention we got from that time on for the next couple of weeks was overwhelming and sometimes even intimidating. The international press conference we arranged under careful guidelines, moderated by Robert Burrowes, turned into a three ring circus with every loose cannon in the big top firing off barrages of unbalanced harangues to the attentive media. The loosest cannon of them all was a gun from New Zealand called John Livesey. His salvoes of hysterical paranoia were greeted with delight by his camera and pencil wielding audience. What he had to say filled lots of negative media space in both North America and Europe. Later two Americans - one who had been at the peace camp and one who had stayed in Baghdad - generated even more negative media. I think John was disturbed and grossly misdirected but I feel sure both of the yanks had secret (were they CIA directed?) agendas.

There were two separate impressions I took away with me concerning the Gulf Peace Team. The first was of a people who could not see the futility (and the moral wrongness) of sitting in a frontier camp in a war zone with their sleeping bags and packs stowed already to leave the camp, while forcing tired and hungry Iraqis to use vast amounts of energy in carrying them into the transport buses which were to take all of us away from the camp and into Baghdad. The question of whether it would have been a good thing to stay on in that camp was never a real one because we had all known for days that inevitably we would be made to leave even if we had to be carried. People performing an inappropriate ritual are usually merely embarrassing. People performing an inappropriate ritual involving tired and frightened human beings as their slaves to carry them onto the buses so that the ritualistic significance of their action could be fulfilled are rather more than embarrassing though.

The second impression I retain is of a group of people who cheerfully volunteered to stay in heavily bombed and nearly starving Baghdad to help with war injuries. The fact that the sort of irresponsibility which had led some Gulf Peace Team members to engage in the ritualistic sit-in also forced these brave people to leave Iraq with the rest of the team takes nothing away from their dedication and courage. Many of those same people stayed on in Amman when there seemed to be a real risk of Israel responding to the continuing Scud attacks by invading Jordan. They have also escorted relief convoys into Iraq both during and after the war.

The strange thing is that some of the people who have performed such good work in post-war Iraq and Jordan and such a heroic role in Baghdad are also some of the same people who did the border camp sit-in. This has caused me to think long and hard about the rights and wrongs of the Ar'ar camp sit-in. But I can't think of any argument to allow me to honestly feel any differently than I do about it. I respect (and in some cases love) many of the people involved, but I do deplore the action.

Nonetheless, it is the dedication and bravery of the group who wanted to stay on in Baghdad and of those who have stayed on in Amman which I believe will be the inspiration for large numbers of people in a future series of peace camps at national borders. It is these people and many others at the camp and in Baghdad who I feel proud and inspired to have spent time with.

The hundred or so people from around the world who were actually at the peace camp, or caught up by the war trying to get there, did not stop this war from happening. Yet, our presence at the frontier and in Baghdad, I believe, did become both a small beacon of light and a strong pointer to the way forward for all those people in the world who actively want to oppose future wars, even at some possible physical cost to themselves. Our presence at the frontier camp also exploded the myth that only heroes can involve themselves in ventures such as this.

As I have indicated above many of us were far from heroic and many I know went forward as tentatively and uncertainly as I did. Yet we, no less than the truly brave people I have referred to above, did all perform a valuable service. I am proud and happy that I was allowed to be part of this historic venture and less uncertain of my reaction the next time I may be called upon to bear physical witness to the fact that all wars are acts of madness and under all circumstances totally immoral and unjustifiable.

Tower of Babel

Agnes Bauerlein

We had come from fifteen different countries, united by only one thing: our commitment to peace. We numbered seventy-three. And for each of us, the decision to join the Gulf Peace Team had been wrenching. We knew it could cost us our lives.

We arrived at the camp - three hundred miles southwest of Baghdad, one mile from the Saudi border - on 14 January. For the next two weeks, with US bombers roaring endlessly overhead, we lived together in ten large tents in a fenced-in compound. And the great irony was this: we could not find peace. Not even among ourselves.

On my first day, I realized this "peace camp" was a microcosm of the world. I was naive to think things would be different there. They were not.

Cultural and ideological differences loomed large. Goals varied. Spirituality was scarce. The biggest egos among us were still trying to solve the world's problems alone. People did not seem to need God. We had long meetings over logistics and what we meant by "nonviolent resistance." Even my affinity group of seven couldn't agree. It was easy to see why we have so many wars.

The Japanese and Indians were quite baffled by our long meetings and need for consensus. And puzzled by the very aggressive behaviour of westerners, particularly the British and North Americans. Day after day, westerners were verbally pushy, always wanting their points adopted. North Americans in the camp had an autocratic approach that never factored in other elements of the picture. Seldom, if ever, would they negotiate. Whatever the issue, they were aggressively certain they were right.

A few lone westerners were always prepared to do it their way, with or without others. In fact, we had several affinity groups of one.

Whatever course of action we chose, the eastern view, articulated by the Indians and Japanese, was to keep the camp as unified as possible. They also emphasized respecting the restraints Iraq had put on our camp.

Slowly, many of the westerners realized how aggressive their behaviour often is. It became clear that the group needed to act out the peace we were trying to manifest. Some of us began to pray together and apply Scripture to our situation. Little by little, the atmosphere changed. The aggressive behaviour became assertive. Our trust level went up. And our fear diminished. Cooperation became evident, and concern for the outside world primary.

Peace is this: we must try to be a silent balancing point in the tumult of life. Whether we are walking the streets of Philadelphia or living on the Iraq-Saudi border in the midst of a senseless and destructive war, or ploughing a garden in the country, if we don't begin to listen to one another with love and compassion, we will fail our mission. Always.

When the Iraqis came to evacuate us, there were three or four people who absolutely refused to leave. Each minute they resisted, they further endangered the group as a whole. If we did not reach Baghdad before nightfall, we would be caught in the bombing. Yet they would not get on the bus.

I was overcome with the sadness of it all - selfish and proud motives disguised as convictions more important than this bus full of lives. When they had to be carried bodily to the bus, I was ashamed.

We had gone to Iraq as a witness for peace, but we did not end up where we had hoped. We did not break out of our individualistic world views or the patriarchal system that feeds our violence.

But we also did not fail. Everyone who was there responded to an urgent, dangerous call to speak for peaceful solutions. I take a lot of hope from the fact that such a wide variety of people and backgrounds came under difficult circumstances to take a stand against violence and for world peace.

Like the world, no one in the camp had their feet on solid ground. All of us were missing points. We were broken people. And we all brought with us that brokenness. In many ways, the camp simply expressed in a more outrageous way our corporate need for healing.

To bring people together is a lifetime job. We are birthing peace; it will always be a long, labourious task. There is no quick fix, though the great danger of this war is that it might make us believe there is.

There is only this gentle, painful working of will, faith, and patience; nothing else is possible.

An unforgettable experience

Ivy Phillips

At the advanced age of 75 and with a disability, I had not expected to be flying out to the Gulf in January 1991. My journey was the result of an appeal for volunteers in The Friend, a Quaker weekly journal. I answered the appeal and to my surprise was accepted. My outstanding impression of the whole expedition was of the wonderful friendliness and hospitality of the Iraqi people. We went in peace and love, and they accepted us in that spirit. It was a long journey from Amman to Baghdad across the desert, in a bus which would probably not have passed the M.O.T. in the United Kingdom. Peace banners hung from the windows and draped the front, and everywhere we went we were greeted by smiling children who, with their fathers, crowded round the bus eager to clasp our hands and bid us welcome. We were offered glasses of tea at the check-points and what I found really moving, we were thanked for coming. We received the same warm welcome even after the war began, when "officially" we were "the enemy"! Differences of race and culture seemed quite irrelevant.

We reached Baghdad at night after a long slow journey in thick mist. As we reached the city the mist cleared and I shall never forget the wonderful view of a great mosque, its golden dome illuminated and reflected in the waters of the Tigris. The following day I went into Baghdad by taxi, with two Muslim friends, Aisha and Karen. While they were visiting the mosque the taxi driver bought me a glass of tea and on our return to the Peace and Friendship Village he refused to accept our fare. Another gesture of hospitality.

Another warm welcome awaited us when we arrived at the camp in the desert. The "campers" represented many different countries with varying religious and cultural backgrounds but all motivated with the same desire for peace in the whole world. This common bond soon welded us into a strong community. It was inevitable that with so many strong personalities in a rather limited space there would be some tension at times but differences were eventually resolved and all had an opportunity to state their views. It was a time when strong friendships were formed and I am grateful to have had the opportunity to meet so many "caring" people and to have formed lasting relationships with some of them.

There was a lighter side to camp life. I remember one evening in which a group of us read "The Tao of Pooh" by flickering candle light, and there were get-togethers for music and circle dancing. Owing to my disability I was unable to use the primitive toilets. That presented no problem and an improvised "loo" was soon provided. The first one was in a tent which billowed in the strong breeze. A later one, in a large shed, boasted a door marked, "Ivy's loo". I have often wondered what the next occupants of the camp made of it! Perhaps someday archaeologists will excavate it and ponder over its significance!

After war was declared we heard "our" planes droning overhead at night as they flew to Baghdad to drop their loads of death and destruction. We felt safe, but we grieved for our Iraqi friends who were suffering. The mosques were full of weeping people, our brothers and sisters, praying for peace.

We were evacuated from the camp on 27 January, and returned to Baghdad, and later to Amman. It was after our press conference in Amman that I experienced deep depression and felt that the whole peace project had collapsed. Edward Poore saw my distress and convinced me that our coming to Iraq was not in vain. He was a man of great integrity and compassion and one of the brave souls who stayed behind to help in the aftermath of the war. Tragically, he died in Jerusalem but he lives on in the hearts of those who were privileged to have met him.

While at the camp we received a welcoming letter from Hasan Kilgour, a former camper. One passage impressed me greatly and I still find great comfort in it. He wrote: "Take heart, because all the work you have been doing in cold, discomfort and isolation is bearing fruit. We could even be on the brink of the greatest revolution in history – the time when the ordinary fragile creatures that we are rose up against the madness of self-destruction and broke the death machines into little pieces, transforming them into food, shelter and tender loving care – the only "new world order" worth contemplating." We pray that the great revolution is on its way. Many death machines are already being broken.

Thirty nine days in the desert

Pat Arrowsmith

I returned from my summer holidays in 1990 to find the Gulf crisis in full swing and opposition to the potential impending war steadily mounting. I felt that members of the peace movement - especially pacifists - should do more than just join in rallies in city centres. We should practice what peace activists have so often preached: we should attempt to prevent the outbreak of war by opposing it nonviolently *in situ* - that is by interposing ourselves as a nonviolent human barrier between the two opposing forces. So I began asking likely people in Britain what they thought about the idea. A sufficiently large number seemed to be in favour of it, so David Polden and I, as individuals, convened an informal meeting to consider the desirability and feasibility of some such scheme.

I saw to it that representatives of appropriate peace organizations were invited to the meeting as I hoped that some suitable body - War Resisters International for instance - would mount the project we had in mind, but in the event no peace organization was able or willing actually to organize the venture, although two or three gave practical help. Our first meeting (held on 1 October), which had been lightly advertised at a recent anti-war rally, was attended by an international assortment of some 20 people, which at subsequent meetings boiled down to a hard core of about 10 individuals determined to plan some appropriate response to the Gulf war. But our ensuing series of more or less weekly meetings seemed to get us nowhere fast.

Initially, we decided not to try to plan anything in Iraq itself, so great was our abhorrence of the current regime there. This meant considering attempting to position ourselves in Jordan near the Saudi border. We also thought of taking action at a US base in Turkey. Meanwhile our letter to the press appealing for support and volunteers to join a peace camp in the area of potential conflict achieved some recruits and funds. However, we made little concrete progress until one member of the team suggested contacting Yusuf Islam (formerly Cat Stevens, the pop singer). It transpired that he had been entertaining a similar idea - a scheme he and his Muslim colleagues called Peace Guards, which they had already been discussing with political leaders in the Middle East.

It was not until Yusuf Islam and colleagues joined "forces" with us that the Gulf Peace Team really took off. Yusuf convinced us that only if we stationed ourselves in Iraq at the Saudi frontier would we be able to carry out our project to form a nonviolent human barrier between the armed forces of both sides. He felt that the idea was sure to be sympathetically received by the Iraqi authorities. After some heart searching we finally decided that the potential importance of our scheme outweighed the problems that would undoubtedly be posed by peace camping in Saddam Hussein-run Iraq.

We sent a delegation to the Iraqi Embassy in London to assess our chances of being allowed to pitch a peace camp near the Saudi border. A delegation visited the Saudi Arabian Embassy too - and even the Kuwaiti Embassy - but our repeated efforts to get permission to pitch a peace camp in Saudi Arabia near the Iraqi border proved fruitless. Receiving a favourable response at the Iraqi Embassy, we thereupon picked a small team of seven to go as an advance party to Baghdad to get final permission for a border peace camp and make the necessary practical arrangements. Visas for the seven were obtained without difficulty and, thanks to several anonymous loans and donations, the group was able to fly to Baghdad on 16 November.

In the event it took a long while and much lobbying of Iraqi officialdom to obtain permission for the camp - so long in fact that we began toying with the notion of simply setting off on foot from Baghdad to the frontier without authorization. Eventually, after a month or so of politicking, press interviews and frustrating time-filling, we got permission to set up the camp in an erstwhile Mecca pilgrims' compound at Ar'ar, two kilometres from the Saudi frontier, opposite (so we were told) French coalition forces. The camp started on Christmas Eve - later than we had hoped and expected. The 30 or so campers that first night were mainly (apart from we seven) members of various foreign peace delegations staying, as we ourselves had been, in the so-called Peace and Friendship Village in Baghdad.

Both the planning of the camp and its running were fraught with difficulties. The seven-strong advance party comprised people who barely knew each other and soon discovered how much they did not have in common. The conflicting approaches and personality clashes that bedevilled the group (to such an extent that it was amazing we ever achieved our purpose) were echoed to some extent in the actual camp later on. Participants in such a project are bound to be strong-minded, not to say obstinate, people. Moreover the total of about 150 individuals who at one time or another joined the camp inevitably included some who were awkward, even eccentric. And the multicultural character to the camp (20 nationalities were represented), although eminently desirable politically, was probably not conducive to extremely harmonious relations or totally shared values. The arguments that erupted at the countless camp meetings we felt obliged to hold were numerous, strenuous and sometimes bitter.

Nor was the situation helped - either then or at the preparatory stage in Baghdad - by deficient communication and some discord with Gulf Peace Team headquarters in London which, among other things, was apt to send us misleading information (even misinformation sometimes) about the number of volunteers waiting in the wings and the amount of funds in the pipeline. There were even occasional, unacceptable attempts to lay down the law to us from London.

An interesting feature of the camp was that by no means all the participants were long-time peace activists: some had been inspired to join simply through consternation about the current Gulf situation. And a high proportion were middle-aged to elderly - a couple of the latter actually being somewhat disabled and afflicted with walking difficulties. Possibly this was because older people are less reluctant to put their lives on the line. Then too, elderly people are less likely than the young to have jobs to lose, partners to leave or children to support. Interestingly, the campers appeared to include only about a couple of couples.

I myself found that the aspect of the project that caused most strain, apart from interpersonal conflicts, was the chronic sense of uncertainty about almost everything - initially as to whether we would ever be permitted to pitch the camp at all, and, if so, whether we would be able to conduct it in an acceptable fashion in the right place. Then we never knew just how many volunteers were standing by; nor could we be sure, supposing the camp ever materialized, that it would be of any real political significance and get properly publicized. We wondered how the project would be financed and whether our funds would dry up. And of course we endlessly debated whether or not war was going to break out at all. Later, when it did, we wondered whether the camp would be overrun by troops and all of us be killed (possibly bombed or gassed); whether US troops might conceivably kidnap us by helicopter; whether the Iraqi authorities would leave us *in situ* for the duration of the war, with diminishing stocks of food, declining water supplies and no more heating oil; whether the Iraqis would forcibly evacuate us (we had endless acrimonious debates as to what we should do in this eventuality), intern us, deport us, or whatever. Partly because of this constant collection of uncertainties I found myself doing what I seldom do - living almost entirely in the present, my personal past and future seeming largely irrelevant. Even my dreams proved to be about day-to-day camp matters such as washing-up, pots and pans, etc.

Many of the frictions, tensions, uncertainties and practical worries that beset this project came as no great surprise to me - back in the 60s I was involved in a somewhat similar, although less successful, nonviolent enterprise in southeast Asia during the Vietnam war, in the course of which we faced many similar problems. The one major lesson I learned was how extremely difficult, indeed all-but impossible, it is to remain totally neutral if you are, like it or not, the guests of a particular country, with whatever type of government. The Gulf Peace Team took a neutral position on the political issues at stake in the conflict, our stance being simply opposition to the war coupled with determination to try nonviolently to resist combat by the forces of either side or both sides. And to be fair, the Iraqi authorities by and large respected our neutrality, did not manipulate us unduly and published our policy statement in the Baghdad English-medium paper. However, if you establish yourselves as a human, nonviolent would-be barrier at a frontier you inevitably find yourselves at least to some extent the guest of the country (or countries) in which you are based - and this poses great difficulties for peace activists not wanting, as a group, to take sides.

In the end the Iraqi authorities were able, regardless of our wishes (and some of us declined, nonviolently, to cooperate), to evacuate us from the camp, briefly intern us in a hotel in Baghdad then deport us to the Jordanian border. The difficulty of remaining wholly neutral prompted a few of us at one stage even to consider transplanting ourselves into the narrow strip of no-one's land between the nearby Iraqi and Saudi frontiers - although in the end this scheme proved to be a non-starter.

So what, if anything, has been achieved by this difficult, problem-ridden project - apart from the friendships that were, of course, forged and connections made despite all the frictions and conflicts? Arguably, our well-publicized presence did in a very limited way achieve its purpose: we just may, in our immediate vicinity, have discouraged overt hostilities. The Iraqi authorities told us that soon after our evacuation there was both a land skirmish in the area and air raids there. This may or may not have been true - we had, and have, no way of telling: but if it were it would suggest that our presence had, for a short while in a very limited area, served as a nonviolent deterrent to actual hostilities.

On quite another level, the project seems to have been useful as a particular ingredient in the general, worldwide opposition to the war: camper after camper reported at discussion groups that their decision to join the camp had served as a catalyst, prompting more strenuous opposition to the war in their own neighbourhoods back home. And useful national and local publicity was of course generated by their joining in the camp.

But perhaps the project's greatest achievement was the precedent it set: never before had quite such an ambitious nonviolent enterprise of quite this sort on quite this scale actually managed to get participants positioned strategically where they wanted to be. But whether really a historic, significant peace movement precedent was set only time will tell. Let's hope that if (gods forbid) in the future a situation similar to the Gulf crisis were to recur many more nonviolent peace activists from all over the world would decide to try to withstand the outbreak of war on the spot - and perhaps this time succeed.

Part 2

The war and after

"*We are in the process of destroying an entire society. It is as simple and terrifying as that.*"

Denis Halliday,
former UN Humanitarian Coordinator in Iraq

An appeal for justice from a black man in Baghdad

Andrew P. Jones

This appeal for justice, written by the only Black American in Baghdad, is aimed at all Americans. Although I must admit the thought that Black Americans, the Red Indians, and the Spanish population are most likely to take it to heart.

Here in Baghdad, as one storyteller might have put it, the rosy fingered dawn caresses the gold minarets with her painted nails. With her comes the heat of day to the hottest capital in the world. Children arise this morning, sleepy after a night on their flat roofs where they slept with their parents, cousins, uncles and aunts under a fine blanket of desert dust and soothing Arabian night breezes.

It is a troubled place this city in the centre of the Middle East. Winter was a time of war. Spring saw an unjust peace. Shortages of food, water and electricity plagued the people like locusts. For a while civil war in the north and south blotted out relief from suffering, although none of the parties involved now seem to want more killing.

The quality of life in Iraq has taken a turn towards the dismal. True, a few of the rich get richer off the war, but many more went broke. An entire middle class has become an underclass and the poor have become a sub-class, if such a class can be imagined.

Visiting hospitals in the south, I have seen case after case of infant malnutrition, the mothers themselves suffering from the same. In many areas due to a mixture of stress, poor diet, bad sanitation and contaminated water, mothers find themselves unable to produce breast milk for their children. Instead they feed their children contaminated sugar water. The babies get gastroenteritis and become even more malnourished. Those who make it to hospitals soon enough get dedicated treatment. Those who do not just die.

A severely malnourished child looks like a tiny old person. The worst cases, and there are plenty, have wrinkles, baggy skin and distended bellies. They have to be cleaned constantly because as soon as they eat they defecate and the flies come round. Pediatric ward windows must be left open because more often than not there is no air conditioning.

Most hospitals are now using small back-up generators. Engineers make do by cannibalizing main generators for the spare parts they cannot import due to sanctions. Even so, the smaller generators cannot produce enough voltage to supply roomy wards with cool air. So mothers fan their children continuously and try to keep their own spirits up by kidding and joking around.

Playfulness tends to be a major part of most Iraqi households. I remember lots of kidding in my own household growing up in the projects of Richmond, Virginia. My mother used to play jokes on us and we played jokes on her and each other all the time. Later, as I entered white society and acquired white friends, I found them to be taken aback at the extent to which I joked about seemingly serious situations. They didn't understand that I had learned to minimalise a problem first by laughing at it and then later dealing with it seriously. Perhaps it is a coping mechanism, a kind of kill switch for sadness. If we cry hard enough, we laugh and if we laugh hard enough, we cry. Such is true all over the world.

It is early evening in Baghdad and I sit interviewing an Iraqi woman who tells me a story that begins with laughter but ends tragically. The day was 19 January, 1991. The time was approximately two o'clock in the afternoon in the Karada section of Baghdad. She says she was in her kitchen preparing to go to her sister's house where the family was gathering for lunch. Big lunches are a tradition in Iraq.

All of a sudden she heard the roar of what seemed to be a low flying jet airplane. She looked up just as a cruise missile was passing right in front of the window. Laughing hysterically she ran into the living room ready to tell everyone about the slapstick sight she had just seen. Imagine, she says, standing in your kitchen in the middle of the afternoon and a cruise comes zooming by right in front of you. Unfortunately, there was no one in the living room. Everyone was outside already.

The missile had struck the home of her sister and brother-in-law, located a couple of streets away. They had been married thirty-three years. Both were killed instantly. Two of their daughters and the older daughter's 18-month old boy were also in the house. The three of them were dead.

Up in the north of Iraq, in the city of Mosul, children play in the now familiar postwar ruins: rows of houses destroyed by army projectiles. They use cardboard to slide down what used to be concrete roofs of homes. Laughing and playing in front of the camera, oblivious to the smell of raw sewage rivulets, they eagerly show me their bombed school. Some of the children weren't so lucky as the ones now playing in the debris. I ask the names of dead children and their surviving peers shout out an honour roll. Sometimes they pause to remember. The adults say nothing.

A surgeon in the general hospital in Mosul tells me that during the war he decided to allow staff volunteers to video the immediate aftermath of the air strikes. He says he did so because of his belief that the hospital should have its own record of the bombing.

The videos include some shots taken in the hospital morgue. The shots show dead children and adults with no visible injuries, looking as though they died in their sleep. He says they died when their internal organs imploded. Often, he says, the force of a nearby explosion will simply push all air out of the body and cause it to collapse on itself suffocating the victim.

I write this appeal from the Diwan Hotel here on Saadon Street in central Baghdad. Before the war this was the city's centre of social and retail activity, sort of like Columbus Circle in New York or the Latin Quarter in Paris. One block west are the world-famous fish restaurants situated along the Tigris River. Tourists used to frequent these establishments to eat the fish caught fresh from the Tigris, now badly polluted due to sewage run-off.

Sewage treatment facilities, once the envy of other Third World countries, were shut down when the power plants were struck during the war. Winter rains clogged drains and sewage backed up in the streets. The only place to put it was in the river. Water sanitation experts estimate that it will take years for the great Tigris to recover.

Now most of the restaurants along the river are closed. The fish that is sold is too expensive for most Iraqi families and there are no tourists. Couples still stroll along the river. Men still sit outdoors, play dominoes, smoke and play pool. But the old atmosphere, so they say, is now gone.

It is difficult to imagine how quickly prices have skyrocketed here in Iraq. The average Iraqi family makes 150 dinars a month. A family of six people, two parents and four children, now have to spend at least 1,000 Iraqi dinars a month for food. It is a wonder how people eat. They eat little and work a lot, something for which Iraqis are famous.

Nevertheless I have been a frequent dinner guest of Iraqis rich and poor. Even during brief visits they never fail to offer me tea or coffee. I have been treated to meals, the leftovers of which will be used for days, I am sure. I have never been asked to pay.

There lives in Iraq a strong Arab tradition of hospitality which Iraqis lavish on foreigners and each other. The tradition is so strong that the majority of the Arabs here would probably rather die than suffer the shame of being inhospitable hosts. Graciousness is in their blood but their blood may be shed again for oil.

Caveat!

It is not my aim to base this appeal on a picture of a perfect or even heroic people. Indeed, the Iraqi people have the same foibles that any other people share and in some ways more so. There is racism here, sexism and what some might call arrogance among the educated classes. Yet what I have not found here, in even the most minute amount, is the blind hatred of the "enemy", historically so prevalent in the United States during the times of war.

Throughout this entire Gulf crisis, there has yet to be reported one incident wherein an Iraqi citizen threatened, abused or insulted a visitor from any one of the countries participating in the war against Iraq. All journalists and relief workers in Iraq have been treated with a collective courtesy and discipline which makes the more ignorant visitor suspicious. Not even the children call us names and children are generally the real barometre of the feelings of any given household.

For example, the surgeon I spoke to in Mosul told me that most children in Iraq now hate the Americans. To them America is Godzilla, a huge screaming flying lizard with flashing red eyes, breath hissing down from the skies spreading fire and destruction. They see Americans as lizard people whom they identify with the planes that sent them into shelters night after night last winter, fearing for their lives. His son, having the idea that the Americans are devils, was shocked when he heard his father receiving aid from American relief organizations. The boy urged him not to accept their gifts. Still, I am absolutely certain that were I to encounter the boy in any situation, he would be courteous to a fault.

Many of us foreigners have travelled extensively throughout Iraq, either alone or in small groups, conspicuous where we have been by our accents, skin colour, dress and behaviour. We have passed through numerous military checkpoints often in or near sensitive areas. In every case, the soldiers have been to a man, nothing but professional, though often armed to the teeth. Indeed, I feel safer here in Baghdad than I did in Boston where a visit to the wrong neighbourhood could attract a racial slur or stray bullet.

Most Americans are not aware of the strong bonds between the Iraqi people and the United States. The two countries have a history of cooperation going back well into the fifties when the Iraqis were coming back and forth to America as students and professionals.

One Iraqi engineer in Jordan tells me that when he was at the University of Denver in the fifties, there were over 3,000 Iraqi students attending school in the area. He says that because of their dark skin, many were mistaken for Blacks or Chicanos and treated accordingly. Therefore, he and many others developed close ties with members of the Black community with whom they often shared eating and toilet facilities downtown. Indeed, in Iraq there is a sizeable Black population, although Iraqis insist that skin colour is not a functional variable in their country.

Over a quarter of a million Iraqis now reside in the Detroit area alone in the United States, working in the auto industry as engineers, managers and technicians. Many others live in Chicago, Boston, San Francisco, New York, Tulsa and even Toledo. Almost every Iraqi I speak to here in Baghdad has a relative or friend in the States.

Now, many countries are refusing to issue visas to Iraqis. Consequently the Iraqi passion for travelling, for sharing the riches of other cultures is once again being stifled by political circumstances. Whereas the Iraqi people

have demonstrated their willingness not to hold travellers to Iraq accountable for the actions of foreign governments, that courtesy is not extended
to them in return. The result is insult added to injury.

So it is another hot day in Baghdad. By noon the temperature will have
reached 100 degrees Fahrenheit. The electricity may go off sometime in the
afternoon at the Hotel Diwan, but it will come back eventually and stay on
for the rest of the day. By tomorrow, prices will have risen slightly, excluding
gasoline, currently the cheapest commodity in the country.

One year ago this time, I had just returned from a three-month
photo-journalism tour of southern Africa. In that time I had spent 32 days
inside South Africa travelling alone, talking to people in various cities and
towns and in the townships.

Almost everyone I spoke to shared the fear that South Africa had developed chemical and nuclear weapons as a result of technical assistance from
Israel. It is already the strongest military force in all of Africa. No one inside
or outside South Africa doubts that South Africa would use the full might
of its military capabilities to quell any real threat from its Black population.
The fact that the United States has tolerated and even condoned the development of this militaristic creature is of utmost concern to all parties struggling for liberation in that country.

South Africa is guilty of everything Iraq has been accused of, including
breaching the borders and threatening the sovereignty of a neighbouring
country. Its record of human rights abuses dwarfs that of any country on
earth. The number of political prisoners languishing in its prisons is second
only to the overall Black prison population in the United States. Three quarters of South Africa's population cannot vote and are regarded as non-citizens
solely on the basis of the colour of their skin.

So why hasn't the United States moved against South Africa? Why haven't
the same kind of sanctions applied to Iraq been applied to South Africa?
Why not deprive South African citizens of food and medicine in their country, then bomb them and rebomb them until they either change their system
or die trying? After all, is that not what we want the Iraqis to do?

One answer to the above set of questions is that it is inhuman to make
war against a population when political remedies are available. Successive
presidential administrations in the United States have stuck to a programme
of constructive engagement aimed at inflicting minimal damage on the in-

frastructure of South Africa while enticing it towards slow but meaningful political change. So why not the same policy toward Iraq?

And why bomb Iraq again? Why rebomb a country that is at this very moment losing infants to typhoid, gastroenteritis and other diseases as a result of sanctions imposed by thirty countries? Why rebomb a country that has already felt the blasts of 109,000 tons of bombs? Why rebomb a country that withdrew from Kuwait, had its retreating army slaughtered from the air, and has accepted the most humiliating set of ceasefire restrictions ever imposed on one nation? Why rebomb one country when everything it is accused of is being perpetrated daily by at least two other countries, both of which are guilty of international infractions far larger than those committed by the country about to be rebombed?

I know now that General Colin Powell opposed the initial buildup of offensive forces in the Arabian Gulf. Having read excerpts from Bob Woodward's book, *The Commanders*, I have learned that he questioned the President's motives and at first argued against George Bush, a mean white man bent on punishing a people whom he probably thinks are "uppity". As a Black man I know what Colin must have felt, which is the same thing that his ancestors in Jamaica must have felt, what any Black man feels when called to wield the whip against his brother. He must have felt revulsion. Yet he did what he felt he had to do and he will most likely do it again. For such is the yoke we must carry for now.

But how many times can we be called upon to do the bidding of a people who have fallen prey to the idea of hate? How many times can we march off and slaughter decent human beings without thought of the long-term impact on the idea of God as love?

Previously we might have been accused of striking out in anger and in anger there is some measure of innocence. But now, before the eyes of the world, our actions can only be deemed deliberate, full of pretense and premeditated.

Therefore all deaths that are the direct or indirect result of military actions started or initiated by the United States on or after 25 July 1991, whether the dead be pilots or children, soldiers or civilians, their deaths must be considered murder in the plainest sense of the word.

So I close this appeal with an appeal for restraint, for mercy from the great nation of America, stumbling around now like a mad giant lost in the dust of its own desert storm.

Be still great beast!

Listen to the voices of the humble people, those whom you robbed and enslaved, those who in turn gave you the idea of freedom and justice for all.

Hear the beat of our drums in the cold Dakotas as we flee the long knives. Feel our fear as we run to escape your hunting dogs, not sure of where we are running to, all too sure of the slavery we are running from. Know now, that we ain't gonna run no more.

Know mad and angry giant, that we do not seek to hurt you, that we simply seek to heal you because your power has made you sick. Just do not strike us. Do not kill us, your brothers.

Sit down blind giant. Have some tea. Enjoy the sweet aroma of Turkish coffee. You are safe here even though you have come to make war. All guests are welcome in the house of God.

Stop the screaming planes before they take off and listen to the soft voices of children here. They call on you for mercy. Please feel the gentle hands of their fate. They will guide you.

Listen to the wailing wind and watch the date palms sway in the summer heat. Yes! It is too hot to fight. Why bother with war when the cool peace makes your angry sweat disappear?

Come here crazed giant. I will comfort you. I was taught to love mine enemy. Yes, you have forgotten that lesson, but since you have taught me so much, it is the least I can do to teach this lesson to you in return. There will be no makeup test tomorrow.

The blood red sun sets daily over Baghdad. The cold fingers of dawn, they fold themselves into the west to become the new twilight.

Rest under the stars of the martyrs, great tired beast.

And don't worry

They died so you can sleep and not worry

So sleep great beast

While the rest of the world watches over you.

And may your dreams bring you

And the people of Iraq

Everlasting peace.

Salaam!

A post-war journey through Iraq

Louise Cainkar

I left for Iraq on 24 March 1991, with a Jordanian Red Crescent Society convoy of relief goods purchased from donations collected by international non-government organizations. The Amman-based Gulf Peace Team was responsible for a significant part of this shipment and facilitated, along with the Jordanian Red Crescent Society, my initial and subsequent journeys. On the road between the Iraq border and Baghdad I saw the first evidence of civilian war casualties - no less than 40 bombed civilian cars and freight trucks and two buses lying on the side of the road, most of them between the border and the 200 km road marker.

The civilian casualties from this war had only just begun. The successful achievement of the mission to destroy Iraq's infrastructure has not only thrown Iraq back at least 100 years, it has forced every single Iraqi to search for a new way to cope with the new circumstances of life: no electricity, no running water, reliance on contaminated water, food shortages, fuel short-ages, transportation problems, for many no work, no income and thus no food, the total absence of access to medical care and medicine, massive inflation, and a real severing of human relations as a result of the difficulties in interpersonal communication both inside and outside the country. Iraq had been a highly developed, technologically sophisticated, and self-reliant country. Now, most Iraqis appeared to be in silent shock, trying to figure out how to accomplish the day's tasks just to feed and clothe their families. Within a period of 45 days they had gone from 1991 to the 19th century; the way things were done in January were not possible in March. We cannot underestimate the psychological and logistical toll of this on human beings, nor the human ability to survive despite these conditions. But biological contamination and famine are forces which no human can stop single-handedly, and no society broken to pieces and without the proper tools to combat it can halt. This is Iraq.

I had travelled from Amman to Baghdad with an 18-year old Palestinian from Ameriyeh named Ghassan Khader. Ghassan's mother and four sisters were killed in the Ameriyeh bomb shelter. Ghassan had invited me to visit and one day I took a taxi to Ameriyeh hoping they were home, wondering on the way how I could walk through the neighbourhood of Ameriyeh if they weren't.

When I arrived at Ghassan's house, he and his father (Mohammed Khadder, a professor of soil chemistry) were washing clothes, something I am sure they had not done before. With no relatives in Iraq, these men were now on their own. "Now we have nothing," Mohammed told me, his will to live gone. He showed me photos of his daughters and wife and then their rooms, clothes and possessions. He said this was the first time he had been able to touch these items. The day after the bombing he attempted to set his house on fire, with himself inside it. A neighbour stopped him.

The scene in Mohammed's home was so unbearably painful that I cannot now adequately reconstruct it and know I will never forget it. I knew then that saying I was sorry was totally insufficient. I was surprised that despite my years of human rights work and all that I had seen before, I could only respond with tears. After a woman who survived the shelter happened to come by the house and joined us, my tears shifted to streams and the agony and shame I felt being an American ate at my stomach. I said only that I had opposed the war from the start. I wondered if the millions of Americans who supported this war, waving flags and yellow ribbons, would feel different about it now if they were sitting in this room...

The southern Iraqi city of Basra and its surrounding district received the most bombs of any areas of Iraq I had seen. The bombing included communications centres, power plants, bridges, water treatment plants and residential areas. I personally visited five different sections of Basra where bombs had hit civilian homes; none appeared to be near obvious military targets, unless the Pepsi plant was a military target.

On the grounds of the Tahir Teaching Hospital of Basra is a large crater about 20 feet in diameter, a characteristic feature of places where coalition bombs landed on soil. Shrapnel from this bomb, which landed on 26 January at 7:30 a.m., hit the 6th floor of the hospital and immediately killed four adult patients in the intensive care unit and one baby. Every window of the hospital was blown-out, much of its medical equipment was rendered unusable, and many of the lowered ceilings collapsed when the hospital was jolted by more than one bombing in the area. All patients were evacuated from the hospital after the 26 January bombing, and it was still incapable of handling patients when I visited in late March.

By the end of April 1991 the primary health problems in Iraq were gastroenteritis, malnutrition, and dehydration. These problems result from the shortage of food, reaching near-famine conditions in certain areas, and the absence of potable water in most of Iraq. While all these illnesses are normally treatable, the shortage of medicines, food and uncontaminated water throughout Iraq makes them potentially lethal. Since the end of the war, at least 100 children have died each day from these illnesses.

The food shortage in Iraq is largely the result of UN sanctions. Iraq imported 70% of its food prior to August 1990, when sanctions were imposed. Since then, the population has been living off existing (pre-August) stocks, minimal domestic production, and a small amount of international relief. Food products cost 20 to 60 times more than they did before August 1990. Adequate quantities and a balance of essential food items are now out of reach for hundreds of thousands of Iraqi families. Transportation problems and a system of internal privilege further aggravate the food shortage, leaving sectors of the north and south of Iraq, and certain sub-groups within these sectors, facing near-famine conditions.

The scarcity of uncontaminated piped water in most of Iraq is an outcome of both coalition bombing and sanctions. Some water treatment plants, pumping stations and holding towers were destroyed by coalition bombing. Others remain standing but have insufficient electrical power (due to the bombing of electrical power plants and stations) and inadequate supplies of chlorine, aluminium sulphate and other necessary chemicals (due to bombing of storage facilities and sanctions) to allow for water treatment and distribution.

Except for some hospitals, it was a rare experience to find running water in any other place I visited in Iraq. Where I found it, it was not safe for drinking and the supply was intermittent. The lack of clean, running water has resulted in abnormally high levels of diarrhoea, dehydration, other gastrointestinal problems, and ensuing malnutrition among Iraqis, especially children, and a dramatic increase in the infant mortality rate.

But the real catastrophe from the lack of running, potable water is expected to begin in May, when temperatures will start to soar up to 130 degrees Fahrenheit (54 Celsius). The population's need for water will increase, causing a rise in the propensity to drink contaminated water, which will further poison and weaken the population. In addition, these hot temperatures provide fertile conditions for the growth of bacteria, resulting in the likely spread of epidemic diseases such as cholera, typhoid, meningitis, and hepatitis. Cases of cholera and typhoid had been clinically diagnosed in most parts of Iraq by April.

I visited hospital after hospital characterized by severe shortages of medicines, clean water, milk, infant formula and food. The availability of electricity varied - some had it nearly 24 hours per day while others had it only a few hours per day and/or in certain areas only (depending upon the capacity of and fuel supply for existing back-up generators). Many hospitals were not functional at all, either because all the windows had been blown out and the structures had been damaged from direct or nearby coalition bomb hits, or because they had been pillaged and ransacked during the post-war internal rebellions, and damaged again by the Iraqi army trying to route the rebels. The town of Zubair in the Basra district had no functioning medical system when I visited it in late March.

Upon arriving at Jumhariyya hospital in Basra, the same scene I was to see over and over again emerged - Iraqi women holding thin, bloated and malnourished children, fanning them from the increasing heat. Doctors said that because laboratory analyses were impossible, their diagnoses were based on a clinical assessment of symptoms. For example, everything appearing to affect mainly the gastrointestinal system was called gastroenteritis.

All hospitals reported shortages of crucial medicines and medical supplies. Doctors also stressed that a consistent source of pure water and electricity was essential to the delivery of proper medical care and that the lack of it was seriously hampering their effectiveness. Hospital staff are unable to wash bedding and sterilize equipment, rendering the hospital environment quite unsanitary. Before the war, Iraq had communicable diseases under control due to a large-scale vaccination program. Now supplies of vaccines are virtually non-existent because of sanctions and infrastructure destruction.

In sum, sanctions and war have created a biological and health disaster in Iraq. The destruction of Iraq's infrastructure by coalition bombing and the ongoing imposition of sanctions have transformed a relatively healthy population into a sick one that is being denied proper medical care and nutrition. Civilian deaths from hunger and sickness, averaging at least 3,000 per month since the war ended, will far outnumber those that occurred during the war. These deaths, however, are not indirect byproducts of the war; they are a direct result of the type of warfare used. Surgical precision destroyed the brain of Iraq and the body has been left to die. A new level of inhumanity, brought about by the development of weapons of precision, has been achieved.

Memories of Kerbala

Detlef Enge-Bastien

Kerbala means "catastrophe sent from God". In 680 A.D. the grand-son of the prophet Al Hussein and his half-brother, Al Abbas, lost their lives here during the Battle of Kerbala. Their grave sites have become important holy shrines in the Shi'ite religion. A magnificent multi-coloured city, it is surrounded by old palm trees and fruit plantations. Kerbala is a town of pilgrims and burial places for the faithful.

It is tragic that this lovely city - close to where the Bible states that Paradise once stood - lived up to its name for the second time in March 1991. Indeed the Shi'ite rebellion in southern Iraq led to a second Battle of Kerbala.

Under the observation of American surveillance planes approximately 4,000 - 18,000 people lost their lives in the heavy combat to retake the city. A medical catastrophe resulted and became a terrible but typical example of the sufferings of Iraqi civilians who underwent the coalition bombing, civil war and UN embargo.

Yesterday, carrying my work permit with me, I arrived at the Al Husseiny hospital in Kerbala. I was warmly embraced by Dr. Karim Obais Elewi and his colleagues from the internal medicine section. Much has changed since my earlier visit in March. The general depression of the physicians seems to have receded. Seventy-five per cent of the building and medical equipment are destroyed but, step by step, the doctors are reclaiming the facilities from the debris.

As far as possible the hospital is kept clean. It is the main local hospital for half a million people and suffers from the expected congestion. We see more than 200 patients daily in the internal medicine ward alone.

For two months there has been no medical care and because of this many people, especially children and the elderly, have simply died at home. Among the former dialysis patients who depended on kidney machines, none have survived. But now there is a chance to reopen the hospital!

Unfortunately, many of the chronically ill have got worse because of the absence of appropriate medicines. Impure water has added many more patients suffering from diarrhoea, typhoid and cholera. Small children and infants suffer the most. Milk formula is among the products banned by the embargo and is therefore almost impossible to obtain. Instead the children receive rice water or sugar water. Normal water can only be obtained from bacteria-infested mud-holes, puddles and rivers. There is still no electricity to run the water plant. Many water pipes are damaged and some of the pumps need replacement parts. Due to the embargo nothing can be repaired.

The results are the tiny patients who are brought daily to the hospital. With imploring eyes the mothers lay down their starving and dehydrated children - and hope for a miracle. Most of them look like small mummies. We cannot help them. In a matter of hours or days they die even if the medical supplies from the Gulf Peace Team or other groups arrive on time, enabling us to treat them with transfusions and antibiotics for a few days. Meanwhile the mother's larger family at home, including sick children, remain unprovided for. For this reason many women resign themselves and don't even bother to bring the small children to the hospital. This way they will at least be at home to care for the older siblings.

For a physician such as myself, fresh out of western Germany with its well-organised systems of hygiene and medical care, it is a horrible experience not to be able to help in so many routine cases. I ask myself where this strength comes from, this strength not to despair. Many of these medical specialists have lost their only means of existence through the destruction of their homes and medical practices. But they go on. And most of them recognize that the root cause of their tragedy lies with their own government.

Yet no one here understands the western insistence on the embargo. Why does Bush do it? Why, now that Iraqi forces have withdrawn from Kuwait? I must endure these questions as a quasi-representative of my government but I am also acting in the name of a large German minority who have collected medical supplies and given money to help these people. I repeat again and again: the whole world does not hate Iraq. Many of us find the West just as guilty for this war as Iraq. And we are trying to extend a conciliatory hand. My colleagues believe me. And I feel that my expression of solidarity with them encourages them somewhat despite my inability as a doctor dependent on western technology to be of much help here.

We try to add new beds, mostly on a provisional basis, in an undamaged building in the adjacent children's hospital. The clinic can use the first floor of the four-storey building for out-patient cases and surgery patients. Despite lack of medical dressings and anaesthetics, there will be surgery again - although for the foreseeable future only in emergencies. Huge challenges lay before them but the doctors have the feeling that slowly, slowly, things are improving. For the last two weeks for example we have had a cardiac intensive station, though it is greatly reduced in technical capabilities. One cannot think, without crying, about the modern standards of this hospital before the war. In the internal medicine department alone they had six endoscopes, visual monitors and all the paraphernalia of a modern hospital. The war destroyed everything. None of the replacement parts for the kidney support systems are functional. Oxygen replacement capabilities for surgery and other necessary procedures are completely lacking. Despite emergency help from the Gulf Peace Team and promised susbtitute parts from Physicians Against Nuclear War, the hospital's work is severely crippled.

And so patients continue to die from illnesses that could be successfully treated under normal circumstances. On my first evening at work I became involved in the treatment of a 20 year-old woman in her second month of pregnancy. She was brought to us extremely sick with high blood acidity. We must make do without any technical or laboratory help. The exact diagnosis must therefore be established by the attending physician on purely clinical observations.

The unconscious woman displays rapid and deep breathing. The relatives give no reason to believe in a possible pain-killer overdose. Could the life-threatening condition of the patient result from a diabetic coma or a loss of kidney function? The pregnancy and other symptoms of bladder involvement argue for a kidney infection. However if we overlook the possibility of a diabetic coma we will not engage in a possible life-saving therapy of insulin. In short, if we are wrong our patient will die tonight.

Sugar and urine tests are impossible because of the loss of the laboratory. Even a simple litmus test would cast light on whether we should orient ourselves towards diabetes or a breakdown of kidney functions. These little litmus strips that cost only pennies in Germany! But they are not available in Kerbala.

But this night I am astounded by the 32 year-old physician, Dr. Shakir Mahmud Hamid, who literally holds us all in thrall. He directs my hands, my eyes, the thermometer and the application of the stethoscope. Most of his colleagues consider him to be the best in his field and we are lucky to have him. But I can imagine how every German professor of medicine would give a deep belly laugh if they had to deal with such a hands-on internist.

The typical diabetic acetone smell was missing in the woman's breath so we concluded that diabetes was improbable. The swelling of her eyelids and pale complexion indicated a failure of kidney function. Ergo - no need for insulin. Instead sugar and salt transfusions with antibiotics to work against the blood acidity and infection. It would be unbelievable in an European hospital to treat such a case without complete blood monitoring and replacement of the basic elements. But that is not possible at this hospital.

Dr. Shakir makes his observations and prescribes medicines according to his clinical experience. He does all this calmly but also aware of the desperate circumstances of his other patients. These he must also tend to.

The young woman survives the night. The next day she can communicate. The results of an outside lab substantiates the diagnosis but also points to neurological symptoms of an optic paralysis.

My relief over the first successful treatment of the symptoms disappears as it becomes clear that the patient requires a kidney machine. The hospital's dialysis capabilities were of course ruined through the war and the embargo against replacement parts. A transfer to Baghdad, where the national kidney centre now is, appears to be impossible in the near future.

What will happen now to the young woman and her unborn child? Will the mother die, the baby come already damaged into the world? Who is guilty for this situation? The western politicians who are still trying to enforce an economic embargo in a probably useless attempt to destroy Saddam Hussein but are thereby causing the Iraqi people abject misery?

In the coming weeks I will see many other patients die from easily treatable illnesses such as stomach bleeding and blood pressure crises. Only because the equipment and medicines are lacking.

The real tragedy of this situation is that it is not a result of blind fate as we would think of a natural disaster. It is the by-product of our politics: our pursuit of a military solution to the Gulf conflict, our bombs, the embargo. We cannot rid ourselves of the responsibility. This generation - my generation - has also achieved a perfect, efficient, apparently quiet, death machine. But I must live with this picture of dehydrated and starving children. These children I hold in my arms but after a few hours of insufficient medical help, must put aside. My pregnant kidney patient looks at me imploringly. I meet her eyes. I must live with this also.

Visit to Ameriyeh shelter

Jim Douglass

Sunday, 23 June, 1991 (5.00 p. m.)

Americans visiting Ameriyeh shelter are like Germans visiting Auschwitz, but in the case of Ameriyeh the victims' families - what is left of them - live in the surrounding Baghdad neighbourhood. They observe the visitors.

They also serve as guides. Four young men led us into the darkness of the Ameriyeh shelter. The candle held by the leader was our only light until we approached the centre. There the huge gash in the ceiling revealed how the two bombs had entered at the target's bull's eye, a ventilation duct. Light streamed into the darkness through the opening, illuminating beneath us a bomb-sealed door to the second level of the shelter.

The incineration of hundreds of people in the Ameriyeh shelter at 4.30 a.m. on 13 Feburary 1991 had been done with an economy of war technology. Only two bombs to seal all the doors: the first blasting open the roof; the second immediately after it, blocking and sealing the basement door; their combination serving to destroy the electrical system controlling the shelter's outer exit doors. Then the 2200 C° heat from the bombs quickly burned up the women, children, and older men of the 400 families allowed in the shelter. Only 30 victims survived, by escaping through an emergency exit in the rear. They bear terrible scars: physical and psychic.

Our guides explained the facts briefly, quietly, the candle lighting their eyes.

In the centre I looked up at the daylight, entering at the same angle as the US bombs did. The light broke through crumbling shreds of concrete, with girders hanging down like petals of a flower.

And beneath our feet must have been the remnants of the people who were trapped inside.

We are silent. These realities, and our complicity in them, enter our consiousness as the bombs did the shelter.

Afterwards, outside in the sun, a man walks up to me slowly. We talk. He is Mohammed, 23 years old. Two of his uncles and two of their children died here.

Mohammed said something I had not heard and I hope is true: "The pilot cried."

He adds, "No honour. Just babies, children and parents."

Mohammed was a soldier in Basra during the Gulf war. Unprotected by so sturdy a shelter as this, he survived.

As we part, Mohammed charges me as a writer to say something specific: "You must write in your book that the Iraqi people are very brave and like the peace."

"I will write that."

"Salaam."

"Salaam."

We shake hands.

Jill Castek, a leader in the student peace movement in Pittsburg during the war, is sitting on a block of concrete, feeling the horror and responsibility of what we have just seen. A neighbourhood girl dressed in red pants and shirt, with blue sandals on, comes to Jill. She puts her arm around her, comforting her.

She is eight or nine years old, less than half Jill's age, a fifth-grader from the Ameriyeh neighbourhood. Her name is Nadia. Like everyone in Ameriyeh, she has lost friends and relatives, but her immediate family is alive. Her little sister, Gina, is nearby. Her father and mother are across the street at the gate to their yard, giving us friendly waves.

From what inexhaustible well do these people draw their forgiveness and compassion?

Jill is sobbing as Nadia talks to her softly.

A boy is crossing the street towards us, bringing a pitcher of water. His brother is with him, carrying a tray with cups on it. They pour cup after cup of cold water for us, to slake our thirst in the Baghdad heat. I remember being warned repeatedly before this trip not to drink the water, contaminated from the US destruction of Iraq's water system. Cholera is a distinct possibility.

These people who have suffered so much from our bombs keep repeating that it was not our fault. They say they understand that. We must not blame ourselves. We drink their water as communion.

A halt at Ameriyeh shelter

Jill Castek

The Ameriyeh shelter neighbourhood in the summer of 1991 was the embodiment of the whole of Iraq in the aftermath of the Gulf war. Its population is solemn, strong, and courageous. At the same time they are filled with hurt and remorse, they are driven with the spirit to go on despite the loss of neighbours, friends, and family members.

When I first saw the Ameriyeh shelter it reminded me of a high school gymnasium made of concrete. Upon closer examination, I realized that the true, bitter, ugly face of war laid beneath the facade of normalcy. The shelter at the time of the attack on 13 February was filled with civilians, women with their children, elderly people, and guests from outside the town. Civilians took refuge in the shelter taking for granted they'd be safe there. They went simply to regain their sanity, to hear themselves think. What else were they to do, with coalition bombers flying over their heads day and night, their water supply hopelessly destroyed, electricity lines down, very little foodstuffs available? These are ordinary people just like us, looking for a place where they could feel safe, relax, sleep for a few hours.

I felt the presence of all their souls as I entered the still standing structure that day. I walked through the large caved-in doors, the same doors they entered and never left. A dark echo clouded my mind and my ears began to ring.

The enormous gaping hole in the three-metre thick ceiling lets in all the light and heat of a Baghdad afternoon. Steel beams protrude from the hole, the inner structure completely broken down.

February 13th, 1991, 4.30 a.m. While civilians slept restfully, two "intelligent" warheads struck, setting ablaze 317 bodies, the remains left unrecognizable. The roaring stench of human combustion hasn't dissipated, it remains there, a constant reminder of the fiery fate of innocent people. I walked outside for some air, my head swimming, full of the memory of people I have never met though I somehow felt their presence. I notice there is an elementary school next door to the shelter, not thirty yards away. Now also vacant, it spews children's school papers on to the shelter's lawn: a picture of an apple, a desk, a teacher, and the words scribbled thick on the line underneath in English. The children who survived are learning other lessons today, how to survive in a fractured family, mother and sisters gone, no more small baby, father tries to fix the meals and the house, afraid to leave the family alone even long enough to go to work. He cries, sleeps on the floor next to the big bed he and his wife used to share, he can't face the flood of memories of her, their children.

The evening call to prayer from the mosque behind the school brings many to their knees in their front yards and in the streets. They pray, all will be better in some future tomorrow, inshallah.

I speak to a woman holding a watering can in one hand, her son's small hand in the other. She leads me to a tree sapling just inside the shelter's fence. "My daughter's spirit is in this tree," she tells me, "I water it twice a day and she speaks to me. It's the only time I walk beyond the gate of my home, for the memory of my lost daughter Rhyida keeps me trapped inside the house. She is this tree, her soul is this little tree."

I sit and bury my face in my hands as I can't stop the tears now. Out of the corner of my eye I notice two young girls giggling at one another shyly. Nadia walks over to me and sits down close, wrapping her thin eight-year old arms around me. I begin to settle, her embrace tells me she is stronger than I could ever be, her smile tells me she's hopeful. I can only imagine what she's seen happen here. She holds out her hand and gives to me understanding, an innocence that will never know hate. I know there is hope. Nadia is in all of our souls.

War crimes

Sunil Arora

After the peace camp was evacuated I did not want to return to India. We had seen the bombed road from Baghdad to Jordan, so, when there was a chance to go to Iraq with the first medical convoy, some of us Gulf Peace Team members went with it as a human shield. But at the Iraqi border we could not get in, only the Red Crescent could. After the war I was able to accompany convoys with milk, cement, and relief materials, and yesterday I came back from my fifth trip: two of them to the south, one to the north.

What most impressed me was so much destruction, whether of government buildings or houses. People were killed because of targets missed, and it was difficult to see children suffering, many from diarrhoea. Yet the Iraqis welcomed the Americans. They would say, "Bush is a criminal", they never said, "Americans are criminal".

I visited the road from the Kuwait border to Basra where we saw a lot of soldier's shoes. We were told that the Americans destroyed the one bridge over the river so all the forces leaving Kuwait were stuck there. And then the Americans bombed.

On the peace walk, the mothers came with photographs of their dead children.[24] They were crying loudly. It was a terrible thing to see; it breaks your heart. It is a scandal that there has been no compensation for these crimes. I don't think America will admit them, because when they do, they will have to pay for them. I remember the time in India, in 1984, when an American Union Carbide factory leaked gas and thousands of people were killed in one night – and still there is no compensation.

I can imagine that Americans still think there were soldiers in the Ameriyeh shelter, but we could see baby milk bottles, a lot of small shoes, small things, not any army clothes. One man from a small village told us that a little bridge just for pedestrians had been bombed. He saw his cousin with a child in his arms, both killed… They were not responsible for the war, and I think the person who saw it was very angry and his anger will come out in one way or another.

---

[24] *Editors*: This is a reference to one of the many peace walks organised or undertaken by Gulf Peace Team members (often with Buddhist monks) in Iraq, Jordan, Israel and the Occupied Territories after the Gulf war.

People are very frightened. Before the war they didn't know about this kind of bombing, but now they have seen it. I don't know what the children will be like in the future. Young boys thought they should also have guns and fight. Older people could not make enough money, so they went into another form of business, like taking bribes. If this society is spoiled, it will be terrible for the future.

But the Iraqi people are recovering very fast. They, not foreigners, are repairing the bridges, and they are all saying that, if the sanctions are removed, it would be easy, because they would have enough money for food and everything else; they don't want to depend on relief.

What message would I give to Americans? I think that as they care for Americans, they should care for other human beings. Then I can imagine there would not be this kind of war. If the American people press their government to lift the sanctions, I am sure it will be effective.

"Every night we sleep hungry"
Bela Bhatia

Faddila lives in a poor neighbourhood called Karamad district, a few kilometres from Mosul city in the province of Nineveh. This neighbourhood, a working-class area, is one of the poorest sections in Mosul city.

We first saw Faddila when we were interviewing her neighbour. She is very thin and suffering seems to be etched deep on her face. We asked Karimha, the woman we were interviewing, who she thought was the poorest household in the neighbourhood. She promptly answered, "It is Faddila. I have never seen anyone who suffered more."

We went to Faddila's home, which is two doors away from Karimha's. Her home consists of one room and a kitchen. This is part of a larger house where several other families live. The house is traditionally-built, with rooms all round and a shared courtyard in the centre. Faddila's home was neat and clean. A flowered curtain covered one wall; a wall hanging with an Arab design covered another. A cupboard with glass panes revealed good-quality cups and saucers, plates, serving dishes and a jug. (This showed as many things do in the Arab culture, the preparedness for guests in the household, in spite of personal adversity.) Mattresses were neatly piled on a wooden rack, and from the nails on the wall hung a few clothes. This is the story that she told to us.

Faddila is thirty years old. She got married in 1981. Three years ago she became a widow, on the day when the Iran-Iraq war ended. As with the people around her, significant events in her life too were recalled in relation to one war or another. Her husband was ill for six months. He had cancer. They took him everywhere for treatment, but he could not be cured.

After her husband's death Faddila was faced with the task of raising her four young children alone. Her husband's family did not want her nor did her own. "This was my *naseeb*" (fate), she said. Karimha explained that the reason why Faddila was regarded with disfavour was because she was a Christian-Arab married to a Kurdish-Muslim. "He used to live in the same neighbourhood as we used to. He was a good man," added Faddila with a sigh. Did she think of getting remarried? "No, there is no question of that for I have to look after my children," she said.

How has she been able to survive in the past few years? She replied, "I am able to survive only because of other people's help. I get 54 dinars a month from the government." A similar pension is given to all widows (excluding war widows who are covered under a separate scheme) as long as they live.

"I started working as an office helper, but was able to do this for only 15 days. I decided to leave, because when I came back home I used to find my little boys on the street. How can I work when my children are so young ? If the children grow older, then I will do some work." We asked her why she said "if"; she replied, "It is hard to see your children growing. They don't grow quick enough."

"In the past, with 54 dinars, I used to be able to manage very well. Now I am not even able to feed my family. My small child wants some meat. What do I tell him? When somebody cooks meat, they sit and cry. In the past few weeks, there have been periods when I was unable to get any food for my children. Every night we sleep hungry. I do not have any cooking oil. The other day, Karimha's mother gave me some and I cooked with that. Yesterday also she gave me some food. If we have some bread we eat something." Karimha said that she had never seen anybody so hungry. "I sometimes come to her house and find her crying."

Faddila continued. "During the war, everybody left. I could not leave. I was cold. We would sit in our one room and cough. Karimha's mother and father used to feed us. Even though the whole household had left for a village in the north, the old couple preferred to stay back in their own home. We used to sometimes go and sleep there."

Karimha reproaches her because she has lost her ration card. Now she will not be able to get her rations. Once lost, a ration card is not reissued. Faddila hopes that she will be able to find it. She has been getting the supplies every month. The government ration lasts her for 10 days. Hunger strikes the household at any time in the 20 days that remain. Faddila is never sure that her children will get food the next day. She is able to buy from the open market only if somebody gives her money. "In the remaining 20 days, people give me half of what I get from the government. Sometimes friends like Karimha come and cook for me or share their meal with us. At other times we are able to get leftovers from other families, or we just go hungry."

People from outside

Caroline Dobson

The hospital director was apologetic. The place was filthy and nearly deserted; the lights were on at the moment, but the air conditioning was not, as most of the units had been ripped out of the walls. It was 14 April 1991, in Kirkuk. Ten days earlier the city had been a scene of battle, and the people we were now talking to had hidden in fear for their lives.

They were mostly Turkomans. There are about a million Turkomans in northern Iraq, and they form a large proportion of the population in Kirkuk. When the fighting began, they had been caught in the crossfire between the Kurdish fighters and the Iraqi army, and accused of treachery by both sides. But now the Kurds had fled to the mountains, and the city was under army control. In the uneasy quiet that followed, interviews were nervously tolerated, and our group - Gulf Peace Team members, a journalist, a photographer, and a team of Japanese engineers - were shown round two of the three main hospitals. Our minder pointed to the wrecked dialysis machines and the holes in the hospital walls, most of them near the roof, and told us how evil the Kurds were. I wondered how much heavy artillery the Kurds had actually managed to get hold of. In our impromptu "press conference" with the hospital director, the question was put: Who actually carried out the attacks? "People coming from outside," he said.

It was a phrase we were to hear often. In the Shi'a city of Kerbala, 150 km south of Baghdad, the blame for the destruction around the two holy shrines and the ruin of the hospital was also attributed to the "people from outside". Depending on who we were talking to, these were either Saudi propagandists inciting the civil war (the American and British influence unspoken but implied), or they remained nameless. We quickly came to understand the term as a code-word for the army.

The phrase had an ironic edge. For here were we, no less "people from outside", from countries across the world, including the USA and Britain; here we were in the mad hope that our drop in the ocean might make a difference, and that our attempts at rebuilding psychological bridges might be as valuable as practical attempts to rebuild concrete ones. Later in the summer, one organization after another carried out medical surveys: there were some attempts to pool information but each group was researching something different. These surveys were viewed with growing cynicism.

People began to talk of "aid tourism". It was a thought that occured to many of us as we discussed itineraries.

Our whole existence became one of multiple translations. The unspoken word often assumed greater significance than the spoken. But all these small transferances of meaning were the means of building relationships, and this, it seemed to me, was the most valuable aspect of all our activity. It was at least as important as the supplies that the Gulf Peace Team was able to muster for its convoys. It let people in Iraq know that there were, for example, British and American citizens who deplored the action taken by their governments against the civilian population of Iraq - governments which had previously stressed that their quarrel was not with the people but with the regime. It highlighted for both sides that it is almost always governments that wage wars: people usually make friendships.

We were attempting to communicate in both directions: with the local people in English or broken Arabic, and also to our own people, to inform and if at all possible to stir to action. To do the latter, it was essential to listen to what people in Iraq were saying to us. We found that they were as free with advice as they were with their increasingly limited resources; their hospitality was sometimes overwhelming - their observations were kindly but to the point.

Iraq had never considered itself to be a "Third World" country. Its standards of education and training were excellent. The expertise of its doctors command worldwide respect. Until the embargo, Iraq had been a giver of aid to neighbouring countries, not a recipient. Now that Iraq had been catapulted back to the previous century, it was as if its very essence had changed to one of basic evolutionary principles: survival of the fittest. As mothers fed their babies milk powder mixed with polluted river water, there was increasing evidence not only of typhoid and cholera but also of such typically "Third World" diseases as marasmus and kwashiorkor. Polio and tuberculosis also rose in frequency.

I had my own opportunities to see this. One day I was invited by a local doctor to accompany him to his surgery in Saddam City, a huge slum township on the outskirts of Baghdad. This was one of the poorest areas I had seen; the unemployment rate was close to 90%. There was a noticeable absence of young men, as many of them had been conscripted for the war and had not returned.

"It will be hot and dark", Dr. Khalid warned me before we left. "We had

electricity yesterday; we won't get any more for another four or five days."
He worked from mid-afternoon until well into the evening, lighting a paraffin lamp as dusk fell. No electricity meant no refrigeration of vaccines, and
there were no antibiotics to treat the increasing numbers of typhoid cases.
Dr. Khalid said that the only effective drug was chloramphenicol, a strong
antibiotic with very unpleasant side effects, including pernicious anaemia in
1-2% of cases. But there was none being brought into Iraq, as far as we
could tell; and it was completely unavailable in Jordan. It was not produced
as it was considered too dangerous.

When a group of women brought in a boy of about ten, who com-
plained of something minor but turned out to be suffering from typhoid
(many cases were discovered in a similar incidental way), I was invited to
return with them to their house, to see their living conditions at close quarters. To enter, it was necessary to step over a gutter full of raw sewage -
evidence of the collapsed pumping systems that had been "taken out" by
coalition bombers. Inside it was tiny: a medium-sized room downstairs and
two smaller ones upstairs, plus a balcony with room for one small girl and a
pot on a fire, in which a kilo or so of greasy meat was cooking.

I was hustled into one of the small rooms and was immediately surrounded by a large number of women and children, the children silent and
staring, the women all talking at once. In the storm of Arabic one word
dominated: *maaku*, none. No electricity, no water, no milk, no fresh vegeta-
bles - the prices had soared beyond belief. No work. No husbands. Maaku.
Then they began to repeat a number: 33. It took me a little while to realise
that was the number of people living in the house.

The meeting was brief, but unforgettable. They held out their open
palms in a gesture that at first looked pleading, but which meant simply
"What can we do?". I was asking myself the same question. My Arabic was
inadequate to say what I could barely express in English, and the meeting
ended.

Individual doctors could perhaps be supplied, through our contacts,
with enough antibiotics to last a couple of weeks, but the problem of sew-
age-polluted water persisted far longer than anticipated for much of the 18
million-strong population of Iraq, especially in the poorer areas. When an
Oxfam team visited the Basra area in November 1991, they found lakes of
sewage outside the main hospital. The reason for this was that once a pump
had become blocked, it was tremendously difficult to free it, and parts of

the mechanism became damaged. It was often impossible to replace these components, since no spare parts were entering the country. Practically everything, including essential materials like cement, was assumed to have potential military significance and either delayed for weeks or refused entry outright. Only under the auspices of recognised relief agencies could supplies be brought in, and such action can never be large-scale.

What was needed to reverse the downward spiral into poverty was a change of attitude at the UN, and particularly in the Security Council. Where relief organizations were helpless, governments could act. So letters were written, politicians lobbied, representations made by such respected groups as IPPNW (International Physicians for the Prevention of Nuclear War, which was awarded the Nobel Peace Prize in 1985). To no avail, however. The sticking point remained, of course, Saddam Hussein. The sanctions that were originally implemented to force him out of Kuwait were maintained in an attempt to remove him from power, however foreign office spokesmen were ambivalent on this point, saying that the embargo served a more oblique purpose (to make Saddam comply with the UN's demands). It came to the same thing in the end. Both George Bush and John Major stated on several occasions that the sanctions would remain in place as long as Saddam remained in power. They were in other words a means of using the misery of the population as a weapon against the regime: something that is expressly outlawed by the Geneva Conventions.

The Gulf Peace Team has reverted to what it was at the beginning of the Gulf crisis: a scattered fellowship of concerned individuals. It is up to such individuals to break the silence: to challenge censorship or self-censorship, to remind people of what they would prefer to forget. Even if these challenges go unheeded, the systems of democracy in which we live make it incumbent on us to continue making them. We cannot allow the situation in Iraq to become so cynically marginalised an issue that it no longer receives much media coverage except in the Asian press. If we allow this, we risk slipping back into the old prejudices we thought we had left behind us: the notion, as Kipling had it, that "East is East and West is West, and never the twain shall meet". When that happens, history will have the nasty tendency to repeat itself.

The silent war

Kathy Kelly

It is 10 August, 1996, a sweltering day in southern Iraq, during one of the hottest summers on record. I sink onto my bed at the Basra Towers Hotel, grateful for the overhead ceiling fan and the promise of slightly less intense heat as evening falls. I don't feel particularly tired, but my companions insisted I take a break because I fainted after visiting the Basra Pediatrics and Gynaecology hospital.

Dr. Tarik Hasim, the brilliant young director of residents, had taken us through several children's wards. "This is gruesome," my friend Brad Lyttle declared, after seeing so many skeletal infants, writhing in pain on blood-stained, rotten foam mats, with no anaesthetics, no antibiotics, and barely any medicine at all to help them. (In Baghdad, even government workers in cabinet-level ministry offices asked us for aspirins, eye drops and other rudimentary drugs.) We saw children with severe malnutrition, respiratory diseases, leukemia, kidney diseases, and other serious ailments. Many faced imminent death for want of basic medicine.

Mothers stay with their children day and night. Dr. Hasim explains that the hospital is very short-staffed. Doctors can't earn enough to feed their families, so some leave to work instead as taxi drivers, street vendors or waiters. Nurses likewise find it impossible to continue practising their skills. This means mothers must remain at the bedsides of their afflicted children, hopefully finding someone else to care for their households and other children.

The temperature in Basra today is 140 degrees. Under these conditions, one should drink at least a gallon of water a day. Because sanctions bar chlorine used for water purification, even most bottled water, for the few who can afford it, is contaminated. At the water ministry, officials showed us rusted, corroded pipe sections with large holes that allow contaminants to leak into Basra's drinking water. The eight-year Iran-Iraq war interrupted construction of the water filtration system and the project was never completed. This compounds the problems residents now face.

I reach for the bottled water that Archbishop Kassab gave us. "Drink this," he said, "and mark your bottles. We call this sweet water, water from Baghdad — I can tell you that if you drink the bottled water here it will make you very sick." I think of the desperately ill children I met earlier today, and put the bottle aside. My thoughts return to Father Kassab.

I first encountered him at Sacred Heart parish in Baghdad. Iraqi friends in Chicago had given me his number and when I called him in March, 1996, on my first day in Baghdad, he invited me to visit that same day. He was sweeping the courtyard when I arrived. He and a few helpers were preparing for a weekly distribution of lentils, rice, sugar and tea which his parish gave to the nearby needy. Later, in his office, he read descriptions of our campaign. "That's good," he stated, "keep doing just what you are doing. You challenge this embargo. But we are a proud people and we don't want handouts — we just want to be able to work again and we can take care of ourselves."

Archbishop Kassab is now in Basra. When we met, I thanked him for encouraging us to work towards ending the embargo. So far, four of our delegations have gone to Iraq carrying nearly $50,000 worth of medical supplies. We are on notice from the US Treasury Department that by failing to receive explicit authorization for our travel and humanitarian cargo, we risk 12 years in jail and $1 million in fines. On moral grounds, we won't acknowledge a veto power over our taking medical supplies, medicine and solace to fellow human beings in dire need. On practical grounds, we cannot accept months of bureaucratic delay for a superfluous stamp of approval.

Suddenly the lights go out and the ceiling fan stops. "Not again," I mutter. I grope my way downstairs, where the hotel staff have already mustered up their spare candles, eager to help foreigners like me. Ferial, at the desk, lights a candle for me. "This is the life," she says, smiling softly. "The electricity goes off, unexpectedly, at least four times a day. Really, we wish we never had oil in this country. Without the oil, we would never have all these troubles." Saad, her co-worker, leans on the counter. "You know, Ms. Kathy," he says, "another thing we say is this: 45 days of bombardment were better than these sanctions. You bomb us, and, o.k., after 45 days we can rebuild. But the sanctions destroy us and after six years we have nothing left to rebuild with."

Basra is Iraq's third largest city. Before the long years of the Iran-Iraq war, the Gulf war and the six-year siege caused by sanctions, it was a thriving oil port. Now, of 300 families interviewed by Archbishop Kassab, only 45 have at least one working family member. Unwillingly idle, frustrated and humiliated, Basra residents trudge through streets fouled with sewage and bordered with piles of human waste. The piles, five to six feet tall, are left to dry, spaced every thirty feet. Adults negotiate residential sidewalks with care, stepping over human faeces, and wastewater spills from the streets into nearby homes.

Meanwhile, amidst it all, smiling children, totally innocent victims of the silent war, rush forth to pose for our cameras.

Back in Baghdad, we visit Qadissiya Hospital, on the outskirts of the city. I am determined to carefully identify some of the women and children we meet, and to note details about their plight. What a grim necessity. Rick McDowell, a carpenter from Akron, Oklahoma is an excellent photographer as well. We team up to snap photos of mothers and children and then, with a translator, question the weary mothers. How old are you? And your child? From what does your child suffer, and since when? Do you have other children? Who cares for them now?

And so the stories emerge. Ana Anba is 27 years old. She looks glassy-eyed, exhausted and on the verge of tears. For 11 days she has been at the bedside of her 9 year old son, Ali Anba. He is listless, barely conscious. Ali's illness began, months ago, with a respiratory infection. Ana has since purchased thousands of dinars of medicine, but Ali's condition hasn't improved. She wonders now if the medicine she bought on the black market was expired. Or, perhaps it was not what he really needed. What's more, she's anxious for her other children, knowing there's not enough food for them. We tell her that we hope her story will help awaken parents and families in the US. "When?!" she asks. The interpreter tries to gloss over her obvious anger. "She is frustrated and tired from six years of sanctions."

Ana interrupts sharply. "In America, would women want this for their children?" Then she turns to Ali and whispers softly, "It is for the children that we ask an end to this suffering, not for us."

Yusuf Asad, 7 months old, suffers from septicemia. A doctor tells us that the pale, gasping infant is very near death. Before coming to the hospital, his parents sold their television and other pieces of furniture to buy high-priced medicines. "Nothing works," sighs his mother. "Since ten days he has been here." Yusuf's father makes a fist and points to his arm, telling us he's already donated all the blood he can, for transfusions.

Their family of four eats sparingly. Each day, they make a soup-like substance of tomatoes and oil which they eat with bread. They share their home with 21 other people. The father's income is 400 dinars per month, the standard retired soldier's benefit. As a soldier during the Iran-Iraq war, he spent one year in an Iranian prison. He is now 34. We asked if there was a message he felt we should carry back to the US. "Look at this child," he said, "and you can decide." With heavy hearts, we take Yusuf's picture.

Resisting warfare

Kathy Kelly

It is 16 January, 1997, and with wind chill temperatures at minus 50, Chicagoans are braced for frigid weather. I arrive breathless but on time for a Religious Studies Class at De Paul University, where my Kenyan friend, Dr. Teresia Hinga, teaches a class on conscience and moral choice. I feel awkward, pulling off boots, scarves, and several sweaters as the class members, bemused, listen to her introduction.

Teresia warmly welcomes me as a woman who went to Iraq during the Gulf war and was part of a peace camp on the border between Saudi Arabia and Iraq, and who returned to Iraq several times since then. Dr. Almaney, an Iraqi citizen who teaches Business Management at De Paul, sits at the back. His kindly nod reassures me.

I tell the students a bit of personal background, hoping they can identify with me on some levels. A few heads nod, with wry smiles, when I describe the neighbourhood where I grew up — a blue-collar, not-quite-middle-class area on Chicago's southwest side. I was blest in those years with a profound sense of security. It seemed that mom, dad, the nuns, the parish priest and the corner patrol lady were bound together in a benign conspiracy to assure that the Kelly kids were well cared for. It was a warm, wonderful, uncomplicated world.

Then an incident occurred which revealed that my apparently safe neighbourhood was, in truth, a crucible of racial and political conflict. My father and a neighbour were engrossed in television coverage of Martin Luther King, who was walking arm in arm with open housing advocates in Chicago's Gage Park. Someone threw a brick at King, striking him in the head. Blood trickled down the side of his face. Our neighbour, normally a calm, quiet man, leapt off the couch and said, "The son of a bitch got what he deserved!" I was stunned. It was one of my first encounters with real fear.

The students seem attentive now. I quickly mention another key moment in my teen years when an English teacher showed us "Night and Fog," a haunting documentary film about the Nazi holocaust. I confess to the students that it would be another decade before I would involve myself in public activism and resistance movements. Yet somehow, at a deep emotional level, I realized even then that I didn't want to pretend I was an innocent bystander in the face of terrible injustice. I began, in those days, to read more about people I admired intensely for having taken risks for love and justice, pacifists like Mahatma Gandhi, Dorothy Day and Martin Luther King.

I quote Rabbi Abraham Heschel on pacifism: "There are no absolute pacifists, only biographical ones." I tell them that now, at age 44, I can at least say that I passionately want to be a pacifist. I explain how impossible it was for me, in 1980, to continue paying for weapons when my closest neighbours were homeless and hungry. At an alternative school in my neighbourhood, I taught youngsters who were gang members. Each year, we would plan at least three funerals for students who were killed on the streets of our neighbourhood. I knew I would never, ever say to a teenage gang member, "Here ya' go, I've just been paid — why don't you take part of my cheque and go buy yourself a gun." Then how could I turn money over to the US government to buy weapons of mass destruction and plan a potential nuclear Auschwitz for the entire planet? War tax refusal was a natural step, one which I never doubt. Since 1981, I've refused to pay all federal income taxes, knowing that over half of every tax dollar is used to pay for weapons or defense-related spending.

I was in Iraq during the first 15 days of the Gulf war, one of seventy-three volunteers from eighteen countries who joined a "peace camp" called the Gulf Peace Team. We intended to sit in the middle of a likely battlefield and call for an end to hostilities.

Author Daniel Berrigan, a Jesuit and human rights activist, once said that one of the reasons we don't have peace is because the pacifists aren't willing to pay the price of peace. Soldiers are expected to sacrifice their lives in the name of war, but peacemakers often decline to make the same sacrifice. The Gulf Peace Team was a diverse assortment of people, but I think almost every person there was motivated by just the willingness that Berrigan spoke of, a readiness to pay the price of peace in order to witness against the war.

On 27 January, 1991, anticipating that the ground war would begin, the Iraqi government decided to evacuate us, by bus, to Baghdad. They sent in a team of civilians to persuade us to pack, quickly, and accompany them to Baghdad. We were divided about whether to stay or to go. A hard argument ensued, followed by a brief but moving demonstration by those who chose to stay but were forcibly removed.

During the remainder of the war, some of us joined medical relief convoys that travelled the road from Amman to Baghdad. In accompanying the convoys, we hoped that the US and British forces would refrain from targeting them out of reluctance to bomb citizens of their own countries. After the war, the Iraqis agreed to let us enter the country with study teams to document the combined effects of war and sanctions. I stayed in the region for the next six months, helping to organise medical relief and study teams.

In March 1991, a Red Crescent vehicle delivered four of us study team members to the Ameriyeh neighbourhood in Baghdad. Local residents told us the tragic story of the bombing of a civilian shelter here on the night of 13 February, 1991, the day of the Muslim feast of 'Id al-Fitr. Families from this neighbourhood had decided to celebrate the 'Id despite the relentless bombing. The Ameriyeh bomb shelter was one of the best in Baghdad, and the whole neighbourhood gathered there in the early evening for a common meal. After eating, the men left to make room in the shelter for as many women and children as possible, including refugees from other areas. Mothers, grandmothers, infants, children and teens hoped to sleep in safety during the blistering explosions. That night, two US "smart bombs" found the ventilation shafts of the Ameriyeh shelter. The exit doors were sealed and the temperature inside rose to 500 degrees Fahrenheit. Of the estimated 500 to 1300 people in the shelter, all but 17 perished.

Staring at the scene, I had begun to cry, when I felt a tiny arm encircling my waist. A beautiful Iraqi child was smiling at me. "Welcome," she said. Then I saw two women dressed in black cross the street. I thought surely they were coming to withdraw the children who now surrounded us. As they drew closer, I spoke the few Arabic words I knew: "Ana Amerikyyah, ana asifa" - I'm American and I'm sorry.

But they said, "La, la, la," "No, no, no," and they explained, "We know that you are not your government and that your people would never do this to us." Both the women had lost family members to the American bombs.

Never again in my lifetime do I expect to experience such forgiveness.

And for just that moment I wondered if they weren't better off without electricity. Wasn't it better for them never to hear on TV or radio what was being said, just then, in the United States? I wasn't there, but I was told about it later. I heard that college students hoisted beers to cheer the war on, shouting "Rock Iraq! Slam Saddam!" Soldiers sang out "Say hello to Allah!" when they blasted Iraqi targets. And the unforgettable words of

General Colin Powell, when asked about the number of Iraqis who died in the war: "Frankly, that number doesn't interest me."

The students shake their heads and feel troubled.

During the Gulf war, US aircraft alone dropped 88,500 tons of explosives on Iraq, the equivalent of 7.5 Hiroshima nuclear blasts. Eighty percent of the so-called smart bombs missed their intended targets, falling sometimes on civilian dwellings, schools, churches, mosques or empty fields. But the twenty percent that blasted on target wiped out Iraq's electrical generating plants and sewage treatment networks. Iraq's infrastructure was systematically destroyed – bridges, roads, canals, communication centres.

I hold up a poster bearing photos from my visit to the Ameriyeh neighbourhood and point to the little girl who welcomed me. I wonder, is she a teenager now? Did she survive the ongoing economic war? Is she lucky enough to get clean water and adequate food in spite of the merciless embargo that has created a veritable state of siege in Iraq?

My poster shows other Iraqi children, giggling and smiling. The headline says, "Faces of War: The 'Enemy' in Baghdad." I stop to take a deep breath. I don't want to cry just now. The students might feel manipulated, although frustrated tears befit these memories.

I don't want these students to latch on to impressions that the Gulf war was a series of surgical strikes that, as modern wars go, was not too destructive. I want them to understand that when you destroy a nation's infrastructure and then cripple it further with punishing sanctions, the victims are always the society's most vulnerable people — the poor, the elderly, the sick and most of all, the children.

I tell them about Taha, a Palestinian driver who had braved dangerous treks along the Amman-Baghdad road to make repeated deliveries of Red Crescent humanitarian relief shipments to Iraq. After the war, in mid-March, 1991, Taha drove our small study team back to Jordan. Along the road, we passed a small, isolated village. Suddenly a group of youngsters ran down the embankment toward our speeding vehicle. They stretched out their arms, touched their lips, then made the motion of forming chapatis, the bread of the poor. They were desperately hungry.

"We cannot stop," Taha said, blinking back tears. "And anyway we have nothing to give." The road had turned into a gauntlet, flanked with wave upon wave of child beggars. Taha shook with frustration, then finally heaved with sobs as we drove on through the desert.

I am pleading with the students now. I want to immunize them from the contagion of residual war hysteria, from the temptation to consolidate all of Iraq into one demonized figure, Iraq's President Saddam Hussein. I want them to wonder whether or not the US in fact wants to keep Saddam Hussein in power until they have carefully chosen a replacement who can control Iraq's military and its resources in ways that serve US interests. There are so many stories I can tell about individual Iraqis who are courageous, hospitable, intelligent and kind...

I show the class a poster made from photos our delegation took in August, 1996 — haunting pictures of emaciated children, infants who look like old men, hairless and skeletal. I remember cradling the fragile body of one of the children and wondering if I was interrupting the final hours, together, for the mother and her child.

I feel that I'm more responsible for Iraq's government than any one of these children whom I met last summer. I come from the country whose oil-consumptive lifestyles helped bring about an oil-rich government (and I don't even have a driver's license). How can we impose collective punishment on children for the actions of a government that western diplomacy and weapons cannot control?

There is only a little time left for questions. At first, the room is quiet. Finally, a student poses a thoughtful question: "What can you tell us about what Iraqi people think?" Teresia's eyes light up as she nods toward our guest, Dr. Almaney. The young man continues, "I mean, they must want things to change. Why aren't they taking some steps?"

I feel protective of Dr. Almaney and quickly say that it's not always so easy, or even safe, to give forthright answers when conditions have deteriorated so badly in another country. I feel a surge of admiration for Dr. Almaney as he turns to the student and proceeds to give a perfectly honest, direct answer. He asks students to understand that while Iraqis are very unhappy over their present condition, it is not so easy for them to make a change. First of all, freedom of speech is not so readily enjoyed in Iraq as it might be in other countries. You can imagine further how sadly diminished free speech becomes when education and communication structures have been gravely weakened. When families are worried about where their next meal will come from, they are not so likely to involve themselves in organizing political movements. What's more, because of sanctions, almost every family in Iraq directly depends on government rationing to get whatever meager food supplies they have. Dr. Almaney explains that many people in Iraq have good reason to fear that if Saddam Hussein's government went out of power the country could sink into a bloody civil war, one which could be exacerbated by hostile neighbours.

Dr. Almaney is kindly and professorial as he earnestly presents each point. In contrast, I feel angry and cynical. I interject that the US has heavily equipped neighbouring states with huge arsenals of weapons, that among the top 10 consumers of US weapons are Egypt, Saudi Arabia, Israel and Turkey. Dr. Almaney suggests that the US might want to keep Saddam Hussein in power until it has carefully chosen a new leader who could maintain control over the military and serve US interests in the Middle East.

A few more students raise their hand. Their questions betray a characteristic lack of awareness of the ground reality. I am reminded of another encounter with the American public, in September 1990 when I joined a hunger strike against military aid to El Salvador. Our banner read, "Fast for Peace in El Salvador". Several times, women approached us with curiosity. "El Salvador - now, is that a province of that country Kuwait, 'cuz my husband is being sent there and I'm really worried!" Those were such telling lines. Young US soldiers, sons and husbands of women who may have never heard of Iraq or Kuwait, would be sent to kill the sons and husbands of women in a land and culture unknown to most US people.

Democracy is based on information. Yet the US military-industrial-congressional-media complex strangles the flow of information about suffering and death caused by US reliance on weapons and military strategies to enforce so-called US national interests. Most Americans remain woefully ill-informed and misinformed about the purposes and effects of US policies throughout the world. When we take dramatic nonviolent actions that risk our health and/or liberty, we hope to bring attention to truths which we think, if understood, would deeply disturb masses of people. We think most people don't want to pay for wasteful, destructive policies that cause innocent people to suffer and die.

As students file out, several say they never knew this was happening, others ask me to please call on them when we need help, almost all of them murmur a word of appreciation. I again recall George Rumens' assurance that when the war hysteria subsided the more lasting response to the war would be deepest regret and remorse for the suffering we've caused. Often his words have been borne out. In the absence of warmongering media barrages that obscured and ignored Iraqi suffering, we've been heard, in classrooms, community rooms, small town papers and radio stations. Consistently, a more sober response grows. "We didn't know. We didn't realize."

Part 3

Viewpoints

"I want the peace camp to go on in our hearts. Peace camp, what does it mean? Staying between two opposing fronts, recognising their different points of view, trying to give them the chance to reconsider their opinions and maybe trying once again to find a non-violent solution to the conflict. This should not happen only in times of war, in political conflicts, but also in our personal relations and often also in our hearts. Such a spiritual peace camp is not a comfortable place. Often we are attacked by both sides and we have to endure it in love. I am so thankful for my experience at Ar'ar - the idea of the spiritual peace camp is now a central point of my life."

Irmgard Ehrenberger, Gulf Peace Team

The Gulf Peace Team: An assessment

Robert J. Burrowes

The Gulf Peace Team, like its historical antecedents, raises several issues which are critically important to the theory and practice of nonviolent interposition. These include vital questions in relation to ideology, politics, strategy, morality and organisation. The Gulf Peace Team experience allows the opportunity for a new and wider round of debate, as well as a critical reassessment. It also provides the opportunity to refocus attention on the fundamental question: is nonviolent interposition a viable and effective nonviolent sanction? Some of these questions are discussed below.

Political questions

The peace camp raised at least three important political questions. The first relates to the camp's purpose.

The existence of the peace camp represented the idea (and the ideal) that a peaceful solution to the Gulf crisis was possible if appropriately selected nonviolent sanctions and problem-solving processes were employed. Was it merely symbolic? Or did it have real potential to intervene? Was the main impact of interposition physical or political?

Was the real aim of the camp simply physical interposition, intended, as the Gulf Peace Team's policy statement and constitution suggested, "to withstand nonviolently any armed aggression by any party"? Was this even realistic (particularly given the numbers involved) or was the aim of the interposition primarily political - designed to help build a global consensus against war?

To the extent that this question had been considered, there were clearly different views in the camp itself. For example, thirteen activists - presumably committed to the importance of the physical nature of their interposition - chose to resist evacuation on the basis that they might be able to physically resist violence by the Iraqi army at least. It was patently clear however that 73 people were not going to be able to physically resist the violence of two military forces totalling a million combat personnel, although, in some circumstances, there would have been clear political and symbolic value in trying to do so. The difference in numbers does not, in itself, make physical resistance impossible nor morally inappropriate. However, it does raise important questions about strategy and tactics and the wisdom of these.

It is evident that the peace camp was primarily a symbol that carried political, psychological and moral weight. And it was clearly the physical location of the symbol which gave it power. It was a symbol of nonviolence that challenged the legitimacy of war. It was a symbol of courage that inspired people to act. And it was a symbol of morality that touched the conscience.

The second question concerns the camp's precise location: Should the camp have been nearer the Kuwait-Saudi border? While the advance party was concerned that such a site might have been seen to be defending the Iraqi occupation of Kuwait, it seems clear (at least in retrospect) that the final site offered and accepted on the Iraq-Saudi border was too far from Kuwait, particularly if physical intervention during the land war was seriously envisaged.

More fundamentally however, did the peace camp's location serve the interpositionary purpose when the war was fought essentially in the air? The early "battles" of the Gulf war were bombing raids on the cities of Iraq and Kuwait; they were not land battles fought across territorial boundaries. Should there have been several peace camps located in Baghdad, Kuwait City, Riyadh and Tel Aviv?

The third question concerns the camp's neutrality. Given that the Saudi Arabian government refused to respond to requests for a camp on the Saudi side, was the Gulf Peace Team genuinely neutral? Was it seen to be neutral?

Neutrality is defined as "(n)ot assisting either party in the case of a war between states" and the Gulf Peace Team's policy statement (see p. 5) made its neutrality explicit: "We .... do not take sides in this dispute".

But the question of neutrality is not a simple one. What constitutes "assisting either party"? The camp was clearly located on the Iraqi side of the border. Did that compromise our neutrality? The Gulf Peace Team was not on the side of any government; but that did not stop various parties trying to use it for their own ends. Did that compromise our neutrality? As a camp, we were clearly not on the side of the Iraqi government, but we were logistically dependent on it. Did that compromise our neutrality?

It is evident that the location of the camp at the Iraqi border post - rather than on neutral territory or in conjunction with a second camp on the Saudi border - was a second-best option given the refusal of the Saudis to negotiate. In itself, however, this did not constitute a violation of our neutrality: it was not "assisting either party".

However, the camp's location did improve its potential as a propaganda tool. While there is little evidence to suggest that Iraqi officials used the Gulf Peace Team explicitly or widely for this purpose, it clearly had some value in this sense. More importantly perhaps, some critics (including some in the media) associated with the UN coalition were keen to discredit the camp on this basis or to use it for wider criticisms of the peace movement generally. It is clear that the camp had propaganda value for both sides; but it is difficult to claim that this constituted "assisting either party" in a sense which seriously suggests that neutrality was compromised.

The most difficult aspect of the neutrality question concerns the peace camp's logistical dependency on the Iraqi government; this was clearly less than desirable. However, while this may have been seen to compromise our neutrality in the opinion of some observers, it did not affect the declared political neutrality of the camp. In practice, the camp was little different from a Red Cross operation: dependent on a host government for a range of services, but politically neutral.

What seems clearer is that once the war broke out, our continued dependency on the Iraqi government for supplies and transport used increasingly scarce Iraqi resources and, in that sense, we were obviously assisting (in a very small way) the UN forces. At this point, it seems clear, the camp was no longer technically neutral.

Strategy

While the Gulf Peace Team had a stated policy of "working for peace... in the Gulf", it never had a precise aim and a clear-cut strategy to focus and guide its efforts. Moreover, the conditions necessary to make the project practicable - including knowledge, skills, independent access to resources, high degree of philosophical cohesion, organizational framework, communication channels (especially links with grassroots networks) and determination - were insufficiently met. And, importantly, the Gulf Peace Team could never boast the critical mass necessary as a rallying point for galvanising substantial numbers of people. How was the Gulf Peace Team supposed to help stop the war?

At no stage did the Gulf Peace Team formulate a strategy of its own or consider how its initiatives fitted within wider peace movement strategies to stop the war. The goal of establishing the peace camp was always the focus of attention. And while the camp itself did have a vaguely worded aim - "to withstand nonviolently any armed aggression by any party" - as the main practical expression of the Gulf Peace Team project, the camp was devoid of strategic guidance.

Nonviolence theory would suggest that the power to stop the war rested largely with the domestic constituencies of nations in the UN coalition. The Gulf Peace Team's power hinged on its capacity to influence and mobilise those constituencies. Lacking a clear-cut strategy for doing so, any successes in this regard reflected the initiative of particular support groups or were incidental.

Despite these shortcomings, the anecdotal evidence suggests that the Gulf Peace Team did have an impact on grassroots consciousness in some parts of the world and that this stimulated greater nonviolent resistance to the war. In the eyes of some people, whatever it lacked in strategic conception, the camp made up for with integrity, courage and vision.

As the history of nonviolent struggle clearly demonstrates, however, while inspirational examples have their role to play in galvanising greater spontaneous resistance to violence or injustice, this is rarely enough to compensate for the lack of a comprehensive strategic orientation. Good nonviolent struggle, like any struggle, requires good strategy.

Organisational Issues

A major shortcoming of previous attempts at nonviolent interposition has been the lack of an organisational infrastructure. The Gulf Peace Team suffered the same shortcoming. In part, this reflects the lack of a well-developed and worldwide nonviolent action network which, it seems clear, is necessary if initiatives such as this are to have a strong organisational foundation.

An organisational infrastructure provides the framework in which ideological, political, strategic and moral questions are resolved. It is also the foundation on which action planning, networking, communication, recruitment, training and financial matters are based.

Without an adequate organisational framework, the Gulf Peace Team had immense difficulty dealing with basic policy questions and various practical matters such as recruitment and training. Moreover, it directly contributed to a range of complications in the camp itself. Consider, for example, the question of camp membership.

It is clear from the historical record that the preferred organisation unit for effective nonviolent action is the affinity group. An affinity group is a group of six to twelve people which performs a range of tasks and personal support in an atmosphere of trust developed through periods of time working together.

By contrast, the peace camp was essentially a collection of individuals from fifteen countries. There was no single language which everyone spoke; few had experience of working in affinity groups; not all had experience of nonviolent action. Moreover, there was neither shared cultural identity nor ideological cohesion to bind camp members together. In addition, and typically of social movements which have a tolerant social milieu, the peace camp attracted its share of people with special psychological needs. Given the complexities of camp life under conditions of war, all these factors were challenging complications.

But the organisational problems did not stop at the camp; consider the problems of communication and finance. It is clear that communication is vitally important and should allow regular contact between members of the organisation and grassroots networks. It requires the use of various types of open channels; accurate and adequate information; and conscientious use.

On all of these points, however, the record of the Gulf Peace Team - and particularly the London office - was poor. For instance, it lacked adequate communication channels (and had none with the camp once the war broke out); it lacked access to grassroots networks; it circulated inaccurate information, particularly in relation to the expected number of volunteers; and it consistently failed to supply reliable information to national support groups.

In relation to finance - given the cost of $2000 to $5000 (depending on their country of origin) to support one activist - there are several important questions to be considered. How do projects such as this raise the necessary money? Is this the best use of money raised to support activist causes? Is this a good use of money for someone who can think of nothing better to do to express his or her anger? How much local activism could be financed with the money? How much equipment or food or medicine could be bought?

Whatever the answer to these questions, it is clear that the financial constraint alone means that such projects cannot involve many ordinary activists, especially those from developing countries.

It is evident that if key organisational problems cannot be resolved, then the action itself must be questioned. Integrity of the action alone is not enough.

Conclusion

Whatever its shortcomings, the Gulf Peace Team was profoundly significant, both historically and politically. Firstly, after decades of proposals and abortive attempts, it was the first nonviolent interposition in history. Secondly, it did constitute a nonviolent presence in the war zone which drew public attention to alternative and peaceful solutions to the Gulf conflict. Thirdly, it did inspire some grassroots resistance to the war. And fourthly, it rapidly accelerated our learning in this vital area of nonviolent struggle.

However, it is equally clear that its shortcomings were legion and that the Gulf Peace Team raised a series of questions in relation to ideology, politics, strategy, morality and organisation which need to be systematically addressed. It is now time for activists and scholars to reflect upon this latest experience in order to attempt to answer the fundamental question: is nonviolent interposition a viable and effective nonviolent sanction?

References

Harbottle, M. ed. 1978. *The Peacemaker's Handbook*. New York: International Peace Academy.

Little, W. et. al. 1972. *The Shorter Oxford English Dictionary on Historical Principles*. 3rd revised edition. London: Oxford University Press.

No, I have not been to the Gulf Peace Camp....

Ulrike Laubenthal

In the summer of 1990, I stayed in the Carl Kabat House in Mutlangen, southern Germany, near the former Pershing II missile base. I had agreed to help with the peace work in the house for some months, as two of the inhabitants served jail sentences after nonviolent blockades of nuclear missile bases.

At the beginning of August 1990, our Iraqi friends used to come to our door every evening: "May we see the news on your TV?" Of course they could. They did not have much at all, as they had fled from Iraq and were now waiting for official asylum. We did not really understand what was going on in Iraq at that time. But as we saw the news with our friends every evening, and as they explained to us what none of the TV channels would say, we soon understood that the danger of a big, possibly world-wide war was emerging.

"Why don't you do something about it?", our friends asked us. "You are the peace movement, aren't you?" Well yes, but what could we do? On one of those days I stayed behind after the daily silent vigil at the US base, and I talked to some of the soldiers there. Yes, one of them said, of course he would go to Iraq if he was told to. When Saddam Hussein intervened in Kuwait, the US could not just let him do that, could they? "No," I said, "I'm not talking about doing nothing at all. But I think a war is not the right thing to do. There are other ways to deal with such conflicts." "And what do *you* do?", he asked in return. There he stood, a young man, ready to risk his life in a war for what he supposed to be the rights of the Kuwaiti people; and he asked me, "What do you do?"

I did not know. Gathering signatures or distributing leaflets would probably not stop George Bush from preparing and leading this war. Should I start a fast in front of the EUCOM, the European command of the US army in Stuttgart, which is responsible for US military actions in Europe, Northern Africa and the Middle East? I was afraid of such a fast - and I also felt it would not achieve much. I knew of absolutely no course of action which would have been appropriate to the situation.

When one of the housemates returned from jail, I left Mutlangen. I joined some friends in the countryside and helped them build their house from straw and clay. It was a calm and peaceful place, with nice people, children and animals around; it was a beautiful work; and every time I listened to the radio news, I expected them to say that the war had started, and that a nuclear bomb had been dropped on Baghdad, or even Tel Aviv, or maybe on London. But the news did not mention anything like bombs, the danger of nuclear war, or the dying and suffering of men, women and children, or a people of 17 million threatened by war. They mostly spoke about a few hundred innocent hostages sitting in Iraq, which seemed to be the only major obstacle in starting a war.

At that time, while I was working on a wall with straw and clay, an idea occured to me which scared me and gave me hope at the same time. What if I went to Iraq? What if I offered to stay in that country deliberately, and so reminded people of the fact that European lives are not worth more than Iraqi lives? And, at the same time, gave a nonviolent answer to Saddam's taking hostages? I soon felt that this idea was not for daydreaming, but something calling for action, and that time was short.

In the first few weeks I was quite alone with this idea, but in September I got an invitation for a meeting in Bell/Hunsbruck about the "hostage exchange idea". This meeting was the beginning of a two-months process which finally led to the presence of "Initiative Freiden am Golf" in Iraq. Many people were involved in this process, many helped us with their critical questions, with their prayers and with their practical support.

Among several other ideas about the shape of our presence in Iraq, we considered the idea of a peace camp between the opposing armies. Some of us had experience of walking right into military training sites during manoeuvres and talking to the soldiers; the idea of doing the same in the Saudi/Iraq desert was fascinating. But we were quite aware that this would not be as easy as in German forests. Considering what we knew about deserts, borders and the military, we soon gave up the idea of mediation between soldiers of different armies.

Still, the symbol of a peace camp between the opposing armies was strong, even without that aspect of direct contact with the sodiers. But we concluded that such a camp would be dependent on at least one side for water and food supply, and could therefore never be an independent buffer. We also considered that a modern war would probably start not with a battle between soldiers in the desert, but with air raids on strategic targets; the first victims would be the people in the big cities. Therefore we gave up the peace camp idea as not being the correct symbol. We agreed we would rather live close to the Iraqi population.

When the first six of us left for Iraq on 18 November 1990, our consensus was that some of us would offer to stay in Iraq in exchange for hostages, some of us would return to Germany to report from Iraq, and others would offer to stay in Iraq, even if a hostage exchange was not possible, as long as there was a chance of helping to prevent war by such a presence. We understood our presence as an appeal to the governments, troops and populations of the countries involved in the crisis to struggle for a peaceful solution.

We had spent some time thinking about what we would do in Iraq. We felt that the most important thing was to be there, not as development engineers or relief workers, nor as diplomats, but as ordinary people who share the risks to which the Iraqi population was exposed. Our main task would be to appeal to the people in our own countries, and to give an impulse for concerted action there against the impending war. Therefore we had agreed that our main activities in Iraq would be fasting and praying for peace, together with people back home.

In a way, I was scared by this idea, even if it seemed to be right. Although I am religious, I am not a member of any Church, and I have reservations about many of the Christian rites and prayers. But that was not the main reason I felt uncomfortable; I hoped we would find ways to deal with our differences, and maybe find time to talk about religious questions which were moving us. What made me feel afraid was the anticipation that fasting and praying would lead to a full and permanent awareness of our own and the world's dangerous situation, and that this awareness would be hard to stand. On the other hand, this awareness would probably be our only chance of creating sufficient energy and finding the right steps to stop the danger of war; therefore I accepted this challenge.

I went to Iraq on 9 December 1990 with Gregor, Ria and Hans Joachim. In Baghdad we met Hans, Kees, Marylene and Eva; Beate and Clemens had already returned to Germany in order to speak about their experiences in Iraq, win more people for a peace presence and draw public attention to the danger of war.

At the World Peace and Friendship Village in Baghdad, where the Iraqi government's Organization for Friendship, Peace and Solidarity (OFPS) had lodged us, we met people from many different countries who had come to

Iraq on a peace mission. The respective aims of different groups included: staying in Iraq for some weeks in order to report back home later, taking hostages home, working for contacts between pupils or congregations, and even showing solidarity with the Iraqi government. Some people just wanted to be there and witness for peace. Some of those groups knew quite well what they wanted to do, others accepted everything the Iraqi government offered them; others still spent most of their time in discussions about what they should do.

From the beginning of our presence in Iraq, we were in contact with the "advance party" of the Gulf Peace Team. Although I felt very close to some of these people, I still had all my reservations about the idea of a peace camp in the middle of the desert. I realised there were conflicts within the group about these decisions as well; while some were very keen to set up the camp as quickly as possible under any conditions, others did at least want guarantees that there would be no fence, no armed guards, and no restrictions preventing camp members from going where they wanted. I felt - and I discussed this with some of the early team members - that a peace camp could be a valuable action, even without any chance for mediation between soldiers. However, if it was supposed to be a peace camp, it could not be fenced and guarded, and look like a concentration camp. I also feared that *if* war did not start soon and *if* thousands of people joined the camp, many of them would soon go mad out there in the desert, huddled behind a fence with nothing around.

I understood that it was dangerous to walk into the desert, especially if there were mines; and that the Iraqi government would not agree to have an open and unguarded camp. But in that case, wasn't it better to have no camp at all? Why not have a peace presence in Baghdad, close to the threatened population, in a place where the first allied bombs would kill in the event of a war? Such a presence in Baghdad also offered much better conditions for international media work and for contact with our support groups at home, and it required less infrastructure.

However, almost everybody was too fascinated with the idea of the camp to consider that it might be better not to do it.

In retrospect, I agree that the camp did get a much better media coverage than the presence of groups in Baghdad. It was a strong symbol, yes - but not a true one. Every time I tell somebody that I've been to Iraq before the war, he or she says: "Oh, you've been to that camp in the desert then?"

No, I've not been camping, and I am tired of this question. This strong idea of the camp really overran our less sensational, but maybe more truthful idea of staying in Iraq, just stay there with the people, to fast and to pray, and to share the danger. Who knows whether this would have changed anything… but I wish we had really tried.

Back to Iraq, December 1990. The OFPS organised a whole programme of visits to schools, universities, hospitals and neighbouring cities (e.g. Kerbala and Babel) for all the international peace groups in Baghdad. With this programme and with all the interviews with Iraqi and international journalists, our days were quite full. We did not find much time for prayer, and we fasted only for some days. In addition, the group soon came back to the idea that we had to "do something". After a long and difficult discussion we agreed to write a letter to George Bush and deliver it to the US embassy in a public event with media coverage. On the evening of 15 December, we had a meeting at our house with people from several international peace groups; we discussed the text of the letter and tried to find a version that would be acceptable to as many people as possible. It was a long and difficult discussion which had to be held in four languages. Most of the people were not used to discussions where every word had to be translated thrice, and not many of us were used to consensus building. Anyway, after two hours we found a version of the text which all of us felt able to sign. We brought the letter to the embassy on 18 December.

To me, it seemed that all these activities were not really what I had come to Iraq for. I began to understand that different people in our group had different interests. Those who were planning to return to Germany quite soon wanted to see as much as possible of Iraq in a short time, in order to be able to speak about it in meetings and interviews. Those who hoped that a presence of thousands of people in Baghdad or in the desert would prevent the war just wanted to stay there, see the country, maybe work with Iraqi people. I soon felt quite alone with my idea that only a strong peace movement in the streets of Europe and the USA could prevent the war, and that it was our task to give impulses for this peace movement.

I also did not find much time to think about what would need to be done in order to create these impulses. I was too busy with all the other things that happened.

Some of us felt that we were living too much like tourists and therefore wished to work or to join the peace camp as soon as possible so as to have a simpler lifestyle. I think we could easily have renounced some of our comforts; we could have cooked for ourselves, and we could have switched off the air conditioning, if that was the problem. Concerning the work, I think it would have been a useful job to carefully evaluate different newspapers and radio programmes, to discuss the developments, to write press releases, articles, leaflets to be published in Europe. That would have been work enough to avoid feeling like tourists. But it was always difficult to arrange for more than one short meeting in the morning, and the rest of the day was reserved for walks, bicycle tours, and the official visit programme.

Today I think that we just could not stand the real situation and so did much to avoid being aware of it. We were afraid. The closer the deadline came, the more people I met who said there would never be a war. In order to escape from being aware of the real situation, we all had to fill our day with all kinds of activities and create that "we-are-so-peaceful, there will-be-no-war" mood. In this situation, the peace camp was a welcome opportunity to celebrate our international peace spirit and win more distance to reality.

I decided to stay in Baghdad. But I could not convince anyone else in my group. At that time, communication had become almost impossible in our group. We had meetings, but were not able to understand different points of view. When we could no longer come to consensus decisions, the group did not take this as an alarm signal, but gave up the idea of consensus building and fell back on majority decision. The decision whether to stay in Baghdad or go to the camp was made individually by each person. I was the only one of our group who stayed in Baghdad - almost everybody left for the peace camp on New Year's Eve.

This situation left me quite alone - not only politically, but also personally. I was glad that a Dutch group had also decided not to go to the camp; I will never forget this New Year's Eve with Sietje and Lineke. But still, I felt disappointed by my own group, which was no longer a group and had perhaps never been one.

On 2 January 1991, I decided to go home as quickly as possible. I had lost any hope that our presence in Iraq, as it was, could help prevent the war. And as soon as I lost the perception of being in the right place, I became very afraid of what I might have to experience there when the war started. Two days later I was back home.

I am still convinced that the peace presence in Iraq was the right idea at the right moment. But the main thing I have learnt from this experience is that it is not enough to have the right idea at the right moment, as well as some courage and goodwill. We also need some skills, and clarity about what we are about to do, and structures that are good for transferring the impulses from such a presence to a wider movement at home.

I know that many of us here in Germany who have been to Iraq have felt deep anguish during and after the war. I guess most of you, people from other countries whom I met in Baghdad, experienced the same. I, too, have been hurt by this war more than by any other war before. It was so close to us, and we saw it coming. It hurts to see that we did not stop it. Maybe we had no chance, but still it hurts. All those children who are still dying...

I am still convinced that we started the right thing, and we have to go on with it. There is much left to do and to learn. After having spent most of 1991 with the coordination of relief work for Misan district (southern Iraq), I will start to work in the office of the German branch of Peace Brigades International in April. My main task will be the development of concepts for preparation, training and performance of international nonviolent intervention in acute conflicts. I look forward to this opportunity to build on what we have learnt in the Gulf, and to continue working with some of the peace activists I met there.

An adventure without return

Jerry Hartigan

August 1990 saw the Middle East falling into a spiral leading towards an inevitably destructive war. The Iraqi invasion and takeover of Kuwait set the tinder alight and, whatever the rights and wrongs of the situation and the causes of and pretexts for the aggression which had taken place, it was plain for all to see that a resolution of the conflict by military confrontation would be attempted.

In a democracy with supposedly accountable government, voters at least collectively carry a responsibility for the actions and omissions of their elected governments. With this responsibility in mind it was inevitable that following the calling of the Gospel one was challenged, in this situation, to contribute to the creation of a just and peaceful outcome for everybody involved.

The talk was soon of the inevitability of war for which a just cause was asserted. Regardless of the justice of the cause, signs indicated that this "inevitable" war would be destructive to an incalculable extent. Signs also indicated that the military option, always billed as "the last resort", was in fact the only option being considered, or at least the only option to be given a fair chance.

For me the moving factor was being conscious that to accept war as "a last resort" carried the moral risk of depreciating other options and removing constraints when it came to exercising the last resort. That, together with the thought of the historical background, the original "drawing" of the frontiers, the economic situation, oil, the Israeli-Palestinian conflict, the military resources with which Iraq had been supplied and encouraged, made it a matter of conscience for me to take whatever action was available to promote a settlement to the conflict which avoided the continuation of a disastrous war.

Whatever the rhetoric, the United Nations was bought with money and military power, evidently the basis of the "New World Order". Failure to act and take responsibility in democratic Britain could only be construed as consenting to a war with the predictable tens of thousands of innocent deaths, vast material and environmental damage, the crucifixion of a country for the sins of its leaders and unknown future political consequences for the Middle East and further afield. Never was it more vital to listen to the crystal clear teaching of the Pope that war was no longer an acceptable way to settle disputes. With these thoughts in mind every opportunity to campaign for a negotiated settlement and an Arab solution and against the drive to war had to be taken. When deployment of the most rational arguments supported by the most morally convincing authorities failed to convince a public that remained unaware, refused to be aware or just surrendered to the call of supposed national self-interest, something more had to be done and an escape was needed.

The idea of interposing a nonviolent presence between two forces preparing for war in the Middle East, a sort of moral barrier, was immediately attractive when it came to my ears in October. My faith in its practicality was not strong until to my surprise I heard that an advance party had gone to Baghdad in November and negotiated arrangements for the setting up of an international peace camp on the borders of Iraq and Saudi Arabia. The Gulf Peace Team, as the organization became known, was to be recognized as neutral and have autonomy in a pilgrims' resting post by the side of the road from Baghdad into Saudi Arabia (two and a half kilometres away), leading eventually to Mecca. Support and volunteers were invited at this stage.

The peace camp at Ar'ar was opened on Christmas Eve and on 9 January the number of residents increased to more than 30, reaching 73 by the 15th. A nonviolent presence had been set up in a war zone.

What did the peace camp achieve? On a personal basis, it certainly changed a few lives. Many who went prepared to offer themselves in sacrifice, found they had acquired riches beyond price. How do you evaluate a prayer? How do you measure an act of faith? How do you delineate an act of hope? How do you account for an act of love? If called to account our returns may not be very good, but our plea will be for judgement in the next world.

We were allowed the opportunity of putting into practice on a small scale a peacemaking, peace preserving exercise in an area of land between two nations in the process of going to war. We sat there. We were a sign. We were a witness. We were an example of people taking responsibility and not leaving it to governments which cannot act otherwise than as a bull in a china shop.

We went as peace pilgrims and, through border posts and check points, our role was never questioned. The understanding we met throughout our journey and the contacts made have enabled the team to carry out fresh work in collecting, sponsoring and escorting convoys of medical supplies into Iraq as well as to assess humanitarian needs in Iraq. We are devastated by the present tragedy that is the Middle East today. We feel guilty that we escaped when so many have not escaped or cannot escape. Yet our experience helps us not to despair about the situation and the eventual outcome.

My own feeling is that the value of the peace camp lay in its simplicity which made its message so clear to all. Of course one does not need to go the Arabian Desert to reject a punitive and genocidal war; but the symbolism of being there is certainly very striking, something that is actual and real, like the hammering of the controls of an F-111 by those who beat swords into ploughshares. It makes a powerful symbol recognizable as such and unmistakable for all. There is always an option to remedy injustice by nonviolent means, which implies acting constructively, avoiding passive acceptance of material and military might, having faith in the message of the Gospel and committing oneself to follow Christ.

The Gulf Peace Team
and nonviolent interposition

Alyn Ware

On 24 December 1990, while western nations around the world prepare for the celebration of the birth of Jesus Christ, a group of 29 people set out from Baghdad for a remote spot in the Iraqi desert, close to the Saudi border.

The group is part of the Gulf Peace Team, and their campsite is between the Iraqi armed forces and the US-led multinational forces which are facing each other in preparation for war. The Gulf Peace Team's mission is to attempt to prevent war or to stop war by placing themselves as a nonviolent interposition group between the opposing armies. They are voluntary "human shields" using the power of nonviolence to oppose and withstand armed aggression by either side.

By placing visible, unarmed, non-threatening people between the armies, a nonviolent interposition force brings to the attention of the soldier, the politician and the public the reality of the act that they are contemplating or engaged in, the fact that they are killing humans, and that these human lives are as sacred as those of our own friends or family. It exposes the veneer of justification that the politician has for the killing, a veneer that is necessary to maintain public support and the political power to continue waging war.

The Gulf Peace Team may be seen as a new and unique initiative in the movement to oppose, prevent and halt armed conflict nonviolently. However, there are a number of examples of similar actions or attempts at them in the past.

Maude Royden's Peace Army

On 25 February 1932, a famous letter by Dr. Maude Royden (a friend of Gandhi), the Rev. H.R.L. Sheppard and Dr. Herbert Gray appeared in the London *Daily Express* calling for volunteers for a "Peace Army" that would throw itself between the warring Chinese and Japanese forces in the city of Shanghai.

The force was offered to an unresponsive League of Nations but eventually the cessation of hostilities in China made it redundant. Although attempts were made over the next eight or so years to resurrect the Peace

Army (in slightly less ambitious forms), the idea eventually faded.

Shanti Sena

The Shanti Sena was established by followers of Mahatma Gandhi as a nonviolent peace army. Groups of Shanti Sena volunteers acted during times of Hindu-Moslem conflict to prevent the outbreak of violence between them.

In 1962, prominent Gandhian leader, Jayaprakash Narayan, proposed to lead a contingent of the Shanti Sena between the warring armies of China and India. This provoked heated debate within Gandhian circles. The Chinese unilaterally withdrew their forces before the pro-interposition members of the Shanti Sena could act.

Northern Ireland Peace Force

In 1971, the Fellowship of Reconciliation put forward a proposal to "explore the need for, and the feasibility of, a fully trained, disciplined and maintained corps for non-violent action in Northern Ireland" *(Peace News,* 10 September 1971).

United Nations and Government Proposals

There have been many attempts to interest the United Nations in the concept of unarmed interpositionary peacekeeping; the de Madariaga-Narayan proposals of 1960 and, more recently, Ray Magee's "peaceworkers" are good examples.

Calls have also come from government circles. With the growing tension preceding the Suez crisis in 1956, British MP Henry Usborne wrote to *Manchester Guardian* urging that the UN recruit a volunteer corps of 10,000 unarmed people to patrol and hold a two kilometre-wide demilitarized zone close to the Egyptian-Israeli border. Usborne suggested that this "peace force" should be "equipped only for passive resistance and designed to ensure that the present border is not violated by force. Its tactics would be essentially those of *satyagraha* (nonviolent action)".

In 1958, former MP, Sir Richard Acland, suggested that Britain take the initiative of setting up a world police force that would eventually be adopted by the UN. It was envisaged that an unarmed component of the force would parachute into trouble spots.

UN Peacekeeping Forces and Observer Missions

The UN peacekeeping operations, while not strictly nonviolent, have been the most widely implemented of the proposals for interposition forces, with over 500,000 people serving in them over their 42-year history.

In 1948, the UN established the UN Truce Supervision Organisation to monitor and observe the ceasefire in the Middle East. In 1956 the first Peacekeeping Force was established (UN Emergency Force in the Sinai I) not only to monitor the situation, but also to act as a buffer force between the conflicting parties. Since then there have been eighteen peacekeeping operations dispatched to conflict areas including the Congo, West New Guinea, Cyprus, Lebanon and Namibia.

UN observers are mostly unarmed while Peacekeeping Forces carry light arms and are allowed to use minimum force if (and only if) attacked. In 1988, the UN Peacekeeping Operations received the Nobel Prize for Peace in recognition of their contribution to peacekeeping. Their use is limited however to situations where all parties to the conflict agree to them being there. Also, the fact that the UN Peacekeeping Forces carry arms and will use them, even if it is as a last resort, maintains and reinforces the reliance which nations place on the use or threat of use of force for solving conflicts.

World Peace Army

Others have deliberately steered clear of governments and international bodies which they see as the agents responsible for war. One recent and shortlived attempt was the World Peace Army founded by New York Quakers in 1981.

Greenpeace

Founded in 1971, Greenpeace has applied the concept of nonviolent interposition to environmental campaigns. By placing themselves as human barriers between hunters and endangered species (such as whales and seals), in front of outlet pipes of polluting industries, on or near nuclear test sites and in front of other environmentally damaging practices, Greenpeace has had success in halting such practices at the site of their actions in the short term, and in generating enough publicity to curtail or restrain such practices over the long term.

Peace Brigades International

Formed in 1981, Peace Brigades International took the form of "a specialised agency dedicated to unarmed peacekeeping and peacemaking". Their main function during the past decade has been to provide escorts to human rights activists in Central America.

Witness for Peace

Witness for Peace was established in 1983 with the aim of protecting Nicaraguans from the violence of the Contras who had launched a civil war against the Sandinista government. Teams of unarmed people from the United States and other countries went to the border zones where the Contras were most active in order to establish an international presence, making it more difficult for the Contras to continue their murders and human rights abuses. Similar teams have also been sent to Guatemala, El Salvador and Panama.

Whilst the concept of nonviolent interposition is therefore not new, the Gulf Peace Team is perhaps the first to have actually moved into position between the armies of opposing nations which are preparing for war.

Initiatives Related to the Gulf War

The proposal for a nonviolent group between the Iraqi army and the US-led armies evolved alongside a number of other ideas of nonviolent direct action for peace in the Gulf which were floated by people involved in War Resisters' International (WRI), Fellowship of Reconciliation (FoR) and other peace groups in Europe, USA, Australia and Aotearoa (New Zealand).

These ideas included people offering themselves as voluntary hostages to replace those held by the Iraqi government, sending delegations to Iraq, and sending peace boats. The hostage exchange idea did not proceed, but others did. WRI, FoR, "Uniting for Peace" (USA), many religious groups and a number of private individuals arranged delegations to Iraq, donated supplies, visited hostages to seek their release, and attempted to generate a dialogue for peace with Iraqi leaders, religious groups and Iraqi citizens.

On 30 September 1990, Itaca, a peace boat, left San Sebastian in Spain bound for the Gulf, with the aim of providing an interposition peace presence in the Gulf waters. Bad weather however hampered its journey and by15 January it had not reached the conflict area.

Combining Nonviolent Opposition to War with Positive Proposals for Peace

In the minds of many people, the peace movement is negative and destructive because it is perceived to be mostly *against* things (e.g. anti-nuclear, anti-war, anti-military), and because it allows appeasement of aggression. An important aspect of the Gulf Peace Team has been the promotion of positive and realistic nonviolent political solutions for opposing the aggression of Iraq, facilitating an Iraqi withdrawal from Kuwait, and resolving long-standing conflicts in the region.

If we lived in a world where reason and humanity reigned instead of lust for power and wealth, the resolution of conflicts could be achieved quite readily through negotiation and mediation, and states would welcome these processes. Present governments are however led more by power and greed, and thus more assertive means are often required to achieve justice and resolution of conflicts.

Although there is a possibility that negotiation could have worked in the Gulf crisis, and leaders should have been encouraged to negotiate a solution, the intractability of leaders in this instance indicate that other methods were probably also required.

Other possibilities which the Gulf Peace Team and other peace groups had also suggested include: (1) Seeking mediation or compulsory arbitration of the oil dispute between Iraq and Kuwait. Such mediation or arbitration could be done by the Arab League, the Secretary-General of the United Nations, or a panel chosen collectively by Iraq and Kuwait. (2) Convening a Middle East Peace Conference, under the auspices of the United Nations, to discuss the ongoing conflicts in the area, and in particular the illegal occupations of Palestine and Lebanon. (Iraq had indicated a willingness to withdraw from Kuwait if progress was made on these issues.)

In December 1990 the Gulf Peace Team established representation at the United Nations in order to encourage implementation of proposals for a peaceful resolution of the conflict, and to provide an additional avenue for publicising these.

Peace proposals were introduced by a number of countries including Jordan, Yemen, Colombia and France, but they were blocked by the United States, which at the time had enough economic and political power to sway most of the 14 other members of the UN Security Council. However, the fact that the United States turned to the United Nations in order to gain credibility for the use of force in the Middle East, when previously they had shunned the United Nations, sets a precedent for gaining greater United States accountability to the United Nations. This could provide an avenue for restricting US aggression in the future.

Effectiveness of the Gulf Peace Team

On the surface one could say that the Gulf Peace Team failed in that it did not prevent the outbreak of war. The forces leading towards war in the Gulf were more powerful than those working to prevent it. However, success is not to be measured by immediate tangible results. To the extent that the initiative has reached people around the world and has had an illuminating or empowering effect, the Gulf Peace Team will affect people's responses to international conflict in other arenas and in the future.

The establishment of the peace camp between the armies has had a deep and significant impact on large numbers of people, possibly because of the novelty factor, the element of risk individuals place themselves in by joining the peace camp and the symbolic power of nonviolent direct opposition to war.

The symbolic aspect of the action is a major strength. Like David, the Gulf Peace Team is much smaller than the Goliath it confronts, but in the bravery of direct confrontation the action draws incredible moral strength and respect from people around the world. It demonstrates a positive form of strength, an alternative to physical force, and shows that peace is not weak.

The Gulf Peace Team is a living expression of our vision for a peaceful world, a world where conflicts are solved through respect and understanding of the other party, a world where nonviolence and conflict resolution are used instead of force. We envisage, as a stepping stone to this world, a time when, if armies are called to war or to prepare for war, then the number of people putting themselves between the armies to nonviolently oppose war will be greater than the number of soldiers. At such a time, war will be made impossible, and peaceful ways of solving disputes will be the norm.

To some degree the Gulf Peace Team has sown, in the minds of citizens around the world, the vision of a peaceful world, that it is possible to act to create such a world. Such consciousness change, though not measurable, is vital in the ongoing evolution towards a more peaceful planet.

Part 4

In memoriam

Kees Koning

(1931-1996)

On 26 July, while the Gregorian chant "In Paradiso" was sung, in a coffin made of salvaged wood and carried by friends, relatives and members of his order, Kees Koning made his last trip to rest in peace in mother earth.

Kees was born in 1931 and became a priest (O.S.F.S.) in 1958. Part of his early priest years Kees spent as a military chaplain with the Dutch troops stationed in Germany. Kees had removed all military hierarchy indications from his uniform and ate with the soldiers rather than in the officers' mess. During the Berlin crisis when he was asked to "sell the use of nuclear weapons" to the troops, he decided it was time to leave the military.

After having worked for some time as a nightporter in a homeless shelter, sleeping in his car and distributing the evening paper, Kees left for India where he worked for five years in a Gandhian project. Kees then returned to take care of his sick father, but after his father's death, Kees was no longer able to obtain a visa for India. He deeply regretted this.

What to do, being exiled back into the rich world? How best to be of service? How to deal with structural violence, with our ignorance and apathy? Kees would struggle hard with these questions until the very end.

He went to Paris and met Abbé Pierre and then joined an Emmaus community in Eindhoven, Netherlands. This community is located in a wing of a monastery of the Sisters of Love. Kees' domicile was a little shed in the garden where he cooked his vegan meals on a woodburner and where, as in India, he rolled out his sleeping bag at night and slept on the floor. Working with the community to recover leftovers from our affluent society, and recycling, reusing and reselling them and using the proceeds for projects, mainly in the so-called third world, was part of his answer to The Questions.

Kees also found his way into the "direct action" part of the peace movement, where he joined our affinity group, called the North Atlantic Defence Movement. Being fully in a group, however, was not really Kees' style - he lacked the patience for it. After we hammered on the cruise missile bunkers at Woensdrecht USAFB, in December 1988, Kees was kept on re-mand as the military police suspected him of participating in a previous action at the same base, when an NF-5 fighterplane destined to be sold to Turkey was painted all over with slogans denouncing NATO's complicity in the genocide of the Kurdish people. While in prison, Kees read the book *Swords into Plowshares* (by Art Laffin and Anne Montgomery). When he was released after two weeks, he knew what to do. Instead of the paintbrush, it would be the hammer: Swords into ploughshares!

So on 1 January 1989, Kees Koning and Co van Melle hammered on an NF-5 fighterplane. The fact that an ex-military chaplain and a physician, both with grey hair, did such an action, and did it openly, really made the news and triggered a campaign against arms shipments to Turkey. The sale of planes was discussed and debated in the media, parliament and in the cabinet, but in the end, the Netherlands remained loyal to NATO and sold the planes to Turkey.

Kees participated in a number of direct disarmament actions, hammer-ing on airplanes, taking down a communication tower at Volkel nuclear (US) airforce base, and so on. He spent about two and a half years in jails and prisons.

An infiltrator eventually penetrated our affinity group and this effec-tively split and destroyed the group in late 1990. Kees had become more cautious, having done six months for a betrayed action. In general Kees did not find his jail time particularly "useful", he did not experience it as a pow-erful witness, more as a nuisace that had to be accepted. He often just "did disarmament" and if he was arrested, no problem, no panic; if he wasn't arrested, it meant he was free to continue disarmament.

When the Gulf war started Kees participated in the Gulf Peace Team, travelled up north into Iraq Kurdistan, and also went several times into Turkish Kurdistan as part of human rights observation delegations. In 1993 and 1994 he participated in the Mir Sada and Sjeme Mira civil interventions in Bosnia.

Once a right-wing group burned down his shed and Kees lost his books and sleeping bag, and last year a molotov cocktail missed his shed, but burned down the Emmaus part of the monastery. Kees more or less put up with the attacks and quietly continued to live as he thought was best.

Living simply, working at Emmaus and in his vegetable garden, direct disarmament and civil intervention in war zones provided only partial answers to The Questions (how to live best in this world full of injustice and suffering), and Kees became more and more silent. I think that his death was perhaps a kind of salvation, a liberation from this big struggle. On 22 July, as Kees was in his garden, he lay down, put a piece of wood under his head, and passed away.

There was a night vigil around his coffin in his shed, and during the funeral service we put ears of wheat – the grain that has to die and fall into the earth – on his body. Someone also gave him a little boltcutter for his journey, and his best buddy gave him the Ploughshares Movement symbol (two people hammering a sword into a ploughshare) cut out in wood. I had the feeling that Kees looked down on us with his big smile.

I hope that Kees' searching for a truthful life will continue to challenge and inspire us, and I am sure that Kees now rests in Peace.

Frits Ter Kuile

Edward Poore[25]

(1948-1991)

Dear John Steel,

... I am trying to put together an album with photographs of my beloved son Edward from birth (22 March 1948) to death (29 June 1991). I still find it difficult to be reconciled to his demise. I believe it was you who offered him accommodation if he returned to the U.K. - it was very good of you but he had here a loving home for as long as he wanted it. I feel I must tell you something of the circumstances.

Edward was a very complex character. You could say he was born with a silver spoon in his mouth. As we all recognise none of us has any jurisdiction over our birth or into which state we are born - it could be the Glasgow Gorbals, an Eskimo igloo or an English country home - the latter happened to be our fate. Both our sons went to a preparatory school near home where they were very happy and Edward went on to his father's public school, Harrow. There he excelled in sports, representing his school at long-distance running, swimming and squash - no mean feat in such a large establishment. He was also extremely intelligent. After leaving Harrow he was sent to Lausanne in Switzerland and later to St Luke's College in Exeter. He then became a schoolmaster, teaching French and Maths. He followed his career until his father's death in 1973 when he inherited our lovely Georgian house in Herefordshire, Coddington Court.

After a while I left and subsequently remarried Doctor Richardson. Edward soon realised he could not afford to go on living at Coddington, and that he must sell; this had a profound effect on him as he adored the place where he had lived nearly all his life. He turned to drink and became an alcoholic - you can imagine how devastated I was. To begin with he was able to carry on as a squash coach; Honah Barrington, four times world champion (with whom Edward worked, and who came to his memorial service), said he was the most *brilliant* coach he had ever known. Edward took his junior teams abroad many times and they were never beaten. Unfortunately his condition became worse as time went by, and he began behaving oddly and often refused to come to see me which of course was very distressing.

[25] *Editors*: We are grateful to Rosemary Richardson (Edward Poore's mother) for her kind permission to reproduce here excerpts of this letter, originally sent by her to John Steel on 13 March 1994.

However the climax came and he was carted off to hospital to be dried out, the doctor telling him he would only live a few more months if he did not give up drink. I have the greatest admiration for his will power because he was cured and for the last five years of his life he never touched alcohol. However, he had suffered some damage. He went abroad a lot and was unlucky in catching various illnesses.

After coming back from one of his trips abroad he found his landlord in Worcester was selling up, so I offered him my large spare room, as I have lived alone since my husband died in 1986. He moved in September 1990 with all his furniture, books, pictures, ornaments etc., which he took great trouble in arranging. He was moody and difficult at times and had been diagnosed as a manic depressive, but in between, he was his old self - thoughtful and kind. One day we had a trivial disagreement and he retired to his room, where I later found a note saying he would not return except to fetch all his belongings. I never saw him again.

Later I heard through the social services that he was sleeping rough in London over Christmas. I never ever stopped loving Edward and when he went with your lot to Baghdad I sent him money there and later to Jerusalem. I spoke only once to him on the telephone in Jerusalem - he said he had no intention of ever returning to England. He only did so in his coffin, a short while later.

I tell you all this to explain the tragedy of Edward's life. He was so gifted and I miss him every day so terribly. "Those the gods love die young". I hope you will understand.

Sincerely,

Rosemary Richardson

John Steel
(1914-1997)

John was a dear friend and fellow peace-campaigner. He was an inspiration for many others and the best tribute that can be made is that the difficult task of achieving reconciliation in a nuclear-free world should continue with enthusiasm and good humour, these being just two of his outstanding qualities.

I'm trying to recall when it was that we first met and suppose that it was through fellow membership of Ex-Services CND in the early 80s. By that time John would already have spent many years diligently working for the peace movement.

John was kindly and modest, but aptly named, steel-like in his integrity of purpose. It was when we both became involved in the Gulf Peace Team in 1990 that our comradeship became a close one. Our time in Iraq and at the peace camp resulted in psychic wounds which are still unhealed. John's qualities were put to the most severe test during that extraordinary period, in a situation where personalities were bound to clash, where fear and uncertainty were other potent ingredients.

It is not overstating the case to describe John as a rock of calm and sanity in that turbulent mixture, for which many of us were profoundly grateful.

I have never known to what extent John's army service in the North African campaign, capture and imprisonment in Germany, were powerful factors in focussing his great qualities. Modesty and reticence precluded idle chat about things past; it was the present task, undertaken with optimism, which focussed his powers and drew others along with him.

My admiration goes beyond words when considering the daunting task, which he took upon himself as a matter of honour, of sorting out the financial mess left in the wake of the Gulf Peace Team. With professional legal advice he singlehandedly brought good order and after several years of complicated figure work, the various creditors were recompensed to the greatest degree possible. It was during that time of great responsibility, which might have broken a lesser man, that he became seriously ill. After a slow recovery, he carried on where he had left off, and "delivered the goods". What a man!

We'll miss you John Steel, and are privileged to have marched beside you.

Richard Crump